AF846422

Research Series on the Chinese Dream and China's Development Path

Project Director
Xie Shouguang, President, Social Sciences Academic Press

Series editors
Li Yang, Vice president, Chinese Academy of Social Sciences, Beijing, China
Li Peilin, Vice president, Chinese Academy of Social Sciences, Beijing, China

Academic Advisors
Cai Fang, Gao Peiyong, Li Lin, Li Qiang, Ma Huaide, Pan Jiahua, Pei Changhong, Qi Ye, Wang Lei, Wang Ming, Zhang Yuyan, Zheng Yongnian, Zhou Hong

Drawing on a large body of empirical studies done over the last two decades, the *Research Series on the Chinese Dream and China's Development Path* seeks to provide its readers with in-depth analyses of the past and present, and forecasts for the future course of China's development. Thanks to the adoption of Socialism with Chinese characteristics, and the implementation of comprehensive reform and opening, China has made tremendous achievements in areas such as political reform, economic development, and social construction, and is making great strides towards the realization of the Chinese dream of national rejuvenation. In addition to presenting a detailed account of many of these achievements, the authors also discuss what lessons other countries can learn from China's experience. This series will be an invaluable companion to every researcher who is trying to gain a deeper understanding of the development model, path and experience unique to China.

More information about this series at http://www.springer.com/series/13571

Yuanzheng Cao

Strategies for Internationalizing the Renminbi

SSAP

Springer

Yuanzheng Cao
BOC International Research Corporation
Beijing
China

ISSN 2363-6866 ISSN 2363-6874 (electronic)
Research Series on the Chinese Dream and China's Development Path
ISBN 978-981-13-0799-7 ISBN 978-981-13-0800-0 (eBook)
https://doi.org/10.1007/978-981-13-0800-0

Jointly published with Social Sciences Academic Press, Beijing, China

The print edition is not for sale in China Mainland. Customers from China Mainland please order the print book from: Social Sciences Academic Press.

Library of Congress Control Number: 2018942623

© Social Sciences Academic Press and Springer Nature Singapore Pte Ltd. 2018
This work is subject to copyright. All rights are reserved by the Publishers, whether the whole or part of the material is concerned, specifically the rights of translation, reprinting, reuse of illustrations, recitation, broadcasting, reproduction on microfilms or in any other physical way, and transmission or information storage and retrieval, electronic adaptation, computer software, or by similar or dissimilar methodology now known or hereafter developed.
The use of general descriptive names, registered names, trademarks, service marks, etc. in this publication does not imply, even in the absence of a specific statement, that such names are exempt from the relevant protective laws and regulations and therefore free for general use.
The publishers, the authors and the editors are safe to assume that the advice and information in this book are believed to be true and accurate at the date of publication. Neither the publishers nor the authors or the editors give a warranty, express or implied, with respect to the material contained herein or for any errors or omissions that may have been made. The publishers remains neutral with regard to jurisdictional claims in published maps and institutional affiliations.

Printed on acid-free paper

This Springer imprint is published by the registered company Springer Nature Singapore Pte Ltd.
The registered company address is: 152 Beach Road, #21-01/04 Gateway East, Singapore 189721, Singapore

Foreword

A New Historical Starting Point for National Development

At the end of the Qing Dynasty, Chen Danran claimed that "It is impossible to have a good plan for the present without any long-term strategy; it is impossible to handle the current situation without any overall planning." The development strategy of a given country is predicated on plans made in tandem with global, local, and historically situated contexts, both contemporaneously and over time. National development strategies must account for scientific projections of the internal and external environment, major conflicts, opportunities, challenges, advantages, and disadvantages facing the country's future development. A good strategy illuminates both the global and domestic environment and establishes a top-level plan for the direction, target, path, principles, and policies outlining the country's future development. With such a strategy, a country is able to develop along with the tide of historical progress, seize opportunities as they present themselves, and to win the initiative, advantages, and the future.

History tells us that properly strategizing is central to a country's development, such that any country without adequate strategic planning will find it very difficult to attain any modicum of global power or success. Successful strategic decision-making is vital to a country's ultimate development. History has shown that the reform and opening-up (改革开放/gǎigé kāifàng) policy has been a significant and successful strategy for China, and, furthermore, promises increased future success.

China's development now stands at a new starting point. After more than 30 years of reform and opening-up and progressive development, China has bid farewell to sustenance and entered a new stage of prioritizing self-development. The existing deep-rooted conflicts and problems associated with 30 years of rapid economic growth, however, together with the current complicated and volatile global economy, challenge China on its road to fair and sustainable development.

Since 2008 and the outbreak of the global financial crisis, the global economy has undergone profound changes. The current global economic pattern is being ruthlessly torn apart and reshaped by an internationally unbalanced economic structure and mounting global financial crises. It is difficult to rebalance the world economy. The task of restructuring the global political and economic order is staggering and often conflicts with national interests. Doubts as to the ability of China to overcome the "middle-income trap" and to achieve just, fair, and sustainable development are at the center of global attention.

If global and domestic circumstances are to be believed, the next 5–10 years are critical to China's development. The strategy undertaken during this critical period will exert a decisive influence over the country's development in the next 20 to 30 years. Therefore, we've asked authors to write 20 books for this collection on China's development strategy. This particular collection focuses on holistic and long-term research trends. Twenty strategic topics—covering the economy, society, political affairs, culture, diplomacy, national defense, reform, and opening-up, and more—have been discussed by experts and scholars, who have also provided their thoughts on actionable and strategic proposals. We expect that this collection of books will serve as a research reference for national development strategies. This collection is academic but readable. I believe that readers' needs will be met.

The authors of this collection are well-known experts and scholars with long-term management experience in their particular areas of study. I would like to express my sincere thanks to all the authors. Thank you for researching and expressing your findings despite all the other work occupying your time.

Due to the joint efforts of China (Hainan) Institute for Reform and Development (CIRD), Study Press, and Hainan Press, this collection has been successfully published. I would like to extend my thanks to Study Press and Hainan Press for their hard work in organizing and editing the essays contained herein.

As the director of the editorial committee, I've invited committee members to closely examine and analyze this collection's framework, contents, structure, and style. Each chapter represents the author's academic findings and opinions. Since the task is urgent and the collection covers multiple fields, shortcomings are inevitable and comments and queries are welcome.

October 2012

Chi Fulin
China Institute for Reform
and Development

Series Preface

Since China's reform and opening began in 1978, the country has come a long way on the path of Socialism with Chinese Characteristics, under the leadership of the Communist Party of China. Over 30 years of reform efforts and sustained spectacular economic growth have turned China into the world's second largest economy, and wrought many profound changes in the Chinese society. These historically significant developments have been garnering increasing attention from scholars, governments, and the general public alike around the world since the 1990s, when the newest wave of China studies began to gather steam. Some of the hottest topics have included the so-called "China miracle," "Chinese phenomenon," "Chinese experience," "Chinese path," and the "Chinese model." Homegrown researchers have soon followed suit. Already hugely productive, this vibrant field is putting out a large number of books each year, with Social Sciences Academic Press alone having published hundreds of titles on a wide range of subjects.

Because most of these books have been written and published in Chinese, however, readership has been limited outside China—even among many who study China—for whom English is still the lingua franca. This language barrier has been an impediment to efforts by academia, business communities, and policy-makers in other countries to form a thorough understanding of contemporary China, of what is distinct about China's past and present may mean not only for her future but also for the future of the world. The need to remove such an impediment is both real and urgent, and the *Research Series on the Chinese Dream and China's Development Path* is my answer to the call.

This series features some of the most notable achievements from the last 20 years by scholars in China in a variety of research topics related to reform and opening. They include both theoretical explorations and empirical studies, and cover economy, society, politics, law, culture, and ecology, the six areas in which reform and opening policies have had the deepest impact and farthest-reaching consequences for the country. Authors for the series have also tried to articulate their visions of the "Chinese Dream" and how the country can realize it in these fields and beyond.

All of the editors and authors for the *Research Series on the Chinese Dream and China's Development Path* are both longtime students of reform and opening and recognized authorities in their respective academic fields. Their credentials and expertise lend credibility to these books, each of which having been subject to a rigorous peer-review process for inclusion in the series. As part of the Reform and Development Program under the State Administration of Press, Publication, Radio, Film and Television of the People's Republic of China, the series is published by Springer, a Germany-based academic publisher of international repute, and distributed overseas. I am confident that it will help fill a lacuna in studies of China in the era of reform and opening.

Xie Shouguang

Preface

Two concurrent monetary phenomena currently characterize the world—the European debt crisis and the internationalization of the RMB. These two phenomena share one common source: the world's political and economic order, including the international monetary system, is undergoing unprecedented change. The current international political and economic order was established after WWII and consisted, until recently, of three pillars: the first being international political order as represented by the United Nations, founded on the Yalta Conference; the second pillar was an economic order founded on the WTO (the original GATT), the central goal of which was to liberalize investment and trade; and the third pillar being the arrangement of the US dollar-centric international monetary and financial system, as organized around the Bretton Woods system. The objective basis of these three pillars has been the establishment and sustenance of the North–South gap. More than 70 years of economic development has followed the end of WWII, and as a result, this objective has shifted over time: In terms of GDP, the North–South gap has narrowed considerably, and in some cases has even disappeared altogether. The world's political and economic order—based on this quickly disappearing North–South gap—has therefore begun to fluctuate, and as a result, the traditional mechanisms of global governance are becoming destabilized. This challenge has only one viable choice—establishing a new political and economic order that better serves the needs of developing countries. China, as the world's largest developing country, the second largest economy, and the largest trading entity, must shoulder the responsibilities and obligations of maintaining world economic stability. The most pressing obligation is therefore to realize the RMB's internationalization.

Initiated by the US subprime mortgage crisis, the global financial crisis spread internationally in 2008. International trade—especially international trade with East Asia—faces difficulties in valuation and settlement due to the shortage of US dollar-denominated liquidity. "The US dollar shortage" intensified the ongoing decline in trade, which itself furthered the financial crisis. At that time, China did not have sufficient conditions for internationalization. In order to meet global demand, however—especially the needs of East Asia for regional economic cooperation—the RMB embarked on the road toward internationalization.

On July 2, 2009, the RMB's internationalization was initiated in several pilot cities. The first region targeted was East Asia, with a focus on applying the RMB in cross-border trade settlement with China. History has shown that the RMB's first step toward this cross-border arrangement provides a new tool for valuation and settlement in terms of international trade, eases difficulties associated with the shortage of US dollar-denominated liquidity, impacts the global economy with a higher demand brought about by China's robust economic growth, and alleviates the negative effects of the global financial crisis. As a result, the RMB's internationalization is welcomed globally, which, in turn, promotes further internationalization.

As time goes on, the pilot program has extended to China as a whole. Its scope is no longer limited only to the trade of goods, but has extended to services and investments. As of the first half of 2015, 29% of trade with China and 78% of investment with China had been settled in RMB. Accordingly, the RMB has begun to serve as a tool for investment and financing, and has therefore been applied in international financial trading. Offshore RMB markets in Hong Kong, Singapore, and London have developed, and as a result, a new model for the RMB's cross-border application has taken shape—namely, the "offshore market + settlement bank." On this basis, the RMB has become an international reserve currency. In other words, the RMB has begun to enter the balance sheets outside of China. Considering the staggering progress of the RMB's internationalization, on November 30, 2015, the IMF officially announced that it would include the RMB in its Special Drawing Rights (SDR) basket. As such, the RMB's internationalization has entered a new stage, moving from bilateral application to multilateral application, and the RMB has therefore become an international currency.

China's economy is an integral component of the global economy, and as such, the RMB's internationalization is good both for the development of the world economy, broadly, and that of China's economy, specifically. The application of the RMB in cross-border trade settlement consolidates the economic relationship between China and neighboring countries, thus laying a new foundation for the China-ASEAN Free Trade Zone and the Shanghai Cooperation Organization. Due to the development of the offshore RMB market and the mechanism for the RMB's flowing back into the country, the reform of China's financial system is accelerating. All of these factors have promoted the development of China's economy and improved its socialist market economic system. Considering this, in 2012, several proposals were raised at the 18th National Congress of the Communist Party of China, to the effect of: "China will steadily liberalize the interest rate and the exchange rate to gradually realize the RMB's convertibility under the capital account"; "China will plan for the bilateral, multilateral, regional, and sub-regional opening-up and will cooperate to facilitate the strategy of a free trade zone, to promote connections with neighboring countries, and to enhance the ability to combat international economic risks"; "China will promote the robust, sustainable, and balanced growth of the global economy through increased cooperation. China is committed to narrowing the North-South gap and supporting other developing countries in enhancing their capacity for self-development. China will strengthen coordination with other major economies on macroeconomic policies and resolve economic and trade frictions with other countries through consultation. China upholds the principle of balancing rights with obligations. We will take an active part in global economic governance, promote and facilitate free trade and investment, and oppose protectionism in all its forms."

In the 3 years since 2012, all of the above proposals have been gradually realized. As of the first half of 2015, China's interest rate regulations have been totally canceled, and the regulations outlining the exchange rate have weakened considerably. Mechanisms for liberalizing the interest rate and the exchange rate have taken shape. Free movement under the capital account has almost been realized, while the process of enabling the RMB's convertibility under the capital account has been initiated. At the same time, the pilot program for establishing the Shanghai Free Trade Zone with Pre-Establishment National Treatment and a Negative List has been fully realized. At the same time, the threshold for foreign financial institutions has been, for the most part, lowered. The process of developing Shanghai into an international financial center has accelerated. Financial products represented by fixed-income products have been continuously forthcoming for some time. The deeper reform of China's financial system and accelerated development of the financial market have created favorable conditions for the RMB's international applicability. For this reason, the Association of Southeast Asian Nations plus three ("ASEAN 10 + 3") countries, the Shanghai Cooperation Organization, and BRICS (Brazil, Russia, India, China, and South Africa) members —while owning and utilizing their own alternative and operative domestic currencies—have, at the same time, correspondingly set up new financial institutions such as the Silk Road Fund and Asian Infrastructure Investment Bank. Under such circumstances, regional economic cooperation has become closer, and the Belt and Road initiative has indicated greater prospects. A new world economic pattern and a new mechanism of global governance have been built.

In just a few short years, significant progress has been made in the internationalization of the RMB. Its development path and future prospects have attracted the attention of the world's academic, business, and political circles, with conflicting descriptions, explanations, speculations, and arguments rising one after another. It is necessary to analyze the rationale behind the RMB's internationalization from a theoretical perspective, in order to better evaluate existing practices and to look into the future. I have long been a participant in, witness to, and strong advocate for the internationalization process. *Strategies for Internationalizing the Renminbi*, which I had written at the request of the China Institute for Reform and Development, was published 3 years ago and has been well-received. In it, we argued that practice in RMB internationalization has already indicated that, in marked departure from the traditional model, opening of capital accounts and full convertibility of the country's domestic currency are separate from each other. Careful design and precise solutions may open up a whole new roadmap for the RMB's internationalization, thus further enhancing global governance and facilitating the reform of the international monetary system. Now that several years have passed, the actual practice of internationalization reforms has validated ideas held at the time of writing. For this reason, the Social Sciences Academic Press (China) expects to publish an English language version of this earlier study by revising the monograph according to the latest progress.

This book aims to present a theoretical framework for the evolution of the international monetary system and the internationalization of the RMB, on which an in-depth analysis of the relevant issues from multiple perspectives has been made by combining theoretical research and empirical study. The first chapter is an overview of the roots of the international monetary system's development, investigating in particular its evolutionary and reform history; the second chapter demonstrates the necessity of internationalizing the RMB for the world economy and discusses the progress and challenges associated therewith; the third chapter looks back into the history of monetary internationalization, summarizes the experience of internationalizing the Deutschemark and the Japanese yen, and explains how the opening of the capital account is a common problem for developing countries in the process of internationalizing their currencies, with the expectation that previous experiences can serve as lessons for the RMB's internationalization; the fourth chapter analyzes China's solutions to Mundell's "Impossible Trinity," and makes an in-depth analysis of possible methods for internationalizing the RMB; the fifth chapter emphasizes the status and functions of the HK offshore financial market in internationalizing the RMB; the sixth chapter explains the "two-step strategy," from the capital account opening to the full convertibility of the RMB; the seventh chapter extends the discussion on the RMB's internationalization based on existing promotional plans; and the eighth chapter predicts a bright future for the RMB's internationalization.

The internationalization of the RMB presents new challenges and paths toward macro-strategies, politics, the economy, diplomacy, and many other areas. The authors acknowledge that the breadth of their knowledge is far from complete and welcome comments and suggestions for improvement.

Beijing, China Yuanzheng Cao

Acknowledgements

After a relatively short gestation period, the *Research Series on the Chinese Dream and China's Development Path* has started to bear fruits. We have, first and foremost, the books' authors and editors to thank for making this possible. And it was the hard work by many people at Social Sciences Academic Press and Springer, the two collaborating publishers, that made it a reality. We are deeply grateful to all of them.

Mr. Xie Shouguang, president of Social Sciences Academic Press (SSAP), is the mastermind behind the project. In addition to defining the key missions to be accomplished by it and setting down the basic parameters for the project's execution, as the work has unfolded, Mr. Xie has provided critical input pertaining to its every aspect and at every step of the way. Thanks to the deft coordination by Ms. Li Yanling, all the constantly moving parts of the project, especially those on the SSAP side, are securely held together, and as well synchronized as is feasible for a project of this scale. Ms. Gao Jing, unfailingly diligent and meticulous, makes sure every aspect of each Chinese manuscript meets the highest standards for both publishers, something of critical importance to all subsequent steps in the publishing process. That high quality if also at times stylistically as well as technically challenging scholarly writing in Chinese has turned into decent, readable English that readers see on these pages is largely, thanks to Ms. Liang Fan, who oversees translator recruitment and translation quality control.

Ten other members of the SSAP staff have been intimately involved, primarily in the capacity of in-house editor, in the preparation of the Chinese manuscripts. It is time-consuming work that requires attention to details, and each of them has done this, and is continuing to do this with superb skills. They are, in alphabetical order, Mr. Cai Jihui, Ms. Liu Xiaojun, Mr. Ren Wenwu, Ms. Shi Xiaolin, Ms. Song Yuehua, Mr. Tong Genxing, Ms. Wu Dan, Ms. Yao Dongmei, Ms. Yun Wei, and Ms. Zhou Qiong. In addition, Xie Shouguang and Li Yanling have also taken part in this work.

Ms. Li Yanling is the SSAP in-house editor for the current volume.

Our appreciation is also owed to Ms. Li Yan, Mr. Chai Ning, Ms. Wang Lei, and Ms. Xu Yi from Springer's Beijing Representative Office. Their strong support for the SSAP team in various aspects of the project helped to make the latter's work that much easier than it would have otherwise been.

We thank Ms. Gu Guan for translating this book and Ms. Virginia L. Conn for her work as the polisher. We thank everyone involved for their hard work.

Last, but certainly not least, it must be mentioned that funding for this project comes from the Ministry of Finance of the People's Republic of China. Our profound gratitude, if we can be forgiven for a bit of apophasis, goes without saying.

Social Sciences Academic Press
Springer

Contents

Introduction

The Internationalization of the RMB and Regional Economic Cooperation in East Asia

East Asia is now the world's most dynamic economic region, with ever-increasing trade and economic cooperation among its member states. Inside China, the Chinese government has signed the Closer Economic Partnership Arrangement (CEPA) with Hong Kong and the Asian Committee for Future Accelerators (ACFA) with Taiwan. As for China's external cooperative ties, the China-ASEAN Free Trade Zone has been established. In addition, the establishment of the China-Japan-South Korea Free Trade Zone is ongoing. Closer economic and trade cooperation of this nature has facilitated the RMB's application in this region. Accordingly, East Asia was the first region in which an offshore RMB market developed, the first region in which frequent official exchanges of the RMB have occurred, and the geographic location where the RMB's overseas application is most comprehensive. For this reason, the RMB's application in this region, prospects for its further application, and its impact on the economic and political order have naturally become subjects of global interest

Reasons for the RMB's overseas application in East Asia

Research has shown that applying a stable currency in trade will help lower associated risks and promote future exchange, thereby promoting economic growth.

East Asia is one of the most important trading partners for China. As of December 2014, China's trade volume with ASEAN countries, Japan, South Korea, and Hong Kong accounted for 36.8% of China's total trade volume, among which ASEAN and Japan were the third- and fourth-largest trading partners with China, just behind the European Union and the United States. East Asia is a popular outbound travel destination for Chinese residents, who enjoy advantages in geographical location, culture, traditions, and facilitated visa issuance. In 2014, the number of Chinese outbound tourists reached 116.59 mn, reporting an annual growth of 19%. Among the ten most popular destinations for Chinese outbound tourists, excepting the United States, all other destinations are in East Asia and Southeast Asia.

For those East Asian countries reporting trade surpluses, the growing Chinese market is their main export destination. Statistics show that China's trade deficits are mainly with other East Asian countries and that China has developed stable trade deficits with ASEAN countries, Japan, and South Korea. In 2011, China's trade deficit with ASEAN reached USD22.4bn, accounting for 6.17% of the bilateral trade volume. In the same year, China's trade deficit with Japan accounted for 13.5% of the bilateral trade volume, while its deficit with South Korea accounted for 32.5% of the bilateral trade volume. In 2012, the bilateral trade volume between China and ASEAN was USD400.1bn, of which, USD204.3bn was China's export volume and USD195.8bn was China's import volume. Here, China's trade surplus with ASEAN reached USD8.5bn, accounting for 2% of the bilateral trade volume. In 2014, China's trade volume with ASEAN was RMB480.394bn, accounting for 11.6% of China's total export and import volume. China's increasing trade deficit has laid a foundation for the RMB's outflow. Due to the development of China's economy and increase in labor productivity, the RMB has a stable currency value and has maintained a trend of appreciation, which creates conditions for applying the RMB in valuing and settling international trade.

In fact, even as foreign exchange was still under strict control in the early 1990s, the RMB's cross-border application had already appeared in the border areas of China. Along China's southwest border, many informal financial institutions had sprung up for the express purpose of cross-border trade settlement, with the RMB being the major currency applied. The "stall banks" facilitated this "cross-border trade" and were popular among neighboring countries. Since then, the RMB has begun to flow outward and has been widely used by China's neighboring countries.

After the 1998 Asian financial crisis, the economic development of East Asian countries became much closer. On the one hand, to cope with the difficulty of making international payments, East Asian countries focused on the importance of accumulating trade surpluses and foreign reserves; on the other hand, China's growing economy has served and continues to serve as a huge market for these countries. The result is that China's trade deficits with these countries have increased annually and—due to increasing international demands for the RMB—what was once unofficial and under-the-table acknowledgement of the RMB's international application has gradually become officially sanctioned.

The 2008 global financial crisis fully revealed the irrationality of the US dollar-centric international monetary system. Due to the subprime mortgage crisis of the United States, the liquidity of the US dollar suddenly shrank, causing East Asian countries to face payment difficulties in the US dollar-denominated trade of goods or services, which, in turn, created further economic shocks. One logical outcome of this instability was that the US dollar would be replaced by domestic currencies. During this process of currency replacement was when the RMB best demonstrated its advantages. To meet international demand, the Chinese government decided to initiate a pilot program for applying the RMB in cross-border trade settlement, which was carried out on July 2, 2009. Since then, the RMB's cross-border application has expanded, namely, the process of internationalizing the RMB. In the first half of 2015, cross-border trade settlement utilizing the RMB reached RMB3.37tn, accounting for around 29% of the total trade volume with China.

The Special Path of Internationalizing the RMB and its Impacts on East Asia

Global experience has shown that the prerequisite for internationalizing a sovereign currency is to realize the full convertibility of this currency (including the current account convertibility and capital account convertibility). The RMB is not convertible under the capital account, however, when it is applied overseas. The RMB's internationalization is a special arrangement under the current account for the purpose of meeting the demands for international trade that are predicated upon full convertibility, especially the demands for trade among East Asian countries. This special arrangement forms a unique path and status quo: the development of the offshore RMB market is proceeding much faster than that of the onshore RMB market.

On July 2, 2009, the RMB began to be applied by 365 companies in five separate cities for settling cross-border trade with Hong Kong, Macao, and ASEAN countries via settlement banks (Hong Kong/Macao model) or via agency banks (Shanghai model). Under the Hong Kong/Macao model, offshore RMB holders will square off their positions with the People's Bank of China (PBOC) via settlement banks. Under the Shanghai model, foreign correspondents will transfer or square off the offshore RMB positions via domestic (Shanghai) agency banks.

Over the past 3 years, both of these two models have reported significant achievements. The progress made by the Hong Kong/Macao model, however, has developed much faster than that of the Shanghai model. According to available statistics, the settlement volume of the offshore RMB in Hong Kong accounted for 70.83% of the total, resulting in an offshore RMB market in Hong Kong. A greater number of financial products have also emerged, including RMB-denominated bond products, RMB-denominated stock products, and derivatives. Such a situation was within the bounds of reason yet beyond expectation. Traced back to the root, one important finding is that in Shanghai's onshore market, even though the RMB can be applied in valuing and settling international trade, the RMB remains inconvertible under the capital account. By contrast, since 2003—when the Chinese mainland and Hong Kong signed CEPA—certain arrangements can be made through the RMB for China's international balance of payments. In other words, in the offshore RMB market in Hong Kong, the RMB is convertible under the capital account under certain circumstances. In this way, overseas holders of RMB-denominated positions under the current account can enjoy the capital account arrangement, thereby boosting the RMB's application in cross-border trade. Due to this development, the Hong Kong-centered offshore RMB market has grown extremely rapidly in comparison to the Shanghai-centered model.

According to a preliminary analysis, the development of the offshore RMB market in Hong Kong is based on objective observations and has followed a measurable trend of development. Hong Kong has a mature financial infrastructure, talents, and appropriate legal environment, and is an international financial center, besides, thus providing ideal conditions for the RMB's international application. What's more, the regulator for the Chinese mainland and the regulator of Hong Kong are able to closely cooperate with each other in matters of economics and trade. Under a framework designated "One Country, Two Systems," there is no conflict of interest between the Chinese mainland and Hong Kong. Regulators of these two locations cooperate under a single common arrangement. It is a solution that respects the reality on the ground, releases each region's potential, and forms the outlines of these two systems' regulatory interactions. In Hong Kong, the regulatory pattern for the RMB is: the RMB's flowing into or flowing out of Hong Kong should follow the rules established by the Chinese mainland, but the RMB itself is regarded as a foreign currency when being applied in Hong Kong and is allowed to be applied in any financial activities where foreign currencies are used. This special arrangement not only meets the requirement that states that the RMB is not convertible under the capital account but also boosts the Hong Kong financial market to satisfy the demands of East Asian countries for the RMB.

As the offshore RMB market in Hong Kong develops, the use of the RMB among East Asian countries for settling trade has increased, particularly in Hong Kong. Take the Bank of China's business of cross-border RMB settlement as an example. In 2011, this business accounted for 30.5% of the total volume Bank of China. Among the total settlement volume for 2011, 73% was contributed by branches in Asia (especially in Hong Kong and Macao); only 7.08% was contributed by Southeast Asian branches (not including Hong Kong and Macao), while 22% was contributed by European branches. The distribution of settlements in RMB was similar during the first three months of 2012, in that Southeast Asian branches accounted for only 7.7% of the total.

The development of the offshore RMB market in Hong Kong serves as an operational foundation for deepening the international applicability of the RMB. On one hand, the currency's geographical range has expanded. On the Chinese mainland, the RMB's cross-border application is no longer limited to certain regions or cities, but is instead broadly available domestically. On the other hand, the scope of the RMB as it relates to business is also increasingly internationally applicable. The current account has covered the service trade while the capital account has covered the ODI. In 2014, the total volume of China's non-financial ODI reached RMB632.05bn, of which 30% (RMB186.6bn) consisted of RMB-related arrangements. In the aspect of regional distribution, most ODI went to Hong Kong. In 2013, investment in Hong Kong contributed 58% of the total. What's more, in 2013, investment in Latin America—which was second only to that of Hong Kong—contributed 13% of the total. Direct investment in ASEAN countries accounted for 6.74% of the total. Investment in Japan and South Korea each only accounted for a small percentage (less than 0.5%, respectively). Except for its investment in Hong Kong, China's ODI has been quite resource-oriented. Most investment in Latin America, Africa, Oceania, and ASEAN was for the purpose of exploiting mineral resources.

As the RMB's overseas applicability in trade and investment becomes more frequent, arrangements for the influx of the RMB have become increasingly challenging. As the offshore RMB market in Hong Kong develops, this market is becoming the main channel for the RMB's domestic flowing back. For example, the RMB-denominated bond is one product that significantly represents this challenge. Aside from China's Ministry of Finance and the major financial institutions on the Chinese mainland, institutions in Hong Kong and foreign countries also leverage this market to raise funds for investing in the Chinese mainland. The issuers of RMB-denominated bonds in Hong Kong are mainly institutions based out of the Chinese mainland or Hong Kong institutions held by the Chinese mainland, contributing 66% and 77% of the total bonds, respectively, in 2011. Institutions of Southeastern countries are not active in issuing bonds. Only four of the total 415 bonds (including certificates of deposits) issued in 2011 came from Southeastern countries (three from Singapore and one from Malaysia), totaling RMB3.7bn (1.9% of the total amount issued). During the same period, European institutions issued 37 bonds, the amount of which accounted for 17% of the total amount issued. The bonds issued by institutions in Japan and South Korea accounted for a large portion of the total bonds issued, proportionally similar to those contributed by European institutions. Since the amount of single bonds issued by Japan and South Korea was relatively low, however, the total amount was lower than that issued by European institutions. Except for those issued through China's Ministry of Finance and the major financial institutions of the Chinese mainland, other funds raised from the RMB-denominated bonds flowed into the Chinese mainland in the form of FDI, thus creating an RMB-denominated FDI.

As the RMB's application expands, the process by which the RMB experiences outflow is likely to accelerate. Since the RMB faces restrictions for flowing back, however, "the pool of RMB" has begun to develop in the overseas market, especially in Hong Kong. Up until this point, the total RMB accumulated in Hong Kong has reached RMB600bn. Due to the enlarging "pool of RMB" in Hong Kong, more RMB resources will be available, but the risks will also be higher. These two factors further facilitate the development of an offshore RMB market in Hong Kong and a correspondingly large number of emergent derivatives. For now, except for the fact that RMB-denominated loan products are in short supply, RMB-denominated products are considered to be relatively complete when compared to other foreign currency-denominated products in Hong Kong. Based on the growing offshore RMB market in Hong Kong, the RMB has almost become fully convertible, thus promoting the exchange rate of CNH. It is worth noting that the development trend of the exchange rate of the CNH is almost consistent with that of the Chinese yuan (CNY) (see Fig. 3). The question now is whether the exchange rate of CNH is guiding that of CNY or vice versa. But one thing is clear: two different pricing mechanisms have one common exchange rate curve, which indicates that the RMB's exchange rate has entered into a range characterized by equilibrium with higher flexibility. As a result, the RMB's exchange rate has become predictable, and the foundation has been laid for the RMB's further application in East Asia. For this reason, the direct convertibility between the Japanese yen and the RMB has been made available as of June 1, 2012, without the need for dependence on an anchored currency (the US dollar). Because of this, other East Asian countries are also likely to directly link their domestic currencies to the RMB. One obvious trend is that East Asian countries are now gradually reducing their dependence on the US dollar, which has profoundly changed the financial pattern of East Asia as a whole.

The Special Path Taken by the RMB Toward International Applicability and its Corresponding Significance for China's Economic and Financial Development

There is no doubt that the RMB's cross-border application toward the trade of goods under the current account was undertaken in order to meet the needs of East Asia for intra-regional trade. Three further considerations of China's conditions include:

Open the capital account. On January 1, 1994, China took steps to reform the country's foreign exchange system and to enable current account convertibility. Encouraged by these reforms' measurable achievements, the original plan was to enable capital account convertibility, namely, the full convertibility of the RMB by 2000. The 1997 Asian financial crisis, however, sharply derailed these plans. The Asian financial crisis demonstrated the fact that if a country loosens its regulations on the capital account, the country's domestic currency will become fully convertible, indicating that international capital—especially short-term capital—can flow in and out without many obstacles, potentially destabilizing the macro-economy. Conversely, any positive development of the macro-economy will further agitate the already-overactive economy and increase inflation, while any negative economic development will trigger an economic downturn and recession, or, in the worst-case scenario, can even result in comprehensive economic and financial crisis. Therefore, after the Asian financial crisis, various monetary authorities have reached a consensus on adopting measures for capital control, including but not limited to "encouraging exports and limiting imports." For this reason, China has also stated that "the opening of the capital account—namely, the RMB's full convertibility—has yet to be scheduled." One thing China is very clear about, however, is that the highly centralized planned economic system of the Soviet Union offers no recourse. Once a market-oriented economic system is adopted, production factors must be liberalized —a prerequisite of which is the opening of the capital account and realization of the RMB's full convertibility, thus liberalizing the exchange rate and the interest rate. The stability of the macro-economy, however, conflicts with the opening of the capital account. Deciding which aspect to pursue—macro-stability or capital account liberalization—is no trivial matter.

The second aspect needing to be taken under consideration in terms of the RMB's cross-border application is China's balance of payments deficit. According to previous international experience, once a country's currency is widely applied in international trade, the country's balance of payments will report a deficit. As the scope of applicability and depth grow, so too will the deficit. As a whole, the balance of payments might not report a deficit, but a deficit should be developed either under the current account or under the capital account under threat of insufficient liquidity on the overseas market. Even if a currency has previously been widely applied in the overseas market, a shortage of liquidity will end its usefulness. The global community's enthusiasm in applying the Japanese yen in the 1990s followed by its rapid decline in this century illustrates the significance of developing a stable mechanism for forming a deficit. China's balance of payments, however, still reports "double surpluses." Huge surpluses still exist under both the current account and the capital account. This is not entirely due to China's "export-oriented" policy; rather, much like in other East Asian countries or regions, these surpluses exist because of industrialization determined by the existing factors—namely, the "flying geese paradigm," which combines low-cost labor with mature mainstream technologies. Under this "flying geese paradigm," can a country develop a deficit under certain economic conditions for a given developmental stage? Assuming a country is able to develop deficit, will a mechanism for stability also be cultivated? More importantly, in this economic development stage, is it necessary to compulsorily develop a deficit for the purpose of achieving an ambitious goal? For China, the challenge is how a middle-income country with a hidden unemployment problem can expedite economic growth in order to achieve full employment. Therefore, the requirement for the RMB's large-scale international application is to foster a stable mechanism for generating a deficit. This requirement conflicts with accelerating economic growth to achieve full employment for the purpose of absorbing foreign capital and expanding domestic exports. Which path the country decides to follow will greatly determine its economic future.

The third aspect under consideration is the reality of China's financial system. For many years, China adopted a highly centralized, Soviet-style planned economy, under which market-oriented resource allocation was replaced by governmental planning. As a result, the free-enterprise system—wherein enterprises are allowed to enter/exit the market without restrictions—was replaced by factories attached to the government's administrative functions. The whole economy was highly fiscalized. Under such a system, functions of finance were inapplicable, or, if they were utilized, their purposes were only to meet fiscal needs. Before the Reform and Opening-Up policy, China did not have a financial market or financial institutions in a real sense. The monetary authority—the People's Bank of China, or PBOC—was, at that time, subordinate to the Ministry of Finance. After the Reform and Opening-Up, China's financial market and financial institutions began to experience long-term development along with a constantly increasing number of financial products. Compared to other industries, however, the financial system was and is not perfect, and reforms to the financial system continue to lag behind similar reforms in other areas. Obvious evidence of this is that the interest rate is yet to be liberalized and the development of the capital market still leaves much to be desired. The result is that a fixed-income market has not yet been established and instruments for derivatives are still in the infancy. What's more, the very effectiveness of the PBOC's monetary policies has not yet been fully revealed. International experience shows that once a domestic currency is widely applied globally, that country's central bank should not only be responsible for the stability of the country's macro-economy, but also shoulders responsibility for the stability of the international economy. The focus of regulations is to leverage the country's financial market in order to affect international financial activities. The interest rate is a major regulating tool employed for just this purpose, such that the country in question is able to exert influence on international financial activities by adjusting the interest rate of the domestic currency. Considering all this, even if China's PBOC were willing to shoulder international responsibilities, the immaturity of China's financial market prevents it from doing so. This represents a new conflict and new economic decisions.

Considering the above constraints, the RMB's international application was initially limited to the trade of goods under the current account. The current account, especially the trade of goods, does not involve the capital account. Due to the small range involved, implementation will be easy and international needs will at least partially be met. East Asia has reported trade deficits and might develop a stable mechanism for generating further deficits, which ensures that a foundation has been laid for the RMB's liquidity in this region. At the same time, considering that Hong Kong is an international financial center and in consideration of the mature financial market and financial infrastructure of Hong Kong (especially the "One Country, Two Systems" arrangement), the PBOC's operations are becoming increasingly feasible. As a result, the RMB's internationalization is proceeding as scheduled by the previously mentioned special arrangement.

As the region's economic policy arrangements evolve, those policy arrangements restricted by initial conditions will follow a unique developmental path. In this process, new conditions will be generated for further evolution, which will determine the direction of the future—something known as "path dependence." In fact, the initial status of the RMB's international application was what has determined today's results—the development of the offshore RMB market is likely to develop faster than that of the onshore RMB market. Because of this, new evolutionary conditions have been further created, thus creating new prospects for the RMB's internationalization.

The RMB's cross-border application, especially the emergence of the offshore RMB market in Hong Kong, offers a solution to the "dilemma" faced by East Asian countries. Under circumstances in which the domestic currency is not convertible, the country will be able to open the capital account. The rationale behind this arrangement is to separate the opening of the capital account from the full convertibility of a domestic currency. Even though it is not possible to separate these two in perpetuity, partial separation at a certain stage is feasible. In fact, the current opening of the capital account of China's balance of payments demonstrates this handily. According to criteria established by the IMF, there are 43 items under the capital account. In China, most items have been open or are essentially open, among which, only three items are related to capital account regulation, and those concern capital behaviors. They include regulations indicating that: foreign direct investment requires examination and approval; Chinese residents should not principally bear foreign debts and the scale of foreign debts should be strictly managed; and that China's capital market, in principle, should not be accessible to foreign capital. For foreign capital to enter China's capital market requires a special arrangement, namely, the QFII. Due to the RMB's growing global application and in addition to previous regulations on foreign currencies, the world economy is opening up to the RMB, particularly RMB-denominated FDI. Chinese residents bear RMB-denominated debts and China's capital market is accessible to the offshore yuan. Since the RMB is one of the principal domestic currencies of this region, the capital account regulation can be quite loose. Reductions in capital account regulations protections have concurrently created conditions for reducing regulations on foreign currencies.

What's more, due to the RMB's cross-border application (and particularly the development of Hong Kong's offshore financial market), China's balance of payments deficit has been generated, stabilized, and institutionalized. The past 3 years have demonstrated a greater degree of RMB-denominated trade settlement under the current account applied toward imports than exports. The reason for this is quite simple: besides the fact that the RMB has a stable currency value and an ongoing trend of appreciation, the status of the importer is higher than that of the exporter during negotiation. As a result, the RMB that flows out has a higher volume than the RMB flowing in. So far, the RMB's cross-border settlement under the current account has covered all provinces in China and the RMB's international payment has been institutionalized. China is still experiencing positive economic development and the revenue of Chinese residents continues to experience sustainable growth, thus laying a solid foundation for expanding exports and stabilizing the RMB's trade deficit. At the same time, as China's economy continues to develop, Chinese enterprises are beginning to make greater overseas investments—a process that is facilitated by the accessibility of RMB-denominated overseas investments. Hence, the proportion of China's overseas investments being settled in RMB to the total overseas investments of China as a whole is increasing, thus creating and expanding the RMB's deficit under the capital account. As mentioned above, even though China's balance of payments is still reporting "double surpluses," the RMB has already indicated signs of deficit. As for China's international balance of payments, changes have taken place not only in its regional structure but have also occurred in the nation's currency structure (in that there is a surplus for the US dollar and deficit for the RMB). It not only adapts to China's economic development at this stage but also meets the needs for the internal applicability of the RMB.

Third, the RMB's cross-border application, especially the development of the offshore RMB market in Hong Kong, provides us with a fresh new experience for improving the financial market and economic system of the Chinese mainland. The financial system of the Chinese mainland prioritizes indirect financing, given that its capital market is not mature. Luckily, however, Hong Kong has a mature financial market that focuses on both direct financing and indirect financing. Therefore, the financial circle of the Chinese mainland has always paid attention to Hong Kong's experiences in developing its finances. The development of Hong Kong's offshore RMB market provides such a solution. As the RMB becomes convertible under the capital account, all financial instruments attached to the RMB will be directly transmitted to the Chinese mainland, thus stimulating and guiding the development of the Chinese mainland's own financial market. Overseas financial institutions are allowed to directly engage in the interbank bond market of the Chinese mainland, which directly or indirectly intensifies domestic competition. With an eye toward enhancing competitiveness, the Chinese mainland's financial market can promote financial innovation by following the example set by the managerial experience of overseas financial institutions. A clear indicator of this is the faster liberalization of the interest rate and greater flexibility on the part of the exchange rate, which lays a foundation for enhancing the effectiveness of the PBOC's monetary policies and enables the PBOC to prudently undertake the obligation of managing global liquidity.

The above conditions have created new prospects for the RMB's further international application. In August 2011, the Chinese government announced the opening of the RMB-denominated FDI under the capital account, allowing Chinese enterprises to raise RMB70bn bonds in the overseas market and allowing foreign capital to make, at most, RMB50bn in investments in the Chinese mainland. In June 2012, the Chinese government announced that it would encourage the country's domestic and foreign enterprises to make mutual investment in the RMB, in order to allow foreign enterprises to go public and issue RMB-denominated bonds in the Chinese Mainland and to enable the direct convertibility between the RMB and the Japanese yen. The road to the RMB's full convertibility is becoming increasingly clear as a result of the government's actions: the first priority is to achieve the RMB's convertibility under the capital account and only then achieve the RMB's full and total convertibility. There is evidence to show that as events unfold, the timetable for convertibility will become more predicable, thus paving the way for the RMB's further application.

The International Application of the RMB Further Facilitates Intra-regional Cooperation Among East Asian Economies

Within the past 3 years, the RMB's cross-border trade application was initiated and now accounts for roughly 29% of China's total export and import volume. In June 2012, the Society for Worldwide Interbank Financial Telecommunication (SWIFT) announced that the RMB had become the world's third largest currency used for issuing credit, gaining a 4% market share. If we extrapolate from this trend, the estimated market share will reach approximately 30% within 5 years. At that point, the RMB will become the third largest trading currency, behind only the US dollar and the euro. The abovementioned prospect is quite promising, but it's worth noting that it applies only to the bilateral application of the RMB. The RMB's internationalization should ideally involve a third party in order to achieve multilateral applicability. Currently, the RMB's application in East Asia is optimistically predictive of the transformation from bilateral application to multilateral application.

The economy and financial situations of many East Asian countries were significantly impacted and damaged by the 1997 Asian financial crisis. In terms of preparing for a crisis, the financing structure of companies and banks in this region is unseasonable. In the short run, there are too many US dollar-denominated foreign debts with relatively few corresponding long-term bonds or equity financing. These countries leverage short-term debt financing to facilitate long-term investment projects, thus generating an inevitable maturity mismatch. In addition, most creditors are foreign investors. If they withdraw funds necessary for meeting the requirements for liquidity, under circumstances in which the domestic currency is fully convertible, the foreign exchange will depreciate, generating currency mismatch. In the face of macroeconomic change, these two mismatches will mutually reinforce each other without addressing corresponding risks, a situation that will easily trigger financial crisis and economic recession. In further analyses of the Asian financial crisis, one fact has been highlighted about the maturity and currency mismatch: East Asia lacks a regional financial market in which domestic currencies can be applied toward valuation and payment. This market needs to attract foreign investors in order to raise funds; however, foreign investors do not have much faith in domestic currencies and prefer to apply the US dollar in valuation. In addition, since foreign investors do not understand or have long-term confidence in local development, they tend only to lend short-term funds, fostering the conditions leading to the original sin of a country being unable to support domestic currency-denominated lending to foreign countries. Small countries' currencies are inherently vulnerable, no matter which foreign exchange policy has been adopted, if the small country in question is financially open and has an independent domestic currency. In other words, floating the exchange rate or accumulating foreign exchange reserves cannot help developing countries to prevent speculation attacks. Monetary and financial cooperation among regional members may instigate the process of applying domestic currencies, but the only real solution is to develop a common financial market.

In order to mitigate the effects of the financial crisis on the region's economies and finances, on May 6, 2000, the finance ministers of ten ASEAN countries, China, Japan, and South Korea reached a consensus on fiscal and financial cooperation in East Asia, particularly on the establishment of a "bilateral currency swap mechanism," namely, the "Chiang Mai Initiative." Under this mechanism, in instances in which Asia's short-term capital shifts rapidly, countries will provide mutual intervention funds, exchange information on the economy and foreign exchange, establish a supervisory institution for preventing monetary crises, and establish a standby fund. The establishment of the "Chiang Mai Initiative" has created a new path for monetary cooperation in this region, enabling each country's central bank to be able to use the foreign exchange reserves of this region's other countries without the need to seek more difficult external assistance, thereby enhancing the region's capacity for dealing with financial crises and laying a foundation for regional economic cooperation. The basis of the swap mechanism at first was the US dollar. Since December 2008, however, when China and South Korea signed the first currency swap agreement, the basis of the "Chiang Mai Initiative" began to shift from the US dollar to domestic currencies, thus creating conditions for the official recognition of the RMB. As of May 2012, China has signed bilateral currency swap agreements with 17 countries and regions, totaling RMB1.58tn, of which 75.4% is with East Asia. Excepting the quota with Hong Kong, the remaining quota is still as high as 50.2%.

In signing the agreement for a currency swap, both parties' central banks were committed to acquiring the other party's currency at an agreed-upon price so as to meet the country's needs for foreign currencies. The currency swap, as a guarantee for trade settlement and the movement of capital, consolidates the confidence of one party in using the other party's currency, and thus creates a channel for the RMB to enter into the list of foreign exchange reserves. So far, 13 countries have explicitly announced their intention to include the RMB in their basket of foreign exchange reserve currencies. Most countries doing so—such as Japan, South Korea, Thailand, the Philippines, and Cambodia—are in East Asia. In this sense, the RMB's internationalization is a significant illustration of the currencies' domestic inclination in East Asia.

As the currency swap goes forward, the prospect of establishing a centralized financial market in East Asia has been given a date. In August 2003, ASEAN "10 + 3"'s finance ministers and central bank governors proposed an initiative to "develop an Asian bond market." Subsequently, the Asian Bond Fund was established, which was expected to encourage the government or governmental institutions to issue bonds and to then encourage large companies to issue bonds and, further, to encourage small- and medium-sized companies to enter into the bond market. The significance of establishing the Asian bond market lies in improving the maturity mismatch of Asian companies and that of financial institutions with the expectation of eliminating the effects of the reversal of capital flow between developing and developed countries. Specifically, East Asia as a region has significantly high savings, most of which flows outwards to foreign countries, most notably, the European and American financial markets. In turn, European and American countries leverage the low-cost capital in order to invest in East Asia. In other words, most East Asian countries are developing countries that require investment *a priori*. Their local savings, however, tend to flow to foreign countries with the expectation that local savings will be applied in domestic investment. The Asian bond market, especially the Asian Bond Fund, has developed rapidly since its establishment. Yet, this region still lacks a common regional currency, which has created numerous problems. In order to properly address these obstacles, in 2006, the Asian Development Bank launched a common foreign exchange indicator for the Asian-Pacific region, namely, the Asia Currency Unit (ACU). The ACU is only an indicator for reference. Unlike the euro, the ACU is not a currency for Asia. There is no one circulated currency in East Asia for trade settlement and financial assets pricing, despite the fact that China is now the world's second largest economy and the largest trading entity with a positive trend of economic development and, for this reason, the RMB has a stable currency value. In addition, since the RMB has initiated its process of international application, the RMB is likely to become the future pricing and settlement tool for the Asian financial market as a whole, as well as the first general currency used in the Asian bond market. Hong Kong, with its mature financial infrastructure and the development of the offshore RMB market, has become the preferred market for application of RMB-denominated instruments, made all the more attractive by the fact that it is already an international financial center.

It seems reasonable to predict that as the monetary and financial cooperation among East Asian countries accelerates, so too will regional economic cooperation. In 2010, China established a free trade zone with ten ASEAN countries. This zone covers a population of 1.9bn and is the largest free trade zone in the world. At the same time, the development of the China-Japan-South Korea Free Trade Zone continues apace. The establishment of such a free trade zone reduces the cost of circulating goods and services among member states and creates a larger market, which is beneficial for the circulation and optimal allocation of production factors. As a result, greater requirements for regional financial and monetary cooperation have been raised.

In 2009, in order to cope with the global financial crisis and to adapt to the new trend of regional economic cooperation, East Asian countries (including aforementioned ten ASEAN countries, China, Japan, and South Korea) began to integrate the development of the Asian bond market and that of the common Foreign Exchange Reserves Fund, a move that was based on the so-called "Chiang Mai Initiative." In May 2012, the scale of the common Foreign Exchange Reserves Fund was expanded to USD240bn, and the kernel of the developing East Asian monetary system began to form. Under this framework, the RMB's international application is likely to gradually change from a bilateral issue to a multilateral one. Due to the unique advantages of the RMB in this region, the RMB will play an important role in regional economic integration and regional monetary integration. In this sense, the internationalization of the RMB is now changing the traditional economic pattern and shaping a new pattern of economic cooperation for East Asia.

Chapter 1
Monetary Systems and the International Monetary System: Evolution and Reform

The drastic changes in the international monetary system over the past 100 or so years present a history filled with turbulence and breathtaking excitement. The United Kingdom's pound sterling was the primary reserve currency for much of the world in the 19th century. WWI then destroyed the pound sterling-centered international monetary system, replacing it with one dominated instead by the US dollar. Later, the old political and economic configuration in the world was completely shattered by WWII, over the course of which, the United States, thanks to its overall national prowess, prevailed over the increasingly war-torn United Kingdom, as the two countries vied for monetary supremacy. As a result, the Bretton Woods agreement was reached in 1944, marking the beginning of a new era in which the US dollar reigned supreme. By the late 20th century, two thirds of the world's total foreign exchange reserves were in US dollars. With the rise of the euro since the start of the 21st century, however, the dominance of the US dollar has been waning. In just a decade, the euro has made significant inroads into the world's traditional US dollar territory. As the competition between the US dollar and the euro countries to intensify, an unprecedented financial crisis has swept the globe, dealing a serious blow to the US dollar, the euro and other forms of currency. When the sovereign debt crisis and the economic and financial depression cast a cloud over Europe, the renminbi, or RMB (Chinese yuan), with its well-deserved reputation and stable value, became increasingly attractive to countries around the world, especially those in Asia. The use of RMB in cross-border trading officially began on July 2, 2009, and has grown rapidly since. The internationalization of the RMB has now become a hot topic around the world. Furthermore, the RMB's growing clout will likely bring new development opportunities to the international monetary system.

© Social Sciences Academic Press and Springer Nature Singapore Pte Ltd. 2018
Y. Cao, *Strategies for Internationalizing the Renminbi*, Research Series on the Chinese Dream and China's Development Path,
https://doi.org/10.1007/978-981-13-0800-0_1

1.1 Money and the Monetary System: Evolution

A traditional theory believes that money has five primary functions, namely: as a common measure of value, a medium of exchange, a storage of value, a standard for deferred payment, and as a world currency (a term referring to a currency that circulates internationally). Historically, money—which has existed as a form of currency for several thousand years—developed as a result of and evolved in the wake of the commodity economy's birth and development.

The legal structure and organization regulating the circulation of currency within a given country is what is referred to by the term "monetary system." Generally speaking, a monetary system consists of four essential factors: those materials used in the production of currency, the unit of currency, the process of currency issuance and circulation, and the system of reserve requirements. Throughout the evolution of monetary systems, two types of currency systems have followed in succession, namely, metallist monetary systems and fiat monetary systems. The silver standard, bimetallism, and the gold standard (including the gold specie standard, gold bullion standard, and gold exchange standard) are typical examples of metallist monetary systems.

The earliest known monetary system—and the one with the longest duration of use—is the silver standard. In this monetary system, coinage was produced in silver, which was taken as the base economic unit. Since silver had a large reserve and was easily smelted, the silver standard, in the past, met the needs of underdeveloped commodity economies. With the development of capitalist economies, however, commodity trading in both urban and rural areas grew exponentially and, later, along with widespread industrialization and the emergence of wholesale business, the silver standard became less reliable.

The silver standard's biggest drawback was its trend towards depreciation, an inevitable result of the mass production that grew out of the combination of plentiful reserves and rapidly-developing mining technologies. Using currencies made of silver-like metals is inconvenient because only metals with stable value retain an unchanging utility in the marketplace. In businesses operating on a large scale, traders had to carry a large amount of silver to make payments. This was neither safe nor convenient, however, in situations where both the transportation and credit system were underdeveloped. As the commodity economy developed further, demand grew for an easily portable currency with a higher and more stable value, in response to which, some countries started to use gold as the standard currency material. In the early 20th century, only a few countries—such as China, India, and Mexico—insisted on the silver standard, while major capitalist counties had already abandoned this monetary system.

With the development of a commodity money system, there was an increased demand for both gold and silver in trading commodities. Silver was primarily used by businesses with significant gross assets while gold was used for large-scale businesses, thus creating a layout wherein both silver and gold were circulated concurrently as standard currencies. Such circumstances constituted the objective requirement for establishing a bimetallic standard. In the early 16th century, in the wake of the discovery of the New World, rich silver deposits were mined in Mexico and Peru while gold was discovered in Brazil. Large amounts of both gold and silver flowed from America to Europe, enabling the establishment of a bimetallic standard amongst European countries. Such a bimetallic standard stipulated that both gold and silver could be used as materials for minting standard money, could be exported and imported without restrictions, could be simultaneously circulated, could enjoy free coinage, and had unlimited liquidity.

Bimetallism, however, is an unstable monetary standard. Since gold and silver are drawn from different reserves and have historically been exploited using different types of exploratory and mining technologies, money made of different materials naturally resulted in different values, resulting in an unfixed exchange ratio between gold and silver. This situation not only hindered economic development, but also caused the monetary systems using it to suffer de facto setbacks. In order to ensure the stability of the monetary system and to better facilitate the country's economic development, the United Kingdom took the lead in establishing a firm, unitary gold standard. At that time, the UK possessed strong economic power on the global scale and enjoyed the resultant advantage in international trade, thus necessitating a stable currency of high value for circulation. In 1816, an act was promulgated by the UK with the intent of adopting the gold standard. Following this act, other European countries—including Germany, France, and Belgium—also replaced their original bimetallic systems with the gold standard. In 1897, Russia and Japan proclaimed a new policy of using the gold standard. In 1900, the US declared that gold was the only metal to be used for minting standard money. At this point, nearly all capitalist countries had completely replaced the original bimetallic standard with the gold standard.

Once the gold standard was able to overcome the shortcomings of the silver standard and the bimetallic standard, it became a relatively stable monetary system and provided a satisfactory environment for economic development. During the more than 100 years during which Western countries adopted the gold standard, their economies enjoyed rapid development. To begin with, a stable currency value ensured the expansion of commodity circulation; assisted merchants in calculating cost, price, and profit while also boosting production; second, a stable currency value maintained the contractual relationship between the creditor and the debtor, further promoting the credit system's development; third, the relatively stable exchange ratio was amenable to the progression of international trade and export of capital, thus stabilizing international economic relationships.

As the economy developed further, however, the contradiction between the limited quantity of gold reserves/output and the expanding commodity production and circulation scale became increasingly acute. On the one hand, further economic development required a larger supply of metallic money, but on the other hand, the available money supply was restricted by the growth of gold output. To cushion the blow of frequent economic deflations, people figured out that deferred payment could be made available for trading commodities if a credit relationship were developed. For instance, sales could be made on credit without the need to deliver goods at the point when the buyer made a timely payment. Such a consideration laid the foundation for the birth of tokens, which were initially made of precious metals below par value, and which were then replaced by paper money. Such is the birth of the banknote. The banknote was a type of promissory note issued by banks and secured by their stock of precious metals. Precious metals functioned as the reserve fund for banknotes. Banks sought to ensure that they could always pay customers in precious metals when those clients presented banknotes for payment. Since the circulation of banknotes was usually larger than that of the reserve fund, the reserve fund system is more properly identified as a partial reserve system. The value of a banknote was determined by both the type of banknote and the type of precious metal backing it.

In the 20th century, as the commodity economy expanded, the contradiction resulting from the limited gold reserves and output became more obvious. Together with the limited gold supply and the unequal distribution of gold among countries, banknotes in many countries could not be absolutely redeemed for the gold they were meant to represent. In order to meet the needs of the gold standard for the storage of the metal itself, many countries set trade restrictions for the export of gold and started to issue banknotes which had value only by fiat. The outbreak of WWI caused many banks to essentially abandon the gold standard, citing the conflict as an excuse. After the end of the war, only the US returned to the gold standard, while other countries started to adopt a modified gold standard that did not rely on the actual circulation of gold—namely, the gold bullion standard. This modified system abandoned the original premise that gold coins could be minted and circulated freely. In this system, banknotes could fully replace gold coins in circulation. Although banknotes were still partially backed by gold reserves and the convertibility of banknotes into gold was still recognized, the government set a high threshold for converting banknotes into gold bullion.

The contradiction between the shortage of gold and the development of the commodity economy was temporarily relieved by the gold bullion standard, due to the fact that such a system limited the usage of gold and lowered the requirement for the gold supply when issuing banknotes. The fundamental contradiction remained, however. Therefore, the gold exchange standard was born. Under this monetary system, a country's currency could not be directly converted into gold, but rather, was converted into bills of exchange drawn on a foreign country whose currency was itself convertible into gold. A nation using the gold exchange standard would be able to guarantee a fixed exchange rate with the currency of another country that also used a gold standard, and would thereby keep a large amount of foreign exchange for sale at any time. A nation using the gold exchange standard, in terms of foreign trade and fiscal and financial work, would of course be controlled by the country which adopted the gold standard. Therefore, the gold exchange standard, by its very nature, was a dependent monetary system that was usually adopted by colonies and satellite states. Before WWI, colonies like India and the Philippines once applied this system to their own economies. After the end of WWI, other countries—including Germany, Italy, Austria, China, and Poland—followed in the rush to engage in this system.

Both the gold bullion standard and the gold exchange standard, however, were far less stable than the gold standard. On the one hand, the value of banknotes often fluctuated due to insufficient gold supply; serious inflation might be caused by currency devaluation. On the other hand, banknotes' looser connection to gold not only conserved its usage, but also generated the possibility that the issuance of banknotes might rid restrictions on the gold supply. As a result, the government could freely adjust the issuance of banknotes without accompanying restrictions imposed by natural resources, thus ensuring that the needs of economic development were met. These steps laid a foundation for a system of issuing banknotes without backing from precious metals. After the Great Depression, for various reasons, many countries started to compulsorily issue "fiat currency" without any physical link to precious metals. Such monetary systems were called fiat systems.

From the perspective of finance, a fiat system, by nature, is a credit-based monetary system, in which a country's central bank or designated monetary authority declares the national fiat currency—namely, paper money—to be legal tender. The fiat money in circulation mainly consists of cash and deposits, with the money being injected into circulation through the business of financial institutions. A country's central bank or designated monetary authority, playing the role of the central bank and ultimate lender, regulates and controls commercial banks through monetary policies. Fiat money is compulsorily issued by a country's government. The money itself is not connected to and cannot be redeemed for precious metals. The foundation of fiat money's issuance is a nation's credit. Usually, monetary issuance is implemented by a nation's central bank and the application depends on a given nation's laws and regulations. Fiat money has unlimited liquidity within the country.

The birth of the fiat system was not only caused by fiat money's physical attributes (fiat money possessed low material value, was more portable than other forms of currency, and could be used on a large scale), but also by the new contradiction brought about by the wide usage of banknotes. Before the introduction of a fiat system, banknotes issued by different banks had different values, due to the banks' disparities in the storage of precious metals. Therefore, once the banks faced difficulties in paying precious metals to customers, inter-bank borrowing became necessary. If the condition arose that many banks had the concurrent need for inter-bank borrowing, however, a serious shortage of liquidity in the market and bankruptcy was risked. To avoid this, the central bank emerged. As the ultimate lender, a nation's central bank would provide the final liquidity for banks, which stabilized the financial system. After the establishment of the central bank, liquidity was no longer based on precious metals—a system that paved the way for the modern credit-based monetary system.

The basis of the fiat system is credit. Borrowing and lending behaviors make up the primary manifestation of credit, which is defined as the delivery of value from one party to another with the necessity of the borrower repaying the principal and interest. To clarify the process of repayment: the owner of a currency or commodity lends his/her currency or commodity to the borrower with an agreed-upon date of repayment and interest. When the agreement comes due, the borrower is obligated to pay back the principal and interest. The essential feature of credit is the necessity of repayment, which distinguishes credit from other formats of monetary movement and is the common feature of credit in all its social forms. Modern credit can be divided and classified as commercial credit, bank credit, national credit, consumer credit, etc. In the modern credit system, the credit of commercial banks has played the most dominant role.

Alongside the development of commercial banks, the bank of banks—central banks—emerged. Both a government authority and a special financial institution, central banks formulate and carry out monetary and financial policies, as well as oversee the financial market on behalf of the nation. *The functions of the central bank are different from those of commercial banks. To begin with, a* central bank is a bank for issuing currency. A central bank possesses a monopoly on the issuance of banknotes (currency) and becomes a country's only agency for issuing currency. Secondly, a central bank functions as the bank of banks. A central bank only has fund transfers with commercial banks and other financial institutions and does not have a direct credit relationship with companies and individuals. Based on this specific relationship, the central bank plays the role of the ultimate lender, thereby stabilizing the financial system. Thirdly, a central bank is the national bank. A central bank formulates and carries out monetary and financial policies on behalf of the nation, managing the nation's fiscal revenue and expenditures, and offers the nation various financial services.

Until the development of a central banking system, the modern monetary system has generally functioned as a fiat system based on credit, which is marked by fiat money (paper money) that cannot be converted into precious metals and is compulsorily issued by the modern financial system—consisting of a central bank, commercial banks, and other non-banking financial institutions—and backed by the security of the nation's credit and implemented by the central bank.

1.2 The International Monetary System: Formation and Evolution

International trade began when production and the exchange of commodities evolved and expanded across a wider geographical area and administrative boundaries. To facilitate international trade, a world currency was required for valuation, settlement, and payment. In cases when the adoption of a unified currency was not yet viable, sets of unified rules were drafted for the exchange of currencies, thus forming an international monetary system. In this sense, an international monetary system is a general term for the rules and institutions established by the world's major trading nations for the purpose of adapting to a world with increasingly frequent economic activities and in order to facilitate currency exchange, exchange-rate regimes, balance of payments adjustments, reserve assets supply, and other economic activities based on common interests and in line with a certain standard or a globally-recognized agreement.

Three important issues will be touched upon in analyzing any international monetary system: first and foremost, the currency standard (which includes information about the selection and supply of an anchor currency or reserve assets); second, the exchange-rate regime (including a currency's relation to other currencies and the underlying arrangements); third, the balance of payments adjustment (which refers to the method of regulating the balance of payment surpluses and deficits). In the same vein, a sound international monetary system should meet three requirements: first, it must have a mechanism for correcting disequilibrium in the balance of payments; second, it must have a mechanism for supplying global reserve currencies, with which the supply will increase within a controllable range as the world's production and trade grows; third, a reserve currency can be qualified to be a standard currency only when it has solid economic fundamentals, thereby ensuring the relative stability of the monetary system itself.

1.2.1 An International Monetary System with Precious Metals as the Standard Foundation

The Industrial Revolution saw the birth of a typical international monetary system, as well as the great development of global economy and trade. The years between 1870 and 1971 represented an era when precious metals served as the standards for international monetary systems. To break the era down into periods, there was the period of the classical gold standard (1870–1914), a period of the gold standard's short recovery (1915–1935), a transitional period from the gold standard to the dollar standard (1936–1945), and a period during which the dollar standard was established (1946–1971).

The world largely adopted a typical gold standard as part of an international monetary system in the period between 1870 and 1914, which is often named by economic historians as the gold standard's "Golden Age". Under the gold standard, if a country faced a balance of payment deficit, gold would be exported as an ultimate solution to disequilibrium; in turn, if a country faced a balance of payments surplus, gold would be imported. Using gold as the payment solution, the global community did not need to worry about any balance of payments surpluses or deficits. In addition, due to the existence of gold export mechanisms, the exchange rate could be stabilized and its range of fluctuation made dependent upon the costs of transporting and safekeeping of gold. A stable exchange-rate regime further facilitated the valuation and settlement of international trade and investment, freeing participants from worries and further boosting the global economy. The adoption of the gold standard (under which gold could be exported and imported freely and goods and capitals could be exported with fewer restrictions) was one of the factors that enabled free trade at that time. If we look into a country's current account deficit/surplus as a percentage of GDP, the average percentage made up of major exporters during the period between 1870 and 1914 was 3.3%. Britain was a major capital exporter at that time, with capital exports accounting for 5% of its GDP, sometimes reaching up to 7–9%. Even now, this is still a considerable figure.

In taking a broader historical perspective, however, the earliest seeds of the gold standard's decline can be seen to have been planted even in its "Golden Age." Some countries—like China—had significant, lasting, and constantly-worsening account deficits even while being offset by capital inflows. In other words, the huge global capital flows covered up the balance of payments disequilibrium. During that time, triggered by difficulties in timely payment and insolvency, financial crises became increasingly frequent. Many countries, such as Brazil and Canada, suffered greatly from debt defaults and banking crises; what's more, Britain, key to global currency circulation, could no longer guarantee a fixed exchange rate of the pound sterling to gold. Sooner or later, the world's holding of a large amount of pounds sterling would pose a serious threat to the cornerstone of the gold standard. When WWI broke out in 1914, the latent inner contradictions of the gold standard surfaced. For the purpose of financing the war, many European countries announced the abandonment of the gold standard.

Yet between 1915 and1935, many countries attempted to recover the gold standard. For example, during WWI, while the majority of European countries abandoned the gold standard, the United States kept it. During the period between 1914 and1917, when the United States remained neutral, those countries engaged in the war exported gold to offset their trade deficits. The external demand for munitions, ships, and foodstuffs accelerated the development of American manufacturing, and as a result, from 1915 on, the United States economy began to expand rapidly. Consequently, by the end of 1919, the United States had shifted from a debtor nation with USD3.7 bn dollars in net debts to a creditor nation with USD3.7 bn net creditor's rights. At the same time, the United States also became a net capital exporter and a net gold importer.

Countries began to rebuild the gold standard at an international scale upon the completion of WWI. In 1924, in order to curb post-war hyperinflation, Germany took the lead among major countries in setting up a gold-backed monetary system. Britain, in order to rebuild London's pre-war status as an international financial center and to protect the interests of pound sterling-denominated bonds, in 1925 recovered the gold parity of the pound sterling at an overrated price. It should be noted, however, that the gold standard of this period no longer resembled the classical model but was, rather, a gold bullion standard or a gold exchange standard. The gold bullion standard is a system in which gold coins do not circulate and fiat currency of a small amount cannot be converted into gold. Instead, only large banknotes can be converted into gold bullion. The gold exchange standard is a system in which both fiat money and banknotes cannot be converted to gold inside the country. The country's government guarantees a fixed exchange rate to the currency of another country that also adopts a gold standard (notably the US dollar), however, thus linking its currency indirectly to gold.

At this point, both the gold bullion standard and the gold exchange standard had nearly come to an end. A worldwide economic crisis between 1929 and1933 followed their collapse. Germany deferred the country's debt repayment in 1931 and announced a total termination of the debt repayment in 1932; in 1931, Bolivia announced its inability to repay its international debt, with other Latin American countries following; in September 1931, France and the Netherlands started a run on the pound sterling, forcing Britain to abandon the gold standard. Another run was spearheaded by the United States during which over 50% of banks declared bankruptcy and large amounts of gold flowed out of the country. Due to the persistent economic depression of the United States, the US government was unable to stop the persistent outflow of gold even by raising the interest rate. Countries such as France dumped the US dollar and initiated a run on gold. On March 6, 1933, then-US President Franklin D. Roosevelt issued a proclamation ordering the suspension of all transfer of gold and foreign exchange—namely, the bank holiday —and initiated the "confiscation" of gold. Subsequently, on February 1, 1934, the US dollar experienced a sharp depreciation at the same time that the gold price per ounce increased from USD20.67–USD35. The depreciation of the US dollar facilitated the ability of the United States to engage in export, thus enabling the inflow of gold and the outflow of the US dollar. In addition, people, notably European Jewish banking communities, based on their anticipation of potential war in Europe, transferred a large amount of capital to the United States. The capital which flowed out from European countries such as Britain and France further reinforced the gold purchase plan of the United States. The significant influx of gold into the US stabilized its failing gold standard. As a result, the US became the only country still utilizing such a system, which, in turn, paved the way for the evolution of the international monetary system to become a US dollar-centric gold exchange standard.

The period between 1936 and 1944 saw a transition within the international monetary system from a semi-gold standard to a US dollar standard. At the end of the 1930s, many countries were forced to abandon the gold standard while the United States maintained it. At that time, the US dollar could be freely converted to gold at a stable rate of exchange with minimal fluctuations. It required the US to peg the dollar to gold and other countries to peg their currencies to the US dollar. From August 1939 on, Britain and its allies started to purchase war supplies from the US with a resultant influx of gold into the States. Meanwhile, the US government issued the Lend-Lease Act to grant loans to the Allied Powers. At the conclusion of WWII, the total loans granted by the US reached USD50 bn. Consequently, Britain and other countries became debtors of the United States. In order to get a loan from the US, Britain had to abandon its Imperial Preference and open its market to the United States. As a result, other than gold itself, the US dollar became the only global currency, thus laying a foundation for the US dollar standard.

The US dollar standard was established and further developed in the period between 1945 and 1970. In 1945, the GDP of the United States represented 40% of the global economy and the United States owned 59% of the world's gold reserves. As the gold reserves held by the United States increased to 72% of total global reserves in 1948, the international status of the US economy peaked. The US dollar became increasingly prominent and its status was further consolidated. As a result, the Bretton Woods Conference was held in order to establish a framework for the post-WWII international monetary system, which has historically been known as the "Bretton Woods system." The underlying feature of the Bretton Woods system can be summarized as follows: first, link the US dollar to gold at a price of USD35 per ounce; second, link all other currencies to the US dollar. A fixed exchange rate with the US dollar was thereafter adopted by all other countries. Since all other countries were bound to contribute to the fixed exchange rate between the US dollar and gold, they had the obligation to peg their currencies to the US dollar at a fixed exchange rate.

The Bretton Woods system can be seen as a US dollar standard system that developed out of the gold exchange standard. The gold exchange standard adopted a "many-to-many" relationship while the US dollar standard adopted a "one-to-many" relationship, under which, the US dollar was the only currency pegged to gold. This pattern is a result of the rise of the US economy and financial system after WWII.

The Bretton Woods system—an institutionalized system marked by the establishment of the World Bank and the International Monetary Fund (IMF)—was a result of the evolution and improvement of the US dollar standard in the years between 1936 and 1944. Compared to the rising economic and financial strength of the United States after WWII, other countries suffered from economic depression and reported a financial deficit. Together with the imbalanced allocation of gold among countries, the US spent less than USD3 bn to hold 27% of IMF quotas and 33% of World Bank quotas, enough on its own to veto all changes. Consequently, the US dollar-centric international monetary system not only symbolized the fact that the US dollar was a global currency, but also indicated that the United States possessed the means by which to establish international economic and financial order.

The Bretton Woods system featuring the US dollar standard brought an end to the economic crisis of the 1930s, terminated the disorder of the gold standard system, stabilized the global economic and financial system, and became an important factor in guaranteeing the prosperity of the global economy after WWII. But an inner contradiction, often recognized as the "Triffin Dilemma," lay hidden within the Bretton Woods system. If the United States maintained a balance of surplus payments, the US dollar supply for the international financial market would be insufficient, thereby impacting the smooth development of the global economy; if the US faced a persistent balance of deficit payments, the supply of the US dollar would be able to meet the world's climbing needs for payments and reserves, but would not be able to maintain a fixed exchange rate with gold, thereby lowering or even leading to the collapse of the world's confidence in the US dollar.

The establishment, development, and decline of the US dollar standard between 1945 and 1970, then, were rooted in the "Triffin Dilemma" of the Bretton Woods system. In the early post-war period, the United States, based on its rich gold reserves and the global availability of the US dollar, established the Bretton Woods system. At that time, the United States was a country with a significant trade surplus, providing the world with liquidity by exporting capital. During the first ten years of the Korean War (which broke out in 1950), the capital account of the

US reported an increasing deficit. In 1961, when the Vietnam War began, the capital account deficit of the United States increased. At the same time, the long-standing surplus registered in the current account of the United States also turned towards deficit. Triggered by the formation of both the capital account deficit and the current account deficit, the inner contradiction of the Bretton Woods system —the "Triffin Dilemma"—surfaced. People began to worry that the United States, under the burden of huge debts to other countries, might no longer be able to guarantee a fixed exchange rate between the US dollar and gold. In October 1960, there was a run on the US dollar, a great undersell of US dollar-denominated securities, and a rush on purchasing gold. The gold in the London market was priced at USD40 per ounce. In 1968, Europe held USD12.8 bn US dollar-backed currencies while the United States had only USD10 bn gold reserves. From that point on, the United States was unable to convert the US dollar to gold at an exchange rate of USD35 per ounce, a price stipulated by the Bretton Woods system. Though other countries still followed the requirements of the Bretton Woods system in order to keep selling their own currencies in exchange for the US dollar to be able to maintain a fixed exchange rate, the depreciation of the US dollar brought on by the country's worsening balance of payments was unavoidable. At the end of 1968, the United States abandoned the use of gold as a currency guarantee and, in 1971, officially announced that the US dollar would neither be pegged to nor maintain a fixed exchange rate with gold. From that point on, no international monetary system relied on a metallic currency standard.

1.2.2 The Fiat System

Since the collapse of the Bretton Woods system, the gold standard has been irreversibly disrupted and a pure fiat system featuring the US dollar followed. Till now, the fiat system has gone through a period of disorder (1971–1973), a period characterized by the Jamaica system (1973–1984), a period featuring the intervention by the US dollar (1985–1998), and a period characterized by the coexistence of currency unions and "in between" paradigms.

1971–1973 was a period of disorder for the fiat system. In 1971, the US had USD11 bn gold reserves but USD25 bn short-term debts. Since the US no longer had the capacity to fulfill the promise made in the Bretton Woods agreement, in August 1971, then-US President Richard Nixon announced that the gold window would be closed—a move that cancelled the direct convertibility of the US dollar to gold and adopted a floating exchange rate. Since foreign governments could no longer exchange their US dollars for gold, they (notably the developed countries) either continued to hold their existing US dollars or undersold them by bearing the cost brought by the US dollar's depreciation. Japan and Europe were in such a "dilemma," and requested an international monetary negotiation, namely, the "Smithsonian Negotiation." On the first day of the Smithsonian Negotiation (held on November 17, 1971), the US requested that Japan and Germany appreciate their currencies (the Japanese yen and Deutschmark,) to the dollar by 19.2 and 6.9%, respectively, while the US itself pledged to depreciate the US dollar by 8.25%. After negotiations, Japan was allowed to appreciate the Japanese yen against the dollar by less than 17%. As a result, the Japanese yen appreciated by 16.9%.

Following negotiations, it was decided in 1971 that the US dollar should depreciate, following which, ten European countries were forced to rebuild a fixed exchange rate system using the US dollar—not gold—as the anchor, a system thereafter known as the "Smithsonian system."

The transition to the "Smithsonian system" from the "Bretton Woods system" was a choice made out of necessity, one which mirrored the decline in the economic and financial strength of the US. The country's strength was no longer able to support its position as a global hegemony; in fact, at this time, the role of the US was declining globally. In addition to its declining political power, the macro policy of the US was also changing substantially, prioritizing domestic economic policies above those aiming for a balance of payments. In order to boost the US economy, the government adopted an expansionary monetary policy which brought low interest rates and adopted a policy of "benign neglect" towards external deficit. As a result, the balance of payments in the first quarter of 1973 registered a negative balance of USD10.3 bn, total to the whole year of 1972 and around 50% of the gold reserves available at that time in the US. In 1973, the US government's total amount of debt totaled seven times that of the available gold reserves. From February 1973 on, the US dollar continued to depreciate at a fixed exchange rate of USD38 per ounce.

The depreciation of the 1971 US dollar to that of 1973 addressed the disequilibrium experienced since the 1960s and typified the negative balance of payments. Such a solution, however, was ultimately ineffective. As such, starting in 1974, the US canceled all restrictions on capital outflow while the Federal Reserve expanded the money supply, thus triggering the most rapid rise in inflation since the Civil War and the accelerated depreciation of the US dollar. Because of this, the conditions that made the international monetary system operative in the first place (i.e. the complicity of all countries involved with international monetary policy) became invalid and the US dollar was no longer able to maintain a credit relationship among currencies. Consequently, the "Smithsonian system" ended in failure and the fixed exchange rate system came to an end.

The years between 1973 and 1984 subsequently were characterized by what was known as the Jamaica system. Following the dissolution of the Smithsonian system and suffering greatly from economic instability, the global economy placed immense importance on the rapid rebuilding of an international monetary system. For this purpose, the Jamaica Agreement was reached in a meeting held in Kingston, Jamaica, in 1976. The distinctive achievement of the Jamaica Agreement and the corresponding Second Amendment to the IMF Articles of Agreement was the announcement that gold no longer remained central to the international monetary system. In other words, the world had entered into an age in which gold was demonetized, officially marking the end of the Bretton Woods system. In the wake of the demonetization of gold, the growth of world currencies, most notably that of the US dollar in the Jamaica system, lacked restrictions based on gold backing. Each country's monetary supply was wholly determined by its macro-economic policy. This ensured that the world had no one unified exchange rate regime, but rather, that all nations had freely-floating exchange rates. The balance of payments accordingly lacked an adjustment mechanism but was passively regulated through regular adjustments to the exchange rate. In essence, it was a US dollar-centric international monetary system of libertarianism. Because of its non-standardization, it was called "an unsystematic system."

A monetary system totally controlled by nations' macro-economic policies—but not restricted by gold—necessarily and unsurprisingly led to immense difficulties in global coordination and effectively rendered the Jamaica system inoperative. In fact, the operating effects of the Jamaica system were far from satisfying. The decade between 1975 and 1985 was one in which the US dollar, Japanese yen, and Deutschmark competed for inflation and fluctuated without coordination. Worldwide inflation and the outbreak of various regional financial crises were frequent. Besides the two well-known oil crises that occurred during this period, nearly all developing countries faced financial crises of various levels of severity. In October 1978, US dollar exchange rates against currencies in major western countries hit historic lows, giving rise to the instability of the major western monetary markets. In October 1979, the Federal Reserve announced an increase in the interest rate to fight against inflation. From 1980 and only ending in February 1985, the US dollar appreciated for five consecutive years. The appreciation of the US dollar temporarily eliminated international fears surrounding a potential crisis of the US dollar. It brought about worsening condition for the US current account in terms of the balance of payments, however, further threatening the smooth operation of the US dollar-centric Jamaica system.

The years between 1985 and 1998 were a period characterized by the intervention by the US dollar. From June 1984 to February 1985, the US dollar further appreciated by 20%, transforming itself into an "irrational speculative bubble." The US dollar's appreciation worsened the performance of the US current account in the balance of payments. To stabilize the nation's economy and to further make the US dollar-centric Jamaica system operative, the US forced other countries—primarily Germany and Japan—to appreciate their currencies as well. In September 1985, the Plaza Accord was signed, setting a target for the US dollar's depreciation to 10–20% within a short time. On the very day the Plaza Accord was announced, the US dollar declined by 4% against other major currencies based on a weighted average of prices. At the end of 1988, the US dollar dropped by 50%, respectively, against the Deutschmark and the Japanese yen.

The Plaza Accord had serious consequences for the international monetary system, most notably that the US only had the need to control its macro-economic policy but had no need to restrict its monetary policy or fiscal policy. Instead, the goal of depreciating the US dollar could be achieved by exerting political pressure on foreign countries with the goal of appreciating their currencies. By depending on the exchange-rate regime, the US was able to meet the goal of regulating the balance of payments, particularly the current account. The US abused the dollar's preponderant status and created a precedent for economic hegemony by saying that "the dollar is our currency, but it is your problem."

In order to legalize this precedent, seven Western countries—under pressure from the US itself—reached what became known as the Louvre Accord in February 1987, stating that the US dollar should "maintain a value around the current level" and agreeing that the US could use an interventionist mechanism in the pursuit of quantitative techniques to set constraints for the exchange rate of the US dollar: if the range was narrow (±2.5%), it must adopt a system of voluntary intervention; if the range was wide (±5%), it must adopt a compulsory global coordination policy. Under the tenants of the Louvre Accord, the US dollar did not face restrictions from either gold or international currencies. Instead, the US dollar's issuance and exchange rate depended almost entirely on the country's macro economy and relevant policies. In the 1980s, with a view towards the US economy's sluggishness, expansionary fiscal policy and monetary policy were adopted, causing or contributing to the depreciation of the US dollar. The international community worried about the US' trade deficit and the depreciation of the US dollar. These issues, together with other economic factors, triggered the country's stock market crash on October 19, 1987. As a result, the US dollar further depreciated.

The US dollar's status as the foremost global currency was endangered by its depreciation. In order to avoid any excessive volatility of the US dollar, the US adopted extensive preclinical interventions targeting the foreign exchange market, thereby boosting the US dollar. As a result, the US dollar appreciated from 1988 to 1989. The appreciation of the US dollar was conducive to the alleviation of inflation, to maintaining interest rates at a low level, and to increasing investment. At the beginning of the 1990s, the key to the macro-economic strategy as carried out by the Clinton Administration was to stabilize the expectation for a strong US dollar. A strong US dollar and investment were the two factors that contributed most directly to the growth of the US economy in the 1990s. No matter when the US dollar depreciated or appreciated, the US government always held an attitude of "benign neglect" towards the trade deficit, resulting in a worsening trade deficit.

Along with the growing deficit in the US current account and boosted increasing = US demands, emerging market economies began to adopt "export-oriented" economic models. This type of model was characterized by a greater investment in export industries in order to fuel economic growth, with one of the central features being the absorption of foreign capital. The maturity mismatch and currency mismatch of the debt portfolio resulted in a structural mismatch, further constituting one of the material reasons for the 1994 economic crisis in Mexico and the 1997 Asian financial crisis. Short-term capital flows represented by that of the US dollar became a central factor in the international financial turmoil. Throughout the 1990s, together with the strengthened US dollar, financial crises among the emerging market economies were commonplace.

The period from 1999 to present featured the coexistence of currency unions and "in between" paradigms. After the 1998 Asian financial crisis, the US continued to adopt the strong US dollar policy of the 1990s, further amplifying external disequilibrium. For their part, however, Southeast Asian countries took lessons from the previous crises and prioritized the task of accumulating foreign currencies. After these countries got rid of the pre-crisis deficit in their current accounts, their trade surplus increased rapidly. The US dollar, however, began depreciating starting in 2002. Together with speculative factors and the increasing global demand for energy and resources caused by the robust growth of the global economy between 2002 and 2007, oil and other bulk cargos reported skyrocketing prices. As a result of these concurrent factors, energy exporters accumulated ample foreign-exchange reserves. A global economic disequilibrium emerged and widened. To be very clear: the first indicator of economic disequilibrium was incurred by the US dollar. The deficits in both the capital account and the current account of the US were in line with the surplus of oil exporters. The trade deficit of the US was in line with the trade surplus of Asian countries. Second of all, the Euro zone registered overall general equilibrium with an internal disequilibrium. The surplus of Germany was in line with the trade deficit experienced by Italy, Spain, and other countries in southern Europe.

The global economy disequilibrium represented by the balance of payments disequilibrium highlighted the fact that the stability of an international monetary system without any attendant gold restrictions rested with that of an "anchor currency." Impacted by globally irresponsible US monetary policies, the "anchored dollar" was unstable, thus damaging the stability of the system as a whole. Under such circumstances, the balance of payments could not be adjusted by simply regulating the exchange rate. Therefore, the issue of a complete reformation of the international monetary system and its operating mechanisms was raised.

1.3 Dilemma Facing the International Monetary System and a Request for Reform

The global financial crisis in 2008 exposed the inner contradiction inherent in the current international monetary system in a comprehensive and systematic way. This crisis occurred in the US—the center of the international monetary system. Due to the crisis of the anchored dollar, the whole system experienced upheaval. As a result, subprime mortgages, themselves an insignificant financial product, led to a much more serious global crisis. People began to carefully review the dilemma of the current international monetary system and the necessity of reform became increasingly urgent.

As described above, the underlying features of the US dollar-centric Bretton Woods system are: first, the US dollar was linked to gold at a fixed rate of USD35 per ounce of gold; second, all other currencies were defined in relation to the US dollar at a pegged exchange rate; the fluctuation range should be within 1%, meaning that all nations' monetary authorities had the responsibility for intervening in the foreign exchange market so as to stabilize their own currencies' exchange rates to the US dollar, further maintaining the US dollar's official price per ounce of gold. Without a "radical disequilibrium in the balance of payments," monetary authorities were not to allow any appreciation or depreciation of their currencies; hence, one can see that the US dollar-centric Bretton Woods system was, in essence, a variant of the gold exchange standard system that became a worldwide "fixed exchange rate regime."

Superficially, the Bretton Woods system was historically similar to the gold exchange standard, but upon further comparison, differences became more obvious. First and foremost, under the gold exchange standard, the pound sterling, the US dollar, and the French franc each constituted world currencies and each had a sphere of influence, while under the Bretton Woods system, the US dollar was the only world currency. Secondly, under the gold exchange standard, citizens could directly convert the pound sterling, the US dollar, or the French franc to gold from their monetary authorities, and, furthermore, the currencies were pegged to gold inside their respective countries; however, under the Bretton Woods system, the US government only allowed other countries' monetary authorities to redeem their US dollar to gold by meeting certain criteria, thus turning the Bretton Woods system into a de facto gold exchange standard with severe limitations on freedom of exchange. Third, the gold exchange standard could safeguard a fixed exchange-rate regime because major currencies could be converted to gold freely, and, what's more, more than one currency could be redeemed for gold. Under the Bretton Woods system, however, the exchange rate experienced inherent volatility due to the fact that the above two requirements could not be met; in order to facilitate international trade and economic interactions, the Bretton Woods system necessitated the adoption of an adjustable pegged exchange-rate regime. It was not only a forced choice, but also the seed for the future floating exchange rate.

Given the aforementioned information, under the Bretton Woods system, currencies were relatively priced against gold as the benchmark. Only the US dollar itself, however, could be directly converted to gold. Therefore, the US dollar was regarded as inextricable from the value of gold itself, and became the major foreign exchange reserve held by many countries. The US dollar's predominance over other currencies showed that the Bretton Woods system was, in essence, a US dollar standard system.

The US dollar standard was primarily demonstrated through two aspects: first, the US monetary authority was both the world's ultimate lender and was responsible for the smooth running of the international monetary system. The US was obligated to provide the world with US dollar currencies and to safeguard the liquidity of the international monetary system. Under such as system, the monetary policy of the US was the monetary policy of the world at large. The Federal Reserve of the US was de facto the central bank of the world, while the central banks of all other countries were just passive performers within US monetary policy. Secondly, the US monetary authority was the regulator of the global financial market. Since all other countries' currencies were pegged to the US dollar at fixed exchange rates, the global financial market was not likely to be volatile. When volatility occurred—since all countries' central banks had the obligation to keep stable exchange rates between their currencies and the US dollar—they had to make interventions by buying or selling their own currencies.

Under such a system, each country held a stable interest rate. Thus, based on a fixed exchange rate and a stable interest rate, risks could be anticipated. As a result, risk management instruments represented by financial derivatives almost lacked the scope for their abilities, leading to an inactive financial market. Since the market did not require innovation, the necessity of regulation was largely mitigated. If anything, it would only be to fine-tuned policies. Consequently, the US financial regulator was the actual policy maker for the regulation standards, and other countries' regulators only served as passive performers of those US policies in place for regulating the financial market.

The Bretton Woods system provided a stable interest rate and exchange rate mechanism that boosted the world economy and promoted the development of international trade. Meanwhile, however, the system's deeply-rooted "Triffin Dilemma" began to emerge. As previously mentioned, the prerequisite for the smooth operation of this system was the fact that the US should have a stable and sustaining deficit in its balance of payments. After WWII, Europe urgently required goods, materials, and money for the purpose of reconstructing its economy. In 1947, then-Secretary of State George Marshall announced an initiative to aid Europe. This initiative was called the "Marshall Plan," established with the goal that within four fiscal years, the US would give USD13 bn in aid to Europe in order to cover funding, techniques, equipment, etc. Besides accelerating the recovery of the European economy, this plan, by adjusting the balance of payments by notably sustaining the deficit in the US capital account, fulfilled the obligation of the US to create liquidity for the world economy and maintained a smooth running of the international monetary system. Yet in doing so, seeds had been planted for change and reform.

In the mid- to late 1950s, the US balance of payments turned from surplus to deficit. Entering into the 1960s, a deficit within the balance of payments was recorded not only in the US capital account, but also in its current account. In the wake of the deficit's increase, in 1966, the debts of the US (balance of payments deficit) exceeded its gold reserves for the first time. The US dollar was oversupplied. Many countries holding the US dollar began asking the US government to redeem their US dollars for gold. As the gold reserves of the US declined and the market turned anticipatorily pessimistic towards the US dollar, currencies' exchange rates against the US dollar became volatile.

In the 1960s, in order to stabilize the foreign exchange market and the gold price and to ensure the convertibility of both the US dollar and the fixed exchange-rate regime, the US requested that other countries cooperate under the framework of the International Monetary Fund (IMF). It, along with 14 other nations from Europe and Japan, signed the "Reciprocal Agreement" (March 1962) and set up both the "General Arrangements to Borrow" (November 1961) and the "Gold Pool" (October 1961) within the IMF. The "Reciprocal Agreement" was a currency swap agreement wherein both parties, for the purpose of stabilizing the exchange rate, agreed to use the other party's currency to intervene in the foreign exchange market within a stipulated term and for a specific amount. In the "General Arrangements to Borrow," G10 countries excepting the US lent a certain amount of capital to support the US dollar, with the US being the largest borrower. The "Gold Pool" was a fund co-built by eight nations' central banks. The US had the largest share in this fund, equal to 50%. Britain's central bank, on behalf of other countries, administered the "Gold Pool." When the price of gold went up, the London market sold gold; when the gold price went down, the London market bought gold. The "Gold Pool" used such an operating mechanism to regulate gold's supply demand within the market and further to stabilize gold's price.

The US' financial situation, however, changed radically as it became more involved in the Vietnam War. The deficit of its balance of payments kept expanding and crises surrounding the redemption of the US dollar for gold occurred frequently. What's more, the above-mentioned arrangements and mechanisms for stabilizing the ratio between the US dollar and gold were powerless to stop this economic change. Following such circumstances, in March 1968, the US announced the adoption of a "two-tiered price system for gold." The price of gold per ounce was USD35 in the official market. In private banks, however, the price of gold against the US dollar was determined by market demand and supply.

The running of a two-tiered price system for gold heralded the collapse of the "gold-US dollar" standard and dismissed the idea of using gold as a stable world currency. The shortage in gold reserves not only restricted the development of the world economy, but was also insufficient to meet the demands of all countries in regulating their balance of payments. In order to overcome the difficulties faced by the balance of payments, the concept of "Special Drawing Rights" (SDR) was created by the IMF in 1969. SDR, usually known as "paper gold," were a type of virtual money that could replace either the US dollar or gold, and, furthermore, can replace gold in terms of global reserve assets. IMF members can use SDR to replace the US dollar in order to settle the balance of payments. SDR and gold shared the same price per ounce of gold, namely, 35 SDR per ounce of gold.

Theoretically, the creation of SDR demonstrates that the international community had begun to recognize that an international monetary system based on a nation's sovereign currency was inherently unstable, and in response attempted to build a super-sovereign world fiat currency with the goal of eliminating this inherent deficiency and thoroughly resolving the "Triffin Dilemma." Practically speaking, however, the establishment of a super-sovereign world fiat currency required the consensus of the international community and the loss of, at least in part, the monetary sovereignty of all countries involved. In a real world constituted by nation-states and not just theoretical entities, however, such a solution faced innumerable obstacles. In response, one feasible choice was to diversify the world currencies. This option opens up broad prospects for and provides experience and lessons for internationalizing the Chinese yuan and other currencies.

In the 1970s, as the problem of the "Triffin Dilemma" deepened, the US' gold reserves could no longer support their increasingly heavy debts. In 1971, the Nixon administration unilaterally cancelled the direct convertibility of the US dollar to gold, ensuring that the US gave up its obligations within the existing system and throwing the international monetary order into turmoil. In January 1976, a meeting was held in Kingston (the capital of Jamaica) by the Interim Committee of the IMF. After a heated debate, the "Jamaica Agreement" was signed by all participating countries. At this point, the international monetary system entered into a period defined by the Jamaica system. The Jamaica system, on the one hand, inherited the legacy of the Bretton Woods system while also, on the other hand, reforming that very system.

In terms of changes and reformations, first and foremost, the floating exchange rate was recognized as the basis for determining the price of one currency against another. The Jamaica system recognized the co-existence of both the fixed exchange-rate regime and the floating exchange-rate regime and empowered member countries to freely choose between the two, thus officially confirming the legality of the floating exchange-rate regime.

Secondly, the system adopted diversified currencies. Each currency's exchange rate and extent of global application relied on each country's economic status and political power in the world, thus weakening the degree of dependence on a single core country and avoiding any further systematic risks triggered by that core country weakening.

Third, gold was demonetized. The system abolished gold's function as a world currency, deleted all gold-related clauses in the rules for the international monetary system, and distanced itself from gold's official price. Member states could trade gold freely at the market price, and gold no longer served as an acceptable currency for settling international trade. Instead, gold became merely a precious metal in which individuals are able to invest.

Fourth, great efforts were applied towards enhancing the status and function of Special Drawing Rights, expanding their application, and increasing their share.

Fifth, the Jamaica system further facilitated developing countries' financing. The IMF used the revenue gained from selling gold to set up a trust fund for the purpose of facilitating developing countries' financing, raising their available credit lines, and stepping up financing in order to compensate for export fluctuations.

The international community did not define a standard currency, a unified exchange-rate regime, or a unified balance of payments adjustment mechanism for the Jamaica system. In fact, the international monetary order as a whole was free from restrictions and only changed in the wake of reforms made to the international economic structure. For this reason, the Jamaica system was considered to be "an unsystematic system." Over a period of 35 years, this "unsystematic system" evolved to the point where it presented the following features:

First and foremost, it presented a multicurrency international monetary structure dominated by the US dollar. The Jamaica system demonetized gold, and, subsequently the global monetary standard as a whole thoroughly severed ties with the concept of its physical value. Gold declined among international reserves while SDR, as a new international reserve, expanded in applicability. The most important roles of world currencies, however, were filled by the fiat currencies of developed countries with significant economic strength. Besides the US dollar and following the economic resurgence of Western Europe and Japan, the pound sterling, what was formerly West Germany's Deutschmark and the Japanese yen all flowed into countries' foreign exchange reserves. The birth and subsequent widespread acceptance of the Euro in 2000 significantly shocked the position of the US dollar as the center in the system, diversifying other countries' foreign exchange reserves, yet the US dollar still held the principal position in this system. In 2008, upon the commencement of the global financial crisis, 64% of the foreign currency reserves held by countries were in US dollars and 50% of international trade was settled in US dollars. The US dollar was adopted by most countries as the benchmark (to varying degrees) of their exchange-rate regime arrangements. The current international monetary system, in nature, is also a de facto "US dollar standard system."

Secondly, diversified exchange-rate regimes have been adopted by those same countries displaying a center-periphery pattern. The Jamaica system did not impose any restrictions on member states' preexisting exchange rate arrangements. Each country can, based on its own status quo, select one exchange-rate regime, from those with a totally fixed exchange rate to a totally floating exchange rate. Subsequently, there was a trend of diversification in the arrangement of the international exchange-rate regime. According to the IMF's means of classification by degree of floating, there are seven types of exchange-rate regimes in the world: (1) exchange arrangements with no separate legal tender (e.g. the euro); (2) currency board arrangements (e.g. the Hong Kong dollar); (3) conventional fixed peg arrangements within margins of ±1%; (4) pegged exchange rates within horizontal bands (i.e. the value of the currency is maintained within certain fluctuating margins of more than ±1%); (5) crawling pegs (i.e. the currency is adjusted in response to changes in predictable indicators); (6) managed floating with no predetermined path for the exchange rate; (7) independently floating regimes. In further consideration of the corresponding monetary policy arrangements, the IMF offers 20 types of exchange-rate regimes. According to the standards described above, the IMF found that of all the types previously listed, independently floating (13%), managed floating (27%), conversional fixed peg arrangements (28%), and exchange arrangements with no separate legal tender (22%) are the most popular exchange-rate regimes among countries and regions. It can be seen from their distribution that countries whose domestic currency are capable of acting as world currencies are few and far between and all such countries have developed economies. In addition, as centers of the international monetary system, these countries adopt a floating exchange-rate regime and independently or jointly float their exchange rates according to their own interests. Since most developing countries are not the centers of the international monetary system and are thus considered to be economically peripheral, this, along with many other reasons, causes most of them adopt an exchange-rate regime wherein the domestic currency is pegged to one major currency (a move referred to as a basket of currencies). Under such circumstances, the countries' exchange rate arrangements present a center-periphery pattern.

Third, global and regional international coordination mechanisms coexist. Since only a few fiat currencies from developed countries can play the role of world currencies, the world's exchange rate arrangements present a center-periphery pattern. As a result, the international coordination mechanism is no longer a unified monolithic whole. Instead, various global and regional coordination mechanisms exist. There are global coordination mechanisms that have inherited the Bretton Woods system (e.g. the IMF) and regional coordination mechanisms (e.g. the Euro zone, Association of Caribbean States, UEMOA, and the eye-catching monetary cooperation in East Asia, represented by the Chiang Mai Initiative). What's more, there are a considerable number of bilateral coordination mechanisms (for instance, China has signed bilateral currency swap agreements with 31 countries and regions).

Fourth, the system for adjusting the balance of payments has various methods of implementation but remains imperfect. Under the Bretton Woods system, the adjustment of the balance of payments disequilibrium is mainly supported by loans granted through the IMF. The loans remain unapproved until the balance of payments faces severe disequilibrium, meaning that they only become effective after the fact. The par of exchange often has changed at the point in which loans kick in, however, meaning that the domestic currency has faced a substantial depreciation and a foreign exchange crisis has broken out. The IMF's adjustment mechanism is rigid, with poor efficiency, and is notorious for its belated actionability. Compared to the Bretton Woods system, in which the international community can only depend on bailout loans under a unified organization and is required to change the par of exchange, the Jamaica system offers rich alternatives. For instance, the international community is allowed to leverage the exchange-rate mechanism, interest rate mechanism, multilateral or bilateral international cooperation and policy coordination, financing from global financial markets, and other related instruments to enable a more flexible adjustment of the balance of payments disequilibrium.

On the one hand, such an adjustment is flexible; on the other hand, it lacks an overall systematic arrangement. The adjustment of the balance of payments relies more on the aspiration and effort of the country facing the disequilibrium, while the means of adjustment relies heavily on the change of the exchange rate. According to earlier international experience, to adjust the international balance of payments by relying entirely on changing the exchange rate of the country facing disequilibrium, the Marshall-Lerner condition should be met. In other words, a country's export and import demand elasticity must be greater than One. Conversely, adjusting the exchange rate will not only exert limited influence, but will also incur strikes brought about by international "hot money"—that is, US dollar-denominated short-term foreign debt—further consolidating the uncertainty of the balance of payments. At this point, the financing arranged by the international financial markets can only serve a mitigating function, but it cannot solve the root problem. The horrible Asian financial crisis teaches us this very lesson. In addition, the proposition put forward in the 2010 G20 Seoul Summit—that the surplus and deficit in the current account should not exceed 4% of the GDP—is an initiative based on the above economic fact. It signifies that the international community has begun to be aware of the limitation of depending on the exchange rate mechanism to adjust the balance of payments.

In essence, the very core of the Jamaica system is to demonetize gold, thus fostering an "unsystematic system." It is labeled as such because without gold as the core, a system cannot be established. Previously, no globally unified exchange rate arrangement existed; each country, most notably the countries with central currencies, went their own way and adopted numerous exchange-rate regimes, thereby producing volatile exchange rates and difficulties in coordination. When a fiat currency-based international monetary order took shape, the system turned towards the systematic. The smooth running and sustainable development of the international monetary system totally depends on the stability of fiat currencies while the latter rests with the macro-economic policies of the world currency countries, especially the stability of monetary policies.

The modern international monetary system presents a pluralistic pattern featuring a central the US dollar. The US dollar functions as the measure against which other currencies to adjust their exchange rates, and is also the de facto anchor currency. Under the Bretton Woods system, since the US dollar and gold had a fixed convertibility ratio, the anchor was stable. Under the Jamaica system, however, the stability of the anchor depends on the macro-economic policies of the US, especially on this country's monetary policies. This implies that the US monetary authority, without any restrictions from gold, ought to act prudently towards macro-economic management, taking responsible for the macro-economic stability of both the US and the world. But, regretfully, the US has shown itself either unwilling or incapable of behaving thusly.

Since the value of the US dollar was not pegged to gold, the US government faced no compulsory restrictions in drafting its monetary policies. The Federal Reserve had no obligations to maintain a certain convertibility ratio between the US dollar and gold, and additionally had no need to sustain the stability of the US dollar's exchange rates with other currencies. This was especially true following the September 11, 2001 terrorist attacks, after which the US's high-tech bubble burst and the economy cooled. In order to boost the economy, the Federal Reserve carried out a quantitative easing policy coupled with low interest rate, greatly increasing the monetary supply. Almost no restrictions were imposed on the issuance of the US dollar. With such a monetary policy coupled with low interest rates, large quantities of US dollars flowed outward through deficits in the current account. In 2008, when the global financial crisis broke out, the deficit recorded in the US current account unexpectedly USD673.3 bn, accounting for 4.7% of total GDP. The expanding issuance of the US dollar not only boosted the US economy, but also brought worldwide excess liquidity and inflation. The 2008 global financial crisis—ignited by the US subprime crisis and the current inflation situation, as represented by the rising price of the bulk raw materials—are the outcome of the US's irresponsible unilateral macroeconomic policy. This situation reveals the fundamental conflict inherent in the assumption that the Federal Reserve should play the role of the world's central bank, but, in reality, can only play the role of a domestic central bank that cannot take responsibility for the global economy.

As previously mentioned, the current international exchange-rate regime presents a center-periphery pattern with diversified arrangements. The US dollar, without any compulsory restrictions from gold, has no obligation to maintain a stable exchange rate between the US dollar and gold, thereby sustaining the US dollar's exchange rate against other currencies. Instead a floating exchange-rate regime serves the country's own best interests. The exchange rate of the US dollar and its backing interest rate experienced a large degree of volatility, thus increasing the risks associated with international economic activities. In order to facilitate these international economic activities and to control for risks, financial derivatives tend to emerge one after another. Originally, the function of derivatives is to manage risks. If we take a 100% reverse investment position, the risk after hedging will be zero. If the percentage is not 100%, the derivatives will function as leverage and can be used as instruments of investment. In the context of economic globalization and taking into account the consistent fluctuation of interest and exchange rates, financial derivatives are found to be available in excess. Numerous hedge fund products and a vast array of financial derivatives flooded the market. For a short period of time, financial innovation became the trend, with leading capital market-investment banking businesses taking the lead in adopting hedge funds, which were then taken by the traditional commercial banking business. Furthermore, industrial and commercial enterprises were unwilling to refrain from participation under the assumption that industrial cost accounting would not be as cost-effective as capital investment. MBA programs teaching courses on financial instruments appeared and became quite popular with CFOs. All of these trends encouraged the growth of certain economic activities that divorced financial development from the real economy. As a result, the global financial crisis was inevitable, highlighting the inherent tension of the US monetary authority between its responsibility to regulate the global financial market and its unwillingness to shoulder such a burden.

In sum, the current international monetary system is a US dollar-centric system that demonetizes gold. The international economic order is highly reliant upon the US dollar to function however, without the restrictions from gold, the US dollar can choose not to assume this responsibility. This results in the following situation: The US holds the rights to issue the US dollar free from the intervention of other countries. The US can adhere to an easy monetary policy long periods of time, a situation responsible for causing worldwide excess liquidity. The US, by issuing the US dollar, is able to finance its trade deficit in order to sustain a domestic economic model consisting of high consumption, low savings, and a high balance of payments deficit. The peripheral developing countries, for their part, have to adopt an exchange-rate regime by pegging their currencies to the US dollar. Changes in the interest rate and exchange rate of the US dollar often follow in the wake of changes being made in international capital flows. The massive flows of hot money pose a serious threat to these countries' economic and financial security. An obvious illustration can be seen in the Asian financial crisis of the 1990s. To avoid these risks and to prepare for contingencies, these countries had to deliberately plan for the expansion of their exports in order to consolidate a surplus, thus accumulating significant stockpiles of foreign exchange reserves, most notably the US dollar. These foreign exchange reserves were then invested in the US capital market for the purpose of maintenance and appreciation, thus further bringing down the interest rate of the US dollar. This situation furthered the habit of US citizens for deficit spending and lowered developing countries' return on assets of the US dollar. What's worse, any hints of the US capital market will be likely to bring losses to US dollar-based assets.

Thus, it can be seen that an international monetary system with the US dollar as the single major global currency has the following fundamental flaws:

First and foremost, the US has the unique capability of being able to transfer crises to other countries. According to statistics provided by the National Bureau of Economic Research, over the past 60 years, the US has faced ten economic crises, both large and small. The country was able to meet and overcome all such crises, however, primarily due to its ability to meet such trials with all the power associated with its dominant role in the global economic system. Many emerging countries believe that the intention of the US in adopting a quantitative easing monetary policy is the leverage of a weak US dollar in order to transfer its economic problems to other countries, especially onto emerging countries.

Secondly, the monetary policy issued by the US central bank runs directly counter to the global responsibilities of the US dollar. Thus, domestic interests are a greater priority than global interests. At the 2010 Caixin Summit, Zhou Xiaochuan stated that, "if a policy is an optimized choice for the US but not one for the rest of the world, the policy might produce side effects".

After the outbreak of the global financial crisis, all countries in the world fully recognize the urgency of reforming the international monetary system. In subsequent G20 summits, all state leaders agreed to accelerate the reformation of the international monetary system. For instance, in the Summit of European Union Leaders, held in Brussels from October 15 to 16, 2008, then French President Nicolas Sarkozy, German Chancellor Angela Merkel, and then British Prime Minister Gordon Brown proposed the establishment of a new international financial order. On October 25, 2008, the 7th Asia-Europe Meeting concluded with a consensus that leaders of Asian and European countries would carry out the effective and comprehensive reform of the international monetary and financial system, to involve all interested parties and international financial institutions for negotiation, and to propose a proper declaration as soon as possible. The G20 Washington Summit on Financial Markets and the World Economy took place on November 15, 2008, in Washington, DC. When addressing the G20 leaders, then Chinese President Hu Jintao delivered a speech entitled, "Making Joint Efforts to Tide over Difficulties" and gave a clear proposition to "improve the international monetary system, to steadily promote its diversity, and to make joint efforts to improve its stability." In January of 2011, then French President Nicolas Sarkozy stated that the reformation of the international monetary system should be promoted through macro-economic level negotiation and cooperation on the G20 platform and that the roles played by emerging countries in the international monetary system should be highlighted. In April 2011, five BRICS countries released the Sanya Declaration, which recognized that the international financial crisis had exposed inadequacies and deficiencies within the existing international monetary and financial system.

The participating countries supported the reformation and improvement of the international monetary system based on a broad international reserve currency system that could provide stability. The five BRICS countries also welcomed further discussion about the role of SDR in the existing international monetary system, including the composition of SDR's basket of currencies. Both in the BRICS Summit in New Delhi in April 2012 and in the summit meeting of the Shanghai Cooperation Organization in Beijing in June 2012, the importance of trading in local currencies was re-emphasized.

1.4 Choosing Which Direction the Reformation of the International Monetary System Will Take

The appropriate selection of a world currency is the number one priority of the reformation of the international monetary system. Both academic and professional circles have held many discussions concerning potential reforms to be made to the international monetary system, with various proposed solutions. Succinctly put, these options generally fall into one of three different categories: (1) set up a super-sovereign currency; (2) form regional currencies; (3) diversify sovereign currencies. All three solutions have their own various theoretical and practical supports.

1.4.1 The Establishment of a Super-Sovereign Currency

The theoretical proposition of setting up a super-sovereign currency has existed for some time. The terminology "world currency" originates in Davanzati's *Lezione delle monete* (1588) of the Florence Academy, in which he explains that, "a country's citizens, as they have done so in the past, can produce currencies with iron, leather, timber, hard leather, leather rope, paper, inkstone or other materials; but these currencies cannot be circulated when they leave the country. These currencies thus cannot be regarded as world currencies."

For the 150 years from the 19th century to the first half of the 20th century, all countries engaged in global trade endeavored to seek monetary cooperation and to reform the monetary system, with significant theoretical contributions being made to economic thought and policy. Karl Marx was one of the most visible contributors during this period. According to Marx, money, as the expression of the value of commodities, is not only an evitable outcome of the production and exchange of commodities, but also results from commodities' inherent contradictions. The money-form of value is only apparently after three preceding stages, namely, the simple form of value, the expanded form of value, and the general form of value. Money, by its very nature, is a special commodity that serves the role of a universal equivalent and is able to reflect certain social relations of production. As such, money has five functions, namely: a common measure of value, a medium of exchange, a store of value, a standard of deferred payment, and a world currency, among which, the first four are domestic functions while the last one is an international function. That is, a world currency is a universal equivalent in the global market that is able to perform all other domestic functions. Only when a country's currency functions as a world currency can it be categorized as a "universal equivalent." In this sense, only world currencies are truly "money" as it has been defined above. The supreme pursuit of the commodity economy is to realize that the monetary unification as the world market has already been integrated.

In order to recover some semblance of order within the international monetary system and to support the Europe's post-war reconstruction, then advisor of British HM Treasury-Keynes and then head of the Monetary Research Division of the US Department of the Treasury-White, proposed the "Keynes Plan" and "White Plan," respectively, within the same ten-year span in the 1940s, raising the concepts known as "bancor" and "unita." These were some of the earliest prominent ideas about super-sovereign currency.

The Keynes plan can be summarized as follows: first, it was necessary to set up a worldwide central bank, namely, the International Clearing Union. A supranational currency named "bancor" was to be issued by the International Clearing Union and would then be used among treasury departments and central banks as a unit of account settlements. Secondly, it was necessary to set up a fixed par of exchange between bancor and gold and, further, to peg all countries' currencies to bancor at a fixed exchange rate. The exchange rates between all countries' currencies and bancor were to be adjustable, but the adjustment would require the approval of the International Clearing Union. Third, each nation's central bank would open a bancor account in the International Clearing Union and then use this account for any and all settlements. Countries with a surplus would bring bancors into this account while deficit countries would pay bancors or overdraw the bancor account. Both surplus countries and deficit countries should assume the responsibility of adjusting the balance of payments disequilibrium.

The Keynes Plan was conceptualized as a central banking system for the international stage at large. As outlined by the plan, the idea for setting up this Union is to generalize the rules for running any isolated systems. If the balance of one creditor can only be cleared within the system, the International Clearing Union will not face the difficulty of being either unable or unwilling to accept the creditor's check. The creditor can grant a loan to any Union members and, furthermore, guarantees that the profit will be transferred to other members' clearing accounts. The only task that this Union has to complete is to ensure that all members operate in accordance with the rules and that every loan granted to members is a prudent one. Such a system should be suitable for the whole Union.

Differing in several respects from the Keynes Plan, the key points of the White Plan are four-fold: first is the establishment of an international monetary stability fund totaling USD5 bn with which member states can subscribe using gold, their own domestic currency, or government bonds. Member states may determine their subscription quota based on their own stockpiles of gold, foreign exchange reserves, national revenue, balance of payments, etc. Voting rights will be determined according to the quota ascribed. Secondly, this international monetary stability fund is capable of issuing a supranational currency named "unita" for the use of settlement among member states. Third, "unita" keeps a fixed par of exchange with gold, and all member states' currencies are pegged to "unita" at a fixed exchange rate. The exchange rates between all member states' currencies and "unita" are adjustable, but any adjustment requires the approval of the international monetary stability fund. Fourth, the fund organization's priority is to stabilize international exchange rates and grant short-term credit loans to member states, thereby solving the problem of balance of payments disequilibrium.

It can be seen that bancor (of the Keynes Plan) and unita (of the White Plan) are, in nature, highly independent supranational currencies that function separately from sovereign countries. Due to the decline of the UK's economic status after the war, the US, leveraging its political, economic and financial advantages, forced the UK to accept the White Plan and to pass the Bretton Woods agreement. The initiative to set up a supranational currency was not implemented, however. Rather, the Bretton Woods system adopted a US dollar-gold standard. Consequently, the sovereign currency of the US became the international reserve currency.

The Bretton Woods system, established in 1944, was a new international monetary system, using gold as the base and the US dollar as the central international reserve currency. Such a system reflects the US dollar's status as the world reserve currency. The establishment of the Bretton Woods system provided guarantees for the rapid development of international trade and the world economy following the end of WWII. The system itself, however, had inexcusable deficiencies, namely, what became known as the "Triffin Dilemma." In the rapidly-growing 1960s, increases in the gold supply were insufficient for the demands of rapid economic development. The international monetary system faced a problem of insufficient liquidity, which required a new type of reserve asset to cover the shortage of the US dollar. Meanwhile, from the end of 1960s to the beginning of 1970s, there were too many US dollars circulating within the market. Because each country held an increasing reserve of the US dollar, it faced a higher risk of depreciation. A new type of reserve asset was required by all countries in order to avoid foreign exchange risks. Obviously, the US dollar-centric international monetary system was fatally flawed. The most efficient solution proposed to recover the global financial order was to set up a new non-sovereign fiat currency, or, rather, a uniform supranational currency. The proposition of a supranational currency was raised by the IMF, which decided to set up SDR to increase international liquidity, thus addressing the issue of insufficient liquidity and unstable reserve asset value.

The SDR, so-called paper gold, was an additional type of reserve asset and a unit of account created by the IMF. Its earliest issuance was in 1970, with a unit value of 0.8887 g gold, equaling the value of the US dollar at that time. The value of the SDR is based on a basket of currencies which were widely used in international trade. Member states, to which the SDRs were distributed, listed the SDRs as their reserve assets and were able to use the SDRs when faced with a balance of payments deficit. The SDR, at least to some degree, follows the spirit of the supranational currency. But the SDR itself also has problems, notably its limited usage and irrational distribution. SDRs are only available among governments, but cannot be circulated for non-governmental commodities or in financial markets.

1.4.2 Regional Currency

Though the theory and practice of a supranational currency has existed for quite some time, given the variations that exist among countries' economic development and differences in political ideology, it is difficult to define a worldwide supranational currency in the short term. In the process of globalization, regional economic integration as a transitional form has proven quite vigorous. This may be defined as when neighboring states with similar degrees of economic development set up a common regional organization and promote individualized economic growth through regional integration. Under such circumstances, theories and practices about regional currencies may emerge.

One of the most representative theories of regional currency is that of the optimal currency region. In 1961, Mundell first raised the concept of an "optimal currency region" and the associated economic criteria for a successful currency union, namely, that of abundant liquidity. Increasing numbers of economist espoused the theory of an optimal currency region thereafter. They proposed criteria necessary for a successfully optimized currency region from different perspectives—considering, for instance, trade's degree of openness, products' degree of diversification, finance's degree of integration, inflation's similarity, etc. All these came to compromise a traditional theory on optimal currency region.

As far as research on the optimal currency region is defined, "optimal" is that which can be achieved based on macro-economic goals for maintaining internal and external balances. In an alternate relationship between inflation and unemployment, the macro economy can maintain an internal equilibrium with an external balance of payments. If all member states within a given currency union—a formation which necessitates the abandonment of their own currencies and exchange rate policies—can both maintain external equilibrium and remain free of inflation or unemployment, such a currency union presents itself as the optimal choice.

One concern of a country considering joining an optimal currency region, no doubt, is the cost to the country of leveraging its macro economy for internal adjustments after abandoning its own exchange rate and monetary policies. This means that when one country joins a currency union, this country, restricted by its economic structure, potentially may be unable to concurrently achieve a balance both internally and externally. Therefore, the price of recovering an external economic balance is usually the country's inflation or unemployment. The cost of leveraging the macro economy upon internal adjustment is largely reduced, since these economies possess certain shared characteristics of their economic structures. These characteristics are what constitute the criteria for an optimal currency region.

As the inherent contradictions of the international monetary system were exposed and theories outlining optimal currency regions became more widespread, the concept of regional currency began to be put into practice. The application of the euro is a typical example. Despite the risks posed by the outbreak of the global financial crisis and the worsening European sovereign debt crisis, the Euro zone is still a prime case study for the evolution of regional currencies.

The birth of the euro has been complex. Upon the publication of the *Maastricht Treaty* in 1992, 62 well-known German economists also published a joint declaration in Frankfurt entitled: *The European Monetary Union—a Crucial Test for Europe,* which stated that the European Union could not meet the criteria necessary for introducing a common currency and any rush for quick results would bring about economic and political disasters. Not long after that, 70 economists from different European countries responded, publishing a joint statement entitled *For the European Monetary Union: a Declaration from European Economists*, in which they argued that a monetary union and a single currency would be the best choice for the European Union's member states. Most economists and lawmakers agreed. This led to arguments over "whether the European Union was an optimal currency region." Though both sides performed an in-depth analysis of the European Union by referring to the theoretical criteria necessary for an optimal currency region, their research results diverged significantly.

Though theorists have not yet reached a consensus on whether Europe was able to serve as an optimal currency region, European governments have been of one mind: the current Euro zone, in its true sense, is not an optimal currency region. As European integration deepens, however, Euro zone countries' economic performance is expected to converge. Consequently, the Euro zone will be able to meet the criteria for an optimal currency region. All economic and political gains and losses considered, the net profit of monetary integration will not be zero or negative, meaning that European monetary integration is a potentially worthwhile solution.

Though the euro's emergence and development has gained the support of European governments, its actual use and application is slow. It has taken more than 20 years from the initial proposal of a unified monetary currency for continental Europe to the official application of the euro in common usage. Looking back even further, however, from the birth of the European Payments Union to the actual application of the euro, more than half a century has passed.

Before the birth of the European Payments Union (EPU), the 1957 Treaty of Rome facilitated the necessary conditions for monetary integration and the promotion of a regional supranational currency. It was in order to solve the post-war payment crisis, however, that the EPU, established in 1950 under the aegis of the Marshall Plan, really pushed forward European monetary cooperation. The 1970 Werner Plan proposed a plan to establish step-by-step a European monetary union within ten years. The 1972 Basel Accord introduced an exchange-rate regime named "the snake in the tunnel," which was an attempt to limit fluctuations between different European currencies while adopting a group floating mechanism against non-European currencies. Besides establishing strict limits, another critical task to the process of monetary integration is to set up an internal fund for monetary cooperation and to define a unit of account. In April 1973, the European Monetary Cooperation Fund (EMCF) was set up to address this issue. The main function of the EMCF was to maintain a stable exchange rate between member states, to extend short-term loans to countries with a balance of payments deficit, and to collect member states' foreign exchange reserves with the purpose of developing a transfer and clearing center. In April 1975, the European Unit of Account (EUA) was born, serving as the weighted value of a basket of European currencies. The EUA was not only a financial accounting tool within the European Community, an embryonic form of later common currencies.

In 1992, the member states of the European community signed the Maastricht Treaty, deciding to set up an Economic and Monetary Union, the ultimate goal of which was to issue a single currency. To do so, it was necessary to first enable the free circulation of capital within the European Union, while the second stage was to set up the European Monetary Institute—a predecessor of the European Central Bank. On January 1, 1999, the euro was conceptualized and on January 1, 2002, it began to circulate. On February 28 of the same year, the currencies of twelve Euro zone countries exited the market simultaneously upon the debut of this new supranational currency. The euro, as the only supranational currency, drives the reformation of the international monetary system, has initiated a global trend towards monetary simplification, and set an example for the formation of supranational currencies.

As an international reserve currency, the euro is second only to the US dollar in terms of widespread use and appeal. After the birth of the euro, the original Deutschmark, French franc, and other international reserve currencies were abandoned. In their place, these countries adopted the euro. According to the statistics provided by the IMF, as of the first quarter of 2015, the euro accounted for 20.72% of total allocated foreign exchange reserve assets. The euro has become an important currency in international financial trade. In the global debt market, euro-denominated money market instruments and bonds are of the largest scales. According to the statistics provided by the Bank for International Settlements, as of the first quarter of 2015, euro-denominated international money market instruments had achieved an issuing scale of USD185.5 bn, accounting for 33.9% of the total, compared to the US dollar-denominated international money market instruments, which had an issuing scale of USD230.4 bn; similarly, euro-denominated international bonds had an issuing scale of USD387.7 bn, accounting for 38.4% of the total. In terms of the global foreign exchange trade and global OTC foreign exchange derivatives trade, the scale of euro-denominated dealings is second only to that of US dollar-denominated dealings. The euro now enjoys increasingly-prominent status in the settlement of international trade. Currently, over 50 countries' currencies keep linked exchange rates with the euro. The euro effectively plays its role as a unit of account and is one of the most important currencies in terms of Special Drawing Rights. In 2015, each currency's weight in Special Drawing Rights was as follows: the US dollar (47.2%), the euro (33.4%), the pound sterling (12.4%), and the Japanese yen (7.0%). In international trade, 50–60% trade between Euro zone countries and non-Euro zone countries were settled in euro.

Coincidentally, along with the euro, the concept of Asian currency attained new prominence in Asia, the region with the fastest economic and intra-regional trade growth in the world. Malaysia's then-Prime Minister Mahathir was the earliest to propose a pan-Asian currency. At that time, East Asian countries, notably the ASEAN countries, directly learnt lessons from the Asian financial crisis, which was primarily triggered by East Asian countries' overreliance on the US dollar. When facing the shock of a large amount of international hot money, these countries' currencies experienced a sharp depreciation against the US dollar. The sudden depreciation of the currency values brought a wave of financial panic to this region, which soon spread to the surrounding countries. This crisis—affecting all East Asian countries—and their subsequent competitive currency depreciation drew East Asian countries' attention to regional financial cooperation. On the other hand, the IMF's indifference to the financial crisis greatly disappointed many East Asian countries and made them aware of the importance of intra-regional financial cooperation, especially the significance and urgency of monetary cooperation.

During the APEC event in 2001, Robert A. Mundell aired his opinion on the future evolution of the world monetary system, believing that in the future, three currency regions would emerge in the world, namely the Euro zone, the US dollar zone, and the Asian currency zone. In the absence of a world currency, it is reasonable for Asia or the ASEAN region to create one common currency. In 2003, Mundell proposed setting up a common currency backed by a set of currencies of Asian countries, which would have resulted in an "Asian currency" that could be broadly circulated in Asia without requiring members to abandon their own domestic currencies. This proposal was enthusiastically embraced by many Asian countries.

At the beginning of 2006, the Asian Development Bank (ADB) proposed the Asian Currency Unit (ACU). Similar to the European Currency Unit, the ACU is not a real currency that can be circulated. Instead, it is a virtual currency the value of which is equal to the weighted value of several countries' currency values, GDPs, and trade volumes. ADB assumed that they could estimate the exchange rates of the ACU against the US dollar and the euro. By publishing the exchange rates on their website, ADB is able to determine changes in the exchange rates and whether market volatility is under control. According to this, relevant countries can adjust their financial and monetary policies to gradually transform their currency regimes into ones approximating the "Asian Currency Unit," thus laying a foundation for the official birth of the Asian Currency. Political and technical arguments over the choice of currencies and their corresponding weights for the ACU resulted, however, such that this plan was ultimately postponed and eventually became invalid.

Though the plan for a pan-Asian currency is somewhat distanced from the political and economic development of Asia, scholars remain keen on it. The countries of Asia and East Asia share geographical proximity, including similarities in culture and common rapid economic growth. Though disparate in many ways, the countries in this region still have the possibility of forming a currency region.

In the late 1990s a number of studies were published on the relationship between trade integration and monetary integration, arriving at the conclusion that East Asia should institute a policy of monetary cooperation and adopt a pegged exchange rate arrangement. Some scholars, examine the prospects, challenges, and obstacles for monetary cooperation in East Asia from the perspective of demographic components and the driving forces behind them. Others focus more on topics including the dynamic constraints on the establishment process of a currency region in East Asia, the impacts of the RMB exchange rate reform, major obstacles, the framework and constitution for stabilizing finances. It has also been proposed that a VAR model might be used for establishing a currency region in East Asian countries at a time when they are facing varying shocks A number of studies have been on the obstacles, feasibility, and the prospects for the integration of East Asian currencies, looking in particular at these issues from the perspective of system improvement, cost-benefit analysis, and system evolution. On the whole, research on the integration of East Asian currencies has tended to focus on trade, the exchange rate, production factors, and economic shocks. This research has contributed toward the development of the Asian currency and enriched and furthered the theory of an optimal currency region.

The current process of globalization (represented by regionalization) is accelerating. The European Free Trade Zone has been established and the construction of the North American Free Trade Zone and Asian Free Trade Zone is progressing rapidly. China-ASEAN Free Trade Area (CAFTA) was fully established at the end of 2015 and is now being upgraded. The Shanghai Cooperation Organization has shifted its position from military cooperation to economic and trade cooperation. As for northeast Asia, the level of economic and trade cooperation among China, Japan, and South Korea grows increasingly close. China and South Korea have reached a free trade zone agreement. BRICS countries, under the new mechanism, have a closer degree of economic and trade cooperation, to the extent that a BRICS Bank has been founded in Shanghai. Under such circumstances, it is possible to reach a regional monetary cooperation. Asia can learn from the experience of Europe to produce its own regional currency, similar to the euro. If the plan for a pan-Asian currency can be implemented, the world will have several regional currencies, namely the Asian currency, the euro, and the US dollar. Among regional currencies, an international coordination mechanism should be established to adjust and control their exchange rates, thus forming a new international monetary system.

1.4.3 The Internationalization of Multiple Sovereign Currencies

In the process of internationalizing multiple sovereign currencies, more countries' currencies will be engaged in establishing a truly international monetary system. For instance, Eichengreen, by comparing sovereign currencies, analyzed the strengths and weaknesses of major currencies such as the US dollar, the euro, the Japanese yen, and the pound sterling, as well as Special Drawing Rights. According to their research, though the financial crisis will affect the US dollar's dominance in the world market, from the perspective of the liquidity of the financial market and the convenience of using this money, the US capital market remains the most developed in the world, especially in terms of having rich short-term bond products, which are able to provide investors with sufficient liquidity. Therefore, the dominance of the US dollar is extremely unlikely to be replaced by other currencies. The status of the US dollar will decline, however, and its international monetary space will be narrowed. Eichengreen also believes that in the future, the trade volume of the Euro zone, Eastern Europe, and Russia will climb. As a result, the euro will become a more pan-European regional currency. Following this path, the Chinese yuan will adopt similar measures in order to remake itself as a regional currency for East Asia or even Asia as a whole, thus forming a monetary system with the US dollar as the center and the euro and the Chinese yuan as two supplementary wings.

Looking into the future, several major currencies (for instance, the Chinese yuan) may experience increased globalization due to their pre-existing high status and broad applicability in the international economic market. It is expected that a gradual trend of diversification within the international monetary system will take place, based on which, multiple international coordination mechanisms will be necessary. The arrangements needed for the internationalization of multiple sovereign currencies are different than those called for by supranational or regional currencies, the reason for which lies in several specific differences. Some regional currencies are also supranational within a certain region while sovereign currencies are currencies issued by nation-states. Difficulties and obstacles in adequately arranging for two supranational currencies are primary drivers for the move to internationalize multiple sovereign currencies at once.

To explore a model of worldwide supranational currency like SDR, after the outbreak of the international financial crisis, theorists discussed the potential applicability of SDR as the supranational currency. Some have argued that it is not an issue of replacing the US dollar with another currency, because supranational currencies do not have political obstacles. Instead, governments would transfer their balance into a certificate representing that they hold a certain amount of SDR, a situation beneficial to all parties. The issuance would be to replace one currency with another. SDR, as a synthetic currency, has the function of diversifying assets and stabilizing value, but the liquidity of SDR must first be enhanced, especially when it is used to value assets. Others believe that as the application of SDR expands, countries will be more willing to shift their diversified reserve assets into a more stable international monetary system. This system allows reserve holders to transfer their US dollar-denominated reserve assets to SDR-denominated assets, thus diversifying. Though the IMF promises to assume the risks brought about by the changing exchange rate of the US dollar, consensus will be reached only under an appropriate risk sharing arrangement.

Jeffrey acknowledges the function of a supranational currency as a world currency. Though some scholars recognize the function of SDR, they are hesitant to make any positive predictions regarding its foreseeable future. According to some proponents of the view described at the end of the last paragraph, the use of SDR seems to be impartial and no country is able to enjoy what might be termed exorbitant privileges. Despite this, its widespread usage cannot expand due to technical obstacles. Reinforcing the central position of SDR will exert limited effects on enhancing system flexibility and on changing the motivation of surplus countries. When countries transfer their existing reserve currencies into a basket of more currencies, SDR might further replace other freely-traded currencies. The current system will accelerate the economic disequilibrium. Therefore, SDR reserves might actually benefit the current strategies of surplus countries.

Following the financial crisis, international cooperation may well grow stronger and an independent central bank might be set up. But the current world is not an optimal currency region (at least, labor forces, goods, and capital cannot flow freely) and the functions of a central bank cannot be diversified. Some research findings show that many difficulties face the expanded applicability of SDR, and increasing its liquidity will be exorbitantly costly because, in reality, the US dollar market and the euro market already have high liquidities and the demand side faces a maturity mismatch. One view holds that due to the huge profits yielded by the US dollar-centric network, SDR is extremely unlikely to replace the US dollar as a reserve currency at any point in time. If the IMF provides liquidity as a marker of the foreign exchange market, the IMF's power should be reinforced. However, the decision to empower the IMF to provide sufficient liquidity to SDR is difficult to justify among member countries. Pietro Alessandrini believes that SDR has two fundamental drawbacks: it is neither a sovereign currency nor indicative of an international institution's creditor's rights. History has demonstrated the deficiencies of SDR as a reserve currency. According to Burak, although SDR is valued based on a basket of currencies and maintains stable purchasing power, it also has many deficiencies. Specifically, SDR lacks the basic functions of money and it is neither a fiat currency nor a physical currency. What's more, SDR faces technical difficulties: SDR is valued based on a basket of four major reserve currencies of which the US dollar accounts for the largest portion. SDR is available only in limited supply, and an extremely uneven distribution exists between developed countries and developing countries. For all these reasons, SDR is far from attractive and it is not widely used in pricing international trade and bulk commodities. In Cooper's opinion, adopting one supranational currency is practical in principle, but under the current economic framework, it is difficult for all parties to reach a consensus on who will be the power behind issuing a synthetic currency and who would have ultimate control over decisions affecting it.

In the opinion of some the feasibility of widely adopting SDR depends on its acceptability among private institutions. Utilizing SDR potentially faces obstacles in non-reserve currency countries. The availability of SDR will be, some have tried to show, enhanced only when the SDR is accepted by private markets under conditions of a higher liquidity.

SDR, therefore, has many advantages, but its functionality depends on the future development of the world economy and the attitudes of major countries, which may prove difficult. The US did not raise any objections, simply because it found that setting up a supranational currency would be unrealizable and infeasible in the short term. In the long term, setting up a supranational currency would necessitate a reformation of the international monetary system, but in the short term, it is not realistic to expect that SDR will play a more important role like physical currencies or that a new supranational currency will emerge.

Secondly, the international monetary system demonstrates significant inertia. While the international monetary system will evolve as the international production system develops, the evolution of the international monetary system will always lag behind developments in the system of international production. One important reason for this is that the central countries of the original international monetary system have historically been unwilling to give up their vested interests when using their sovereign currencies to play the role of world currencies. The historical inertia of the international monetary system resulted in the evolution of the international production system, thus giving rise to a mismatch between the evolution of the international monetary system and that of the international production system. According to an empirical analysis of the US dollar conducted by Eiji Ogawa and associates, even if the US dollar depreciates at an average level, the US dollar's status in playing the role of an international currency will not decrease and the US dollar will continue to maintain its status as a key currency, demonstrating inertia. The inertia extant in the process of currencies' internationalization is a result of the attributes of the currencies themselves. Once a system is established or formed (e.g. the emergence of one international currency or the establishment of its dominance), "path dependence" or even "locking status" can be expected. An international currency, as a systemic arrangement, is no exception. As the inertia of the current international currency grows, this currency will exert pressure on the birth of a new international currency and the internationalization of non-international currencies, thereby delaying the process of internationalizing other sovereign currencies. According to a research in 2000, an international currency's inertia will result in a mismatch between the currency's status and the corresponding country's economic status, both in terms of time and space.

Considering the mismatch in time, at the beginning of the 20th century, the US undoubtedly rose in international prominence to become the largest economic power in the world. Profits derived from WWII further consolidated the hegemony of the country's economy. It took another 50 years, however, for the US dollar to replace the pound sterling as a hegemonic international currency. As to the mismatch in space, once a currency becomes a hegemonic international currency, the corresponding country's status in the international monetary system will be much higher than its place in terms of global economic power. This theoretical research also shows that currencies' internationalization will be affected by the broad trading network generated by cross-border trading activities and further by external issues arising in the economic network. Any possession and utilization of a given currency depends on the willingness of the man to accept this currency as payment. If a currency is accepted across a wider range of potential situations, the value of using and holding this currency will be higher. In economic terms, the currency creates a positive network externality. Meanwhile, the network externality revealed in the process of internationalizing currencies has the feature of self-enhancement. If a currency is adopted in trade and valuation across a wider range, it will play the role of an international currency for a longer period of time. All these features explain why, as the international production system develops, the international monetary system cannot keep up with its pace.

Third, due to the divergent economic development of different countries throughout the world, the birth of one supranational currency was beset by immediate, innumerable difficulties. The euro's success depends on the fact that the member states of the European Union share an extremely consistent economic and social development, as well as similar historical and cultural backgrounds. Even so, after the most recent outbreak of the global financial crisis, the Euro zone's very existence proved precarious. Since 2011, Spain, Italy, and other major European countries have been beset with the euro debt crisis, so much so that the Euro zone has almost fallen apart. It is thus clear that a balanced global level of economic development is the basis for setting up a worldwide supranational currency, but this basis must be further consolidated in order to remain stable.

Fourth and finally, it is difficult to maintain the stability of a supranational currency' value. In order to play the role of a supranational currency, a specific unit is priority is to maintain a stable value. If a new supranational currency is created ex nihilo, its value should be pegged to a basket of reference currencies. These references could be member states' currencies or typical commodities. If the value is the weighted average of all member states' currencies, too many disparate parameters and complications may arise. If we use commodities as the reference, the challenge will be selecting one typical commodity that can adequately represent the unit is fair value. Therefore, the most realistic choice is to learn from the method of pricing used for the euro or SDR: that is, selecting several currencies of countries whose GDP and trade volume account for a large percentage of the world's total and then calculating the weighted average of these selected currencies and gold in order to form a basket. When SDR were initially created, their exchange rate against the US dollar equaled the weighted average of five major currencies, namely, the US dollar, the Deutschmark, the Japanese yen, and the French franc. Now, however, major developed counties have largely adopted a floating exchange-rate regime. Under the floating exchange-rate regime, SDR changes together with the changes in other counties' exchange rates. Therefore, the value of a supranational currency is still unstable. The instability of the currency value caused by the floating exchange-rate regime will, of course, bring down the enthusiasm of people towards the global supranational currency. Therefore, in the course of a supranational currency's development, one of the most important issues is how to appropriately deal with this contradiction.

Theoretically, a regional supranational currency can be the transitional form of a global supranational currency. Yet many obstacles preclude this. On the one hand, the very theory of an optimal currency region tells us that it is difficult to find another region suitable for setting up a currency zone. Asia's failure in setting up the Asian currency serves as a prime example. On the other hand, after 2011, the European sovereign debt crisis continues to worsen and the Euro zone is still currently facing significant issues. Consequently, many have begun to rethink the possibility of developing a regional supranational currency.

In conclusion, the three potential options facing the reformation of the international monetary system are: a supranational currency, regional currency, and/or the internationalization of multiple sovereign currencies. Theoretically, creating a global supranational currency would be the most ideal option, but would realistically take too long and be too difficult to implement. As for the option of creating a regional currency, excluding the European Union as an optimal currency region, Asia, due to the significant economic and political differences among countries, is not likely to adopt one common regional currency within the near future. Yet the push towards the reformation of the international monetary system remains extremely urgent. As the second-best choice, the internationalization of multiple sovereign currencies can serve as an alternative for pushing forward the reformation of the international monetary system. Under such circumstances, the Chinese yuan will begin process of internationalization. In this sense, the internationalization of the Chinese yuan is a product of the evolution of the international monetary system. Its emergence at least partially meets the urgent need for the development of international trade and finance and serves as a new foundation for the evolution of the international monetary system in the future.

Chapter 2
The Internationalization of the RMB: Origins and Challenges

It can be inferred from the previous discussion that, after the onset of the global financial crisis, the necessity of reforming the US dollar-centric international monetary system has become increasingly urgent. Although the three aforementioned methods—namely, the supranational currency, the regional currency, and the internationalization of multiple sovereign currencies—have theoretical and pragmatic foundations, it is the internationalization of multiple sovereign currencies that is the easiest and most pragmatic choice.

After the onset of the 2008 global financial crisis, the global economic community began to review the then-prevalent US dollar-centric international monetary system. Theoretical research has been done on the feasibility of the internationalization of multiple sovereign currencies. Bergsten believes that the exorbitant privilege of the US dollar will facilitate the United States in its global financing. If the US dollar fluctuates, the world economy will become unstable. Much like the adoption of English as the world's lingua franca, however, adopting the US dollar as a single global currency comes with many associated benefits, such as a reduction in trading costs. At present, if the United States reduces or terminates the deficit of the current account, many countries will be forced to adjust their export-oriented development strategies—a process which promises to be quite lengthy and painful. In addition, according to Bergsten, the huge deficit of the United States, the dominant status of the US dollar, and the huge inflow of capital are no longer aligned with or conducive to the interests of the United States. The United States should encourage China and other countries initiate their own plans for reforming the international monetary system. The United States should support any feasible reforms and further enhance the multi-currency system. Differing sharply from the view that the United States will only yield profits predicated upon the dominance of the US dollar, According to some, the excessive monopoly of the US dollar in the international monetary system earns revenue for the United States from seigniorage (USD10 bn), reduces the interest rate of the US dollar due to foreigners' purchasing of US Treasury bonds, and facilitates borrowing on the part of the American people (a net profit of around USD90 bn) at a heavy cost. For

© Social Sciences Academic Press and Springer Nature Singapore Pte Ltd. 2018

Y. Cao, *Strategies for Internationalizing the Renminbi*, Research Series on the Chinese Dream and China's Development Path,
https://doi.org/10.1007/978-981-13-0800-0_2

instance, foreign capital's inflow into the United States in 2008 has driven the exchange rate of the US dollar up by 5–8% (a net loss of around USD30 bn–USD60 bn for the United States). Therefore, the reformation of the international monetary system towards a multi-currency system is likely to be aligned with the interests of the United States as well as all other parties.

Because theory often aligns with practice, when it was widely believed that a multi-currency system was likely to be the world's most realistic choice for success, this concept was put into place: namely the internationalization of the RMB. On July 2 2009, the RMB started to be officially used in cross-border trade for valuation and settlement as a result of the newly-arisen needs that grew out of the global financial crisis.

2.1 The Internationalization of the RMB Is the Necessary Outcome of Rebalancing the Global Economy

The global financial crisis was caused by certain long-standing global economic imbalances. Before the outbreak of the global financial crisis, the world economy was composed of three distinctive economic sectors, each of which was interdependent on and with each other. First among these are the emerging economies as represented by China that are engaged in the process of globalization with their strengths in low-cost manufacturing. On the one hand, these countries, as "the world's factories," gained huge trade surpluses and were able to share the dividends of globalization; on the other hand, these countries, with their low costs, drove down global price levels and increased overall levels of consumption. Secondly, developed countries—as represented by the United States and relying on their advantages in providing financial services and taking advantage of various financial innovations—kept their costs at a low level, thereby facilitating the overall prosperity of the global economy, sharing the dividends of globalization, and enabling the United States to further expand its debt-based consumption economy, which deepened the degree of deficit spending. Third, energy resource exporters (most notably members of OPEC), driven by the industrialization of emerging economies (like China), had a larger volume of exports and raised the price of resources. They not only utilized their resources to facilitate globalization, but also shared the dividends of globalization, thus accumulating huge foreign exchange reserves.

Growing organically from a rapid cyclical pattern wherein global economic development proceeded rapidly, the world's economy was composed of three sectors (see Fig. 2.1). Developed countries like the United States imported commodities and necessary resources from Asian countries while using the US dollar. Products flowed into the United States while the US dollar was earned by exporters. Under the well-developed financial aegis of the United States, the US dollar would ultimately return to the United States via other countries' purchasing of US Treasury bonds and other financial products. The United States, under such

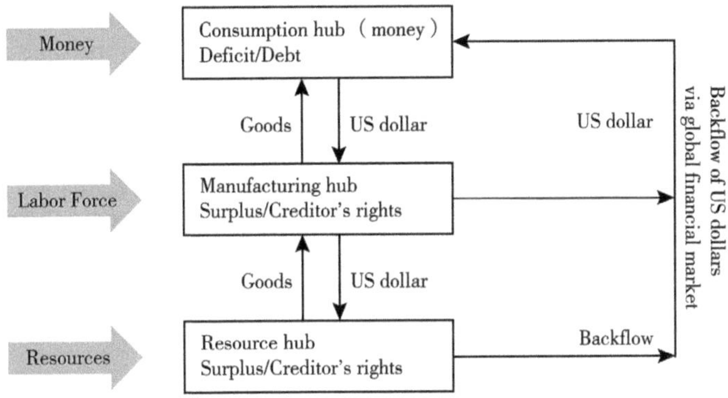

Fig. 2.1 Balanced structure of the world economy

circumstances, was able to keep consuming its credit while maintaining the entire cyclical economic pattern.

In a balanced globalized economy, the "export-oriented" economic development typical of Asian manufacturing centers was based on the stability of the US market's consumptive abilities. Before the outburst of the global financial crisis, two material factors propped up the high consumption of the United States:

First of all, the unique status of the United States within the international monetary system ensured that the country was able to continue with the process of debt-fueled consumption. Since Asia adopted a "US dollar standard system," the goods manufactured by Asia were exported to the United States, forming a huge US dollar-denominated surplus. The US dollar reserves—brought about by the surplus created through Asian countries' purchasing of the US Treasury bond and other financial products—finally flowed back to the United States, enabling the United States to continue consuming its credit. This debt-based model, in turn, stimulated the expansion of the US consumption market, further increasing the volume of imports from Asian countries and growing the surplus held by Asian countries. Once these Asian countries earned sufficient quantities of the US dollar, they would use the US dollar to purchase US Treasury bonds, thus forming a production-consumption loop between the Asian and the US markets.

Also of some note are the structural changes taking place in the household income of the United States at this time. Over the preceding few years, asset consumption contributed significantly to the expansion of total US consumption as a whole. Traditional theories held that household consumption is restricted by household income, and, furthermore, that the marginal propensity to consume decides that changes in consumption patterns are sensitive to income fluctuation.

Due to financial innovations taking place since the 1980s in the United States, however, asset-based income actually occupied a large portion of total household income. For instance, the proportion of financial assets income (represented by real estates and stocks) to total US household income increased from 7% in 1950 to 17% in 2007. With the establishment of an asset-based economic pattern, US household consumption was no longer restricted by income-based consumption. Furthermore, housing prices and the prices of stock also became important influencing factors, manifesting in the wealth effect. According to various estimates, the correlation coefficient between the consumption growth rate and the housing price growth rate is 0.67. Taking only household income and housing prices into consideration, once the price of housing increases by 10%, the actual growth rate of the household consumption will increase by 1.4% points; stocks' rate of return is obviously related to the actual growth rate of the next-year consumption, with a correlation coefficient of 0.44. Therefore, as the asset price of the United States increases continuously, the net wealth effect drives the growth of US consumption overall.

Asset consumption can be said to serve as an important basis for the US consumption market. If the bubble of asset prices burst, US consumption would be unsustainable. The outbreak of the 2007 sub-prime crisis in the United States manifested as the collapse of the asset price bubble, particularly in terms of housing prices. As a result, the asset-based consumption of the United States was heavily shocked. When the market demands outlining US consumption shrank, under the current globalized economic cycle, the "export-oriented" Asian economies were also negatively affected. When the export capability of Asian countries declined in tandem with insufficient overseas and domestic demand, the global economy soon slumped. Because the decline of Asia's manufacturing centers would further reduce the demands for resources, resource suppliers (represented by Russia) earned less and were also subject to decline. As a result, such a globalized economic cycle proved to be unsustainable, ultimately resulting in the global financial crisis.

After China became the new global manufacturing center, insufficient domestic demand from China and other Asian countries coupled with the developed economy of the United States and the status of the United States in the international monetary system created the ideal situation for a consumption market. Consequently, China depended on overseas demand market—the United States—to follow the production-consumption cycle.

In the production-consumption cycle as set against a background of globalization, China imported intermediate goods from Asian countries and exported manufactured goods to consumption markets such as the United States, thus forming both trade deficits against Asian countries and a trade surplus against the United States. Figure 2.1 lists the current account balance of the United States and those of other countries. We can see from this Figure that the current account deficit of the United States reached USD410.6 bn in 2014 (around 23.72% of the US GDP). Figure 2.1 also demonstrates that the current account surpluses of Japan, China, and other East Asian countries were relatively large; one of the more outstanding features visible is that both developed countries and developing countries, in most situations, had a varying current account surplus while only the United States registered a persistent large-scale current account deficit (to which China was the main contributor) (Table 2.1).

China's trade with the United States registered a growing surplus, resulting in external imbalances in both China and the United States. Since China's entry into

Table 2.1 current account of the US and that of other countries or regions

Country/ region	2006	2007	2008	2009	2010	2011	2012	2013	2014
US	−806.7	−718.6	−686.6	−380.8	−443.9	−459.3	−460.7	−400.3	−410.6
Euro zone	34.9	20.6	−97.9	22.0	48.3	53.9			
Japan	171.1	211.7	142.1	145.7	217.5	126.2	59.1	34.1	24.4
China	231.8	353.2	420.6	243.3	237.8	136.1	215.4	182.8	

Unit bn US dollar
Source IMF
World Economic Outlook, Statistical Appendix, September 2005
Note (1) The current account here mainly refers to the import and export of goods and services. (2) Other developed countries refer to economies other than the United States, 12 euro zone countries and Japan; (3) emerging East Asian industrial economies include: South Korea, Hong Kong of China, Taiwan of China and Singapore; (4) the bracketed data are current account deficit of the United States as a percentage of GDP

the WTO in 2001, China's trade surplus has grown rapidly. Particularly, the expansion of China's trade surplus with the United States is one of the most significant factors behind the global imbalances that have emerged since 2003. Another similar case was can be seen in the global imbalances of the early 1980s, featuring Japan's trade surplus with the United States. As shown in Fig. 2.2, the rapid growth of China's trade surplus since 2003 follows the same track as that of Japan's trade surplus.

China, as the center of the international manufacturing system, was too dependent on its exports to the US market, a situation that ultimately triggered global imbalances (as represented by the China-US trade imbalance).

Such global economic imbalances, undoubtedly, were not sustainable, requiring specific adjustments once they reached a certain level. Since these global economic

Fig. 2.2 Trade balance of China and Japan (US dollar) (2006–2014) *Source* UNCTAD COMTRADE database

imbalances manifested in the expanding trade surpluses of Asian countries—most notably, the trade surplus of China with the United States—the pressure of monetary appreciation on the RMB emerged. On July 21, 2005, the Chinese government announced the reformation of its exchange-rate regime for the RMB from a fixed regime to a managed floating regime. On that day, the exchange rate of the RMB against the US dollar, for the first time, appreciated by 2%. As shown in Fig. 2.3, during the subsequent decade, the exchange rate of the RMB against the US dollar sustained a rising trend, experiencing a total growth rate of over 30%.

In short, as the new round of the US current account deficit deteriorated and extant global economic imbalances deepened, the focus on global imbalances switched to China and other East Asian countries. It can thus be seen that the global economic imbalances were due in large part to the balance of payments disequilibrium of China and other Asian countries against the United States. In this aspect, Japan shared the same story in the 1980s. When facing the mismatch between the evolution of the global manufacturing system and that of the international monetary system, China, as the center of Asia's manufacturing system, finally appreciated the RMB as a solution to the global economic imbalances.

The outbreak of the global financial crisis not only revealed that the global economic cycle fostered after China became the center of the global manufacturing system was unsustainable, but also indicated that China's strategy of "export-oriented" economic development had come to an end.

It is urgent for China, the largest developing country in the world, to force the process of industrialization forward. According to the Development Economics Theory, in order to achieve industrialization, a country's citizens should spend less but save more for investment. In the early days of New China, when the country adopted the Soviet model of economic development, such a model of investment

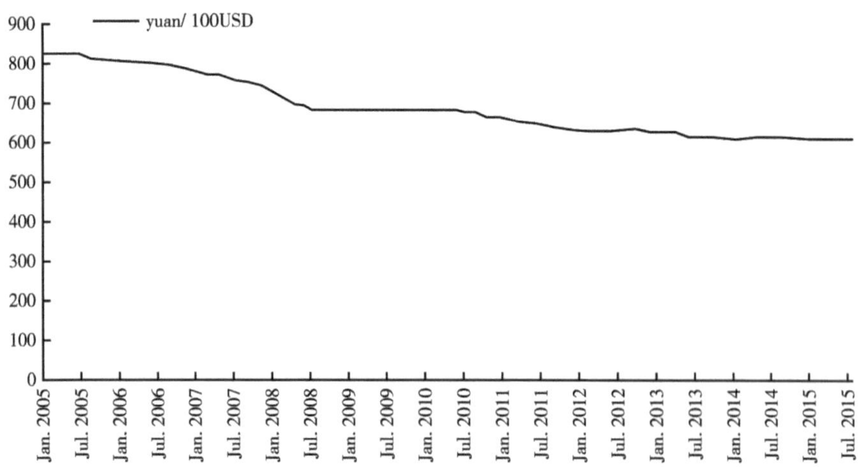

Fig. 2.3 CNY to USD exchange rate *Source* Official website of China's State Administration of Foreign Exchange

towards industrialization was pursued. In addition, since China lagged behind in science and technologies, an extensive investment-driven model for economic growth finally came into being in order to compensate. This type of directed investment boosted the demands for intermediate products. Together with the country's high savings ratio, China, in pressing ahead with industrialization, had insufficient domestic demands. After China adopted its policy of reform and opening-up, the country gradually became the world's manufacturing base. When domestic demands proved insufficient for production and consumption, China's dependence shifted to the overseas market and ultimately developed an "export-oriented" economic strategy. As a result, China's import and export as a percentage of GDP reached up to 9%, far above the universal upper limit (3%). Correspondingly, China's domestic consumption as a percentage of GDP was only 42%, which was lower than the world's average level (over 60%). This was an important factor in explaining why China, in contrast to the UK (the first generation of the world's manufacturing centers), and the United States (the second generation of the world's manufacturing centers), was able to play the role of the world's manufacturing center without being the world's tech or trade center. This was also the very factor that most significantly contributed to today's global economic circulation pattern.

As China fulfilled its industrialization target as scheduled—especially having experienced such rapid growth during more than 30 years since the period of reform and opening-up—the extensive economic growth mode that depended on exports and was driven by investment started to show its weaknesses. When China became the world's manufacturing center, its extensive growth required a greater injection of resources. Along with the development of its domestic manufacturing, China's demands for global resources were growing. As a result, the prices of oil, ores, and other resources skyrocketed, which, in turn, struck at the advantage China possessed in terms of low-cost manufacturing. This development shocked China's export-oriented processing and manufacturing industries. At the end of last century and in light of growing awareness of this problem, China attempted the radical change from an extensive growth trajectory to one characterized by intensive growth. Due to underlying systemic factors, however, no obvious results have come to pass. Furthermore, after China joined the WTO in 2001, the demands of the overseas market were robust. Such a shift in the demands of globalization temporarily masked the urgency of adjusting the country's domestic economic structure and enabled the temporary maintenance of an extensive economic growth driven by both investment and exports.

Factors such as the appreciation of the RMB and the sharp rise in price for raw materials since 2015, started to have a measurable effect on this extensive growth, one which was temporarily masked by the processes of globalization. At this point, adjusting the economic structure and once again changing the economic growth pattern became important tasks for the country's macro-economic control. Unfortunately, the global financial crisis in 2007 seriously impacted the demands of the overseas market on which China's economic growth depended while simultaneously experiencing a lack of any effect on the economic structure adjustment by the previously-implemented macro control polices. As a result, the contradictions in China's economic growth pattern and foreign economic strategy became pressing.

When the global financial crisis broke out, countries adopted macro policies to stimulate the economy. From the second half of 2009 on, the global economy started to recover. This process of recovery was not balanced, however, notably demonstrating disparities between developed economies and emerging economies, between economic recovery and employment growth, and between the actual strength of recovery and that which was hoped for.

Many imbalances were thus created for the world economy as a result of a globally inconsistent process of recovery. These imbalances constituted new risks and became the principal contradictions inherent in the global economy, and it was vital to strengthen the coordination and management of policies addressing such imbalances during the process of global economic recovery. If the original imbalances in the world economy were aggravated by policy imbalances, trade frictions would have the potential to become trade wars and exchange rate frictions could potentially rise to become exchange rate wars. Financial and political wars were likely to be inextricable. A "de-leveraged" financial crisis would de-globalize the economy. To avoid this situation, it was objectively required that the rebalance of the world economy should be the central focus of international attention.

Facing difficulties in the aftermath of the 2009 global financial crisis, China adopted an unconventional macro-economic policy, with which a large-scale fiscal stimulus package was launched in order to maintain its rapid economic growth. By carrying out this policy, China not only insulated its economy from the worst of the crisis, but also created new demands for a real economy. Following the implementation of these policies, China became the second largest importer and the largest trading country in the world. As the global economy shook off the effects brought about by the crisis, China's own economy stabilized and recovered, with its trend towards growth and industrialization playing a decisive role in its ability to recover. Although in the long run, the trend of industrialization and urbanization indicates that China's economic growth will continue to perform well, the global financial crisis indicates that the current globalized economic cycle itself will not be sustainable, and, as a result, China's extensive economic growth and export-oriented foreign economic strategy must end. The expansion of domestic demand is ultimately more important for China's economy when the overseas market becomes unreliable. At present, China's per capita income has reached USD7700. As defined by the World Bank, China belongs to the above-average income level. Previous international experiences can provide precedent for the fact that method—even an effective one—adopted to promote economic development during the low-income period is not necessarily the right solution during the middle-income period. The so called "middle income trap"—slow economic growth and stagnant per capita income—might arise if this warning is not heeded. For this reason, increasing people's income with the aim of growing domestic demand, adjusting the economic structure, and changing the mode of economic development is likely to be the most strategic choice for the future development of China.

A dynamic mechanism for transforming China's mode of economic development is now taking shape. On the one hand, as the labor force in rural areas is gradually decreasing, their income is continually increasing; on the other hand, as the aging population grows, the saving ratio and the investment ratio face greater pressure towards decline. These factors determine that an economic growth driven by the expansion of domestic demand based on people's consumption has begun developing and will gradually replace the economic growth previously driven by investment-based supply. In fact, as domestic demand expands, imports increase. During the period between 2010 and 2014, although China's exports undeniably increased, the import rate grew even faster. As a result, the current account surplus as a percentage of GDP may potentially drop from 10% in 2007 to 4% or lower and continue to decline. While 4% was once a goal pursued by the IMF, this change in the economic pattern of China is of worldwide significance. It indicates that China is contributing to rebalancing the world economy and, as time goes on, its global contribution is expanding. Under the background of rebalancing the world economy, the RMB has begun its journey of internationalization.

2.2 The Internationalization of the RMB Begins Under Specific Conditions

The RMB's internationalization began under certain specific conditions, the particularity of which was fully embodied in the process of the RMB's evolution. The RMB was born in 1949, when the People's Republic of China was founded. After many years' efforts, China overturned the country's feudalism, imperialism, and bureaucratic capitalism, and afterwards was able to plan and develop the economy on a new socialist basis. "Being economically poor and blank" meant that the country's economic development lagged behind the rest of the world's, and additionally that there was a shortage of appropriate economic systems or policies. After the founding of the new China, for a variety of reasons, the country adopted a planned economy, which was popular at that time, and also adopted a highly-centralized economic system that followed the Soviet Union and other Eastern European countries. As opposed to a market economy, under a highly-centralized planned economic system, resources are allocated according to a planned quota instead of according to competitive market prices. In terms of the micro economy, a free enterprise system where only the fittest survive was replaced by bureaucratized factories; when considering the macro economy, the financial market, as one of the most significant means of market-oriented resources allocation, was replaced by the government's fiscal control. As a result, under the planned economy, the government planned everything, including labor forces, properties, production, supply, distribution, etc. Under this system, money was only an accounting tool or a medium of exchange. In China at that time, the RMB was even not a medium of exchange in its true sense because it was not available for use without certificates such as food coupons, cloth coupons, manufactured goods coupons, etc. In view of this, the RMB was not what is typically considered money. Instead, the RMB was a certificate or an accounting tool.

The RMB's role as an accounting tool was particularly obvious when it incorporated external functions. Under a planned economic system, all things are pre-arranged, with the essential requirement being that the system should be a closed loop without exceptions. Since two or more countries involved in mutual foreign trade cannot be completely controlled under one country's plan, a planned economic system would ideally seek to minimize foreign trade as much as possible. Because of this, China decided to take the path of self-reliance in terms of the economy, wherein the purpose of foreign trade would be to regulate any surpluses and deficiencies of goods and materials. Specifically, the only purpose of imports was to obtain necessary goods and materials that could not be domestically manufactured by the country itself, while the purpose of exports was to earn foreign exchange in order to pay for these imported necessities. The sole principle that China held at that time was to earn foreign exchange through exports. On this occasion, the RMB evolved to be a cost accounting tool for export the purpose of which was to earn foreign exchange. Here, the so-called exchange rate of the RMB was the accounting price of the foreign exchange cost, which was far from the typical par rate of exchange.

Since China's reform and opening-up, the RMB has, in a very real sense, become a widely-accepted and circulated form of money. In 1973, for example, China initiated its market-oriented economic reform and the corresponding opening-up policies. First, the free enterprise system—which was mainly adopted by private companies—developed gradually and drove the reformation of state-owned companies at large, thus significantly changing the micro basis of China's economy. Secondly, together with the gradual improvement of the market price mechanism, the marketization of resource allocation became a trend. Reflected at the macro level, the fiscally-oriented economy turned out to be a finance-oriented economy. During this process, the RMB began to transfer its role from an accounting tool to a full-function currency, and played an increasingly important role in China's economy. One of the most significant symbols of this process was the measurable development of monetization, which continually enrolled more financial institutions and more high-performing functions of the financial market.

The RMB's internal functions recovered while its external functions became more prominent. After the mid-1980s, the RMB, in its role as an accounting tool for trade, not only generated the cost of the exchange rate, but also began to put a price on foreign exchange spots, and, gradually, was implemented for the use of spot foreign remittance, which signified that the RMB was starting to take on a typical exchange rate. Based on spot remittance, the RMB's dual exchange rates merged at the end of 1993, while convertibility of the RMB has been available under the current account since 1996. In this century, especially after China's entry into the WTO in 2001, the convertibility of the RMB under the current account became more widely available. So far, according to the criteria given by the IMF, most of the 43 items under the capital account of the RMB have been completely or are basically convertible. Only three items are under control, since they are related to the subject of the capital market. These threefold requirements are: (1) Projects of foreign direct investment should go through the approval procedure; (2) the scale of the foreign liabilities held by Chinese residents (individuals or groups) should go through the approval procedure; and (3) China's capital market is not totally open to foreign investors and the only access is through QIFI.

The gradual recovery of the RMB's external functions also set in motion its own internationalization process. Since China's policy of economic opening-up took effect in the 1980s and construction of special economic zones began, non-mainland residents, mostly Chinese in Hong Kong, Macao, and Taiwan, started to hold RMB-denominated assets and to carry RMB in cash to foreign countries. Black markets (for RMB) soon began to appear in foreign countries as a result. In the 1990s, the process of opening the sea-shore cities, the river-shore cities, and the border-shore cities began. Meanwhile, the RMB continued to make gains in both the geographical area in which it was accepted and the purposes for which it could be used.. Most prominently, in the process of opening the border-shore cities, the RMB not only plays a role of valuation and accounting tool within the structure of international trade, but also serves as an instrument of liability and investment, earning both official and unofficial recognition from both countries along the border. In some countries or regions such as Laos, Myanmar, and the northern region of Vietnam, the RMB is now a virtual anchor currency, determining the rate of exchange of the RMB against other foreign currencies.

Since the beginning of the 21st century, the international use of the RMB has grown in both variety and scale. Before the outbreak of the global financial crisis, the RMB was used internationally in three ways, which we will detail here.

The first channel in which the RMB was used was as the "stall banks" for frontier trade. The growing scale of frontier trade drove the RMB's means of settlement from cash to non-cash, thus stimulating the outflow of the RMB through "stall banks." "Stall banks" took shape differently depending on the region and procedure in question. In Yunnan Province, for example, where frontier trade took place frequently, China had a settlement model with Vietnam, with Laos, and with Myanmar, respectively. The models shared one common feature: a "stall bank" was not part of the official financial system. Instead, it was an open grey channel. The volume of business might differ between different countries and regions, but the general trend was towards the rapid development of "stall banks."

The second channel concerns the economic and trade arrangement that exists in Hong Kong and Macao. In Hong Kong and Macao, the RMB was once traded unofficially. Following the outbreak of the Asian financial crisis, the Chinese mainland initiated a closer economic and trade arrangement with Hong Kong and Macao (through CEPA, for example). Central to this arrangement was the shift in application of the RMB from informal to formal channels. After November 2003, those financial institutions in Hong Kong mainly constituted by commercial banks such as the Bank of China (Hong Kong), were allowed to run the business of the RMB within a limited scope. The Bank of China (Hong Kong), as the exclusive clearing bank, arranged RMB clearing services for the People's Bank of China. As the application of the RMB in Hong Kong expanded, the RMB could be used in both the current account and the capital account. From June 2007 on, both domestic financial institutions and the Hong Kong-funded financial institutions on the Chinese mainland began to issue RMB-denominated bonds in Hong Kong. Notably, in September 2009, China's Ministry of Finance initiated the issuance of RMB-denominated bonds in Hong Kong, and the Hong Kong market served as a benchmark for the overseas RMB-denominated bond market thereafter.

Third concerns currency swaps among countries. In a currency swap, both parties exchange currencies of equivalent amounts at an agreed-upon exchange rate. When the agreement expires, both parties re-exchange their currencies. Currency swaps exchange a loan in one currency for an equivalent sum in another currency, with the purpose of reducing the cost of fundraising and preventing one country from those losses triggered by the exchange rate's fluctuation. In 2000, the ASEAN countries, China, Japan, and South Korea reached what became known as the Chiang Mai Initiative. Under this framework, as of the end of November 2008, the central Bank of China signed six bilateral currency swap agreements with Thailand, Malaysia, the Philippines, Indonesia, Japan, and South Korea, respectively, for a total value of USD16.5 bn. Currency swaps at the national level were initiated by the monetary authority after it learnt this technique from commercial banks, thus increasing the supply of RMB-denominated funds to overseas markets. To deal with the financial crisis, between December 12, 2008—when the central bank of China and the central bank of South Korea announced a bilateral currency swap framework agreement—and March 2009, China signed bilateral currency swap agreements with countries like South Korea, Malaysia, Belarus, and Hong Kong to the tune of RMB650 bn. The hope is that as time goes on, the currency swap agreement will develop and extend beyond frontier trade to become part of a country's official trade and investment. In other words, if both parties' traders and investors agree to use the RMB to make settlements and payments, then commercial banks can be required to borrow RMB-denominated funds from the country's central bank at the same time that the central banks of the two countries involved will source RMB-denominated funds through a currency swap. At present, China has currency swap agreements with eight countries/regions—including South Korea, Argentina, and Iceland—with a total value of RMB800 bn. Among the regions with currency swap agreements, Hong Kong has been an active participant since 2010.

In the meantime, sufficient conditions arose for the internationalization of the RMB. Let's begin by looking into the internal conditions for the internationalization of sovereign currencies. Global experience historically indicates several factors:

First, the basis for the internationalization of a given sovereign currency is the country's relative economic strength. The relationship between the evolution of the international manufacturing system and that of the international monetary system must be investigated when considering economic strength. For example, when the pound sterling became a global currency, the UK had, for some time, already been the world's first-generation manufacturing center, with whom national economic strength and percentage of trade were incomparable. According to statistics, at that time, 5% of global GDP was contributed by the UK alone. When the United States replaced the UK as the world's manufacturing center, the US dollar grew to be a world currency after WWII, and, subsequently, 27% of the world's GDP was contributed by the United States. Similarly, when the Deutschmark became a world currency, its GDP accounted for 5% of global GDP; when the Japanese yen became a world currency, its GDP accounted for 7% of that of the world. It is clear that only the sovereign currencies of major economic countries are likely to play the role of a world currency.

Secondly, one of pre-conditions for internationalizing sovereign currencies is economic opening-up. Import and export trade volume directly determine overseas demands for a single sovereign currency. When the pound sterling initially began the process of internationalization, a quarter of the world's imports and exports were contributed by the UK. After WWII, when the US dollar served as an anchor currency, the import and export volume of the United States as a percentage of the world's total reached 15%. The sovereign currency of the former West Germany or Japan were not internationalized, however, until the country's import and export trade volume accounted for nearly 100% of the world's total. In other words, only the sovereign currencies of major economic countries which are already deeply engaged in international economic activities are likely to play the role of world currency.

Third, the internationalization of a sovereign currency depends on a sound macro economy and a stable currency value. Generally, when the macro economy is in good condition, the rate of inflation will be relatively low at the same time that the currency value is stable. If the currency has a stable value, the cost of holding this currency will be low and willingness to hold it in the first place will be strong. In addition, a stable currency value guarantees a stable exchange rate. As a result, it is more convenient for people to use this currency in international trade and investment for valuation and settlement, thus expanding its international use. All of the above factors are conducive to the internationalization of sovereign currencies.

The process of internationalizing sovereign currencies indicates that only the sovereign currencies of global powers with sound economic development and international involvement have the possibility of becoming global currencies. Thirty years after the country's reform and opening-up, China's economy has advanced rapidly, to the point that it experiences an annual average double-digit economic growth. We can see from Figs. 2.4 and 2.5 that, as of 2010, China has replaced Japan as the world's second largest economy. Furthermore, since the reform and opening-up and particularly following China's entry into the WTO, China's economy has been deeply integrated into the world economy. China's import and export volume as a percentage of GDP—a figure that represents this country's degree of economic openness—has reached over 70%, the highest among major countries in the world. Between 2001 and 2010, China's foreign trade as a percentage of the world's total international trade increased from 3.69 to 8.39%. This percentage exceeded that of Germany in 2009. As a result, China grew to have

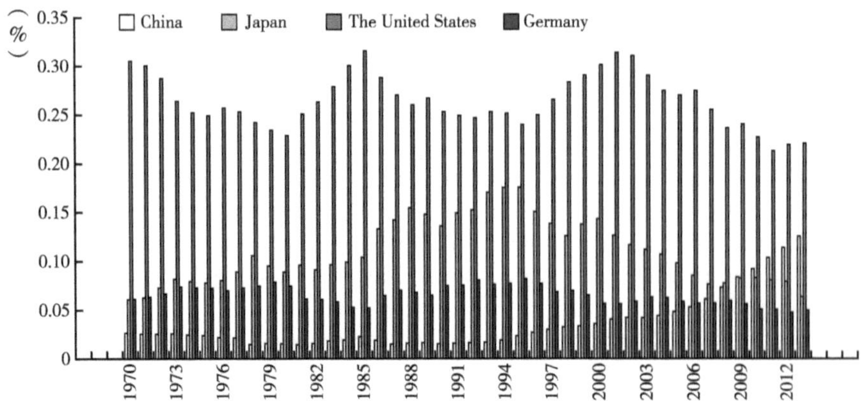

Fig. 2.4 GDP of China, the United States, Japan and Germany as a share of world total *Source* The World Bank

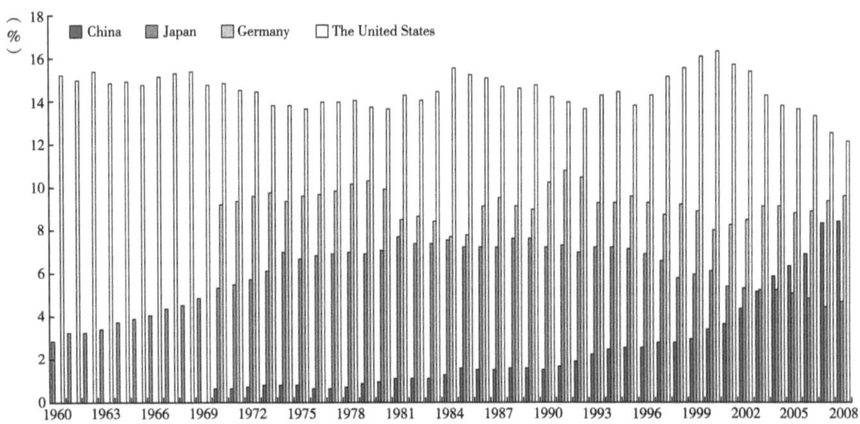

Fig. 2.5 International trade for China, the United States, Japan and Germany as a share of world total *Source* The World Bank

the world's largest percentage of international trade. What's more, since the country's reform and opening-up and especially after the 1990s, China's economy no longer experienced notable fluctuations and has been continually improving. The result is, the RMB has a stable value and trends towards appreciation. All these factors have served as domestic foundations for the internationalization of the RMB.

Next, examined from the perspective of external conditions, the internationalization of sovereign currencies often occurs when the world is badly in need of a new monetary instrument for stability due to a rapid change within the international monetary system and the resulting chaos of the world economy. The RMB's internationalization is an objective requirement for developing the new world economy. That is, the RMB's internationalization is not an intentional action undertaken by China alone, but, rather, is a historical choice by market forces brought about by the international monetary system being subjected to reformation and restructuring and resulting in the need for a new global currency.

First in our consideration of the issue is the need to promote the reformation of the international monetary system. The current international monetary system is a US dollar-centric one. Any instability in the US dollar may result in the instability of the whole system. Therefore, the international monetary system requires reformation: specifically, the establishment of a supranational currency. Existing restrictions make this goal unrealistic at the present moment, however. For instance, the fluctuation of the US dollar's exchange rate challenges the valuation and settlement of international trade. The intrinsic value of the US dollar itself shows a trend of depreciation. As a result, there is a move towards diversifying existing international reserve currencies, which is somewhat more attainable than establishing a fully independent supranational currency altogether. China's status in the world's economy and trade determines that the internationalization of the RMB would be the best choice for this push towards diversification.

Secondly, the need to strengthen pragmatic cooperative ties among emerging markets and developing countries is central: as previously discussed, following the Asian financial crisis in 1997, trade volume across Asian countries and regions (and particularly with China) has continually increased. All intra-regional trades, however, are valued and settled in a third country's currency. After the outbreak of the global financial crisis, the US dollar was in short supply, causing problems inter-Asian trade. If these countries promote settlement with their own currencies, undoubtedly the fluctuation of non-Asian currencies would have less impact on the region's trade. To meet this need, the progress of internationalizing the RMB has begun. More importantly, if Asia has a supranational currency, there will be more cooperation within this region. Pragmatic cooperation among emerging markets and developing countries will be consolidated. Investment within this region can be completed without depending on a third party—a process known as the so-called monetary cooperation mechanism of East Asia.

The third part concerns the need to engage in rebalancing the global economy. Following the outbreak of the global financial crisis, economic globalization has been seriously challenged. Due to imbalance in the world economy and the conflicts concerning upgrading within international trade, individual countries now each exhibit increasingly competitive macro-policies. China has made overtures towards solving the problems apparent in development (imbalances, inconsistency, and unsustainability). One of these proposals is to change the international trade pattern in China. Aside from the fact that China needs to import more resources, as citizens' income increases, China plans to import more consumer goods. In addition, as China's economy develops, overseas investment marked by the global capacity for cooperation will grow rapidly. The potential application of the RMB in cross-border settlements is predicted to facilitate a positive global equilibrium between investment and consumption.

2.3 The Progress of the RMB's Internationalization

The RMB began to internationalize under specific, unique conditions. The distinctiveness of these conditions manifested in the special economic structure and historical background of the process. Through an examination of internationalization precedence, the internationalization of sovereign currencies usually requires three preexisting conditions to be realized. First, a sovereign currency should be a fully convertible currency. At present, most countries' currencies are convertible currencies. Even though a convertible currency is not necessarily a global currency, the reverse is not true: a global currency *must* be a convertible currency. Secondly, a country issuing a sovereign currency should have a stable mechanism for generating deficits in terms of the balance of payments. The country's balance of payments deficit is the pre-condition for non-residents owning this country's currency. It is not necessary to reach an overall balance of payments deficit; however, the deficit should have a long-term prospects in either the current account, the capital account, or both, thus fostering a mechanism for providing the world market with this currency's stable liquidity. Third, the internationalization of a sovereign currency must be capable of developing the financial market. A sovereign currency's ability to function as a world currency means that this country's monetary policy is also capable of serving as a monetary policy for the world at large. The implementation of this policy requires a developed financial market, especially a capital market that is mainly constituted from fixed income products. The RMB is not likely to meet the requirements for internationalization from this perspective, despite the fact that the RMB is currently applied as a world currency. This presents a paradox arising from the currency's special role in the economic structure of developing countries, especially those of East Asian countries.

As previously mentioned, from the late 1950s on, Japan followed the precedent set by the UK and the United States to become the world's new manufacturing center. Centered on and propelled by this country, the so-called "flying geese paradigm" was fostered in East Asia. Within this paradigm, Japan played a leading role in the region while other East Asian countries constituted a trailing group of flying geese in the industrial chain. As a result, a huge intra-industry trade developed among the "geese." Regardless of whether the trade was between Japan and Europe, Japan and the United States, or among East Asian countries, however, the US dollar was applied towards valuation and settlement of intra-industry trade. As a consequence, the supply chain was led by Japanese industries even while the US dollar was applied in valuation, settlement, and payment, a phenomenon known as currency substitution. We can observe the process of currency substitution from three perspectives. The first perspective constitutes a substitution of assets—that is, a country uses a foreign currency to replace the domestic currency in order to serve the function of valuation and settlement as well as to play the role of a medium of exchange and a store of value. The second perspective is a substitution of liabilities —namely, that a given country's government owns substantial liabilities that are denominated in foreign currencies. The third perspective is one of a complete substitution. To be specific, a foreign currency is used as a settlement currency for the final payment. Within the East Asian region, only Hong Kong currently uses a currency board system registering a feature of complete substitution. With the exception of Hong Kong, other East Asian economies still utilize a relatively independent monetary policy, and the currency substitution in these countries is mainly reflected as a substitution of assets or of liabilities. As a result, is the region as a whole exhibits a serious trend towards dollarization.

First and foremost, when considering assets, we must be cognizant that in spite of the fact that Japan was once the world's second largest economy and one of the major players in intra-regional trade, nearly all intra-regional trades except for direct trades with Japan have been and continue to be valued and settled using the US dollar. Even for those trades between Japan and other East Asian countries, the US dollar exerts a larger influence than the Japanese yen as a money of account. For example, although Japan and South Korea have close trade and investment ties, South Korea's 85% exports and 80% imports with Japan are valued and settled in the US dollar, causing the existing currency mismatch.

Second of all, when seen from the aspect of liabilities and for a variety of reasons, it is difficult for East Asian countries to raise adequate funds from overseas markets using their own sovereign currencies. Before the outbreak of the global financial crisis in 2008, all bonds denominated in Asian countries' currencies accounted for less than 5% of the world's total number of bonds. This figure was even lower than the number of bonds denominated by the currencies of South America, a continent that had traditionally been within the sphere of influence of the United States. Many East Asian countries attract foreign capital using all available means for the purpose of accelerating their economic development, resulting in the fact that the proportion of foreign currency liabilities to total liabilities is quite high. These liabilities are mainly short-term, an issue responsible for further triggering the maturity mismatch based on a currency mismatch.

For a long time, the currency mismatch and the maturity mismatch brought about by currency substitution has perplexed East Asian countries.

For example, first of all, the practice of currency substitution brings with it the rapid fluctuation of the exchange rate. In East Asian countries, foreign currencies cannot be directly circulated, but should initially be converted to local currencies. When capital controls are not strict, however—especially when the domestic currencies in question are fully convertible—available liquidity in the market will be quite strong. Any tiny change in the rate of return will bring about a huge currency substitution effect, thus giving rise to significant fluctuations in the exchange rate.

Secondly, currency substitution restricts the effectiveness of existing monetary policies and renders regulation far more difficult. It is true that it is difficult for a country's monetary authority to directly manage the liquidity of assets and liabilities in foreign currency. When large amounts of foreign currency are exchanged for domestic currency or when a domestic currency needs to be exchanged for foreign currency, the monetary authority of the issuing country will be forced into a passive position in regards to controlling the monetary base and even the overall money supply.

Third, "currency's effect on assets" and "currency's effect on liabilities" are likely to be brought into the equation when a currency substitution restricts the circulation of foreign currency within a given country. When increasingly strong currency substitution leads to the depreciation of the currency involved, more foreign currency assets will be subsequently purchased. Accordingly, the expenses drawn from the domestic currency account will be reduced. Such circumstances initiate "currency's effect on assets." Likewise, when currency depreciation and currency substitution occur alternatingly, the balance of the domestic currency necessary for paying both the principal and interest of foreign debts will increase. Correspondingly, domestic demands will decrease, which will further drive down the domestic output and give rise to "currency's effect on liabilities." If a country's monetary authority upgrades the money supply, the shortage in the currency balance cannot, in most cases, be solved, but will, conversely, fuel further inflation. This fact was manifestly visible in the Asian financial crisis of 1997.

The Asian financial crisis urged people to take stock of the situation outlining currency substitution. Targeting the economic deficiencies of East Asia that had been exposed in the crisis, East Asian countries and regions—within the framework of ASEAN + China, Japan, South Korea (10 + 3)—attempted to solve the problem by consolidating increased economic and financial cooperation across the region. On May 4, 2000, at the 9th ASEAN + China, Japan, South Korea (10 + 3) Summit, 13 countries' Finance Ministers signed an agreement concerning the regional currency swap arrangement, namely, the Chiang Mai Initiative (CMI), thereby establishing a bilateral liquidity rescue mechanism. In 2009, this mechanism evolved into a USD240 bn. foreign exchange reserve pool for East Asia, showing a multilateral trend. What's more, by creating a mechanism for monitoring the economy and communicating about related policies, this agreement was able to identify the potential risks within East Asia and rapidly enforce remedies. Third, it was able to leverage the Asian Bond Market Initiative (ABMI) in order to boost the domestic currency-denominated bond market, to reduce regional overreliance on financing via banks, and, finally, to overcome the financial risks brought about by the maturity mismatch and the currency mismatch common to the region.

When considering the above-mentioned efforts, it is worth paying particular attention to the ABMI, whose purpose is to promote the transference of foreign currency to domestic currency. In August 2003, when the ASEAN + 3 Finance Ministers' Meeting was held in Manila, participants reached a consensus on the ABMI. This Initiative attempted to develop an efficient bond market with rich liquidity and to lay a foundation for transferring foreign currency to domestic currency, thereby better leveraging Asian deposits to provide the region with appropriate investment services. At the most basic level, the mission was to diversify both issuers and investors and to develop the infrastructure of the Asian bond market. To achieve this, six working teams were established to take responsibilities for the new tools of securitizing debts, for the credit guarantee and investment mechanism, and for foreign exchange transactions and clearing; multilateral development banks, foreign governmental institutions, and Asia's multilateral corporations were made responsible for issuing domestic currency-denominated bonds, for rating systems, and for technical assistance and coordination. In order to promote the development of the Asian bond market, we note that the Asian Bond Fund (ABF) proposed by the Executives' Meeting of the East Asia Pacific Central Banks (EMEAP) in June 2002 has contributed to increasing regional demand. The first and second phase of the ABF were officially initiated in June 2003 and April 2015, respectively. The purpose of the ABF is to leverage part of the foreign exchange reserves within the region in order to invest domestic currency-denominated or US dollar-denominated bonds issued by entities within the region, thus increasing domestic demand with the goal of boosting the development of the Asian bond market. The scale of ABF1 (Asian Bond Fund phase 1) is USD1 bn, which is the same with that of ABF2 (Asian Bond Fund phase 2). ABF1 is only accessible to EMEAP members, and will be invested in US dollar-denominated sovereign bonds or quasi-sovereign bonds issued by the member states excluding Japan, Australia, and New Zealand. By contrast, ABF2, through listing, is accessible to all other public or private investment projects, and will be invested in the domestic currency-denominated sovereign bonds or quasi-sovereign bonds issued by the above-listed member states.

The Asian bond market had developed to a significant extent before the outbreak of the global financial crisis in 2008, indicating a large push towards the conversion of foreign currency into domestic currency. Take China's panda bond market as an example. A panda bond is a Chinese RMB-denominated bond issued by non-Chinese governments, financial institutions, companies, or international multilateral organizations that is sold in the People's Republic of China (similar, for example, to the samurai bond of Japan and the Yankee bond of the United States). Since October 2005, the World Bank' International Finance Company and the Asian Development Bank have issued bonds in China four separate times, totaling RMB4 bn. The maturities of these bonds range from seven to ten years and their rates of return are between the rate of a one-year deposit and that of the money market. Therefore, these bonds are attractive to both issuers and investors. As the economic cooperation in East Asia increases, regional economic integration will also correspondingly take shape. An agreement on the terms of investment and trade liberalization was signed between China, Japan, South Korea, and 10 ASEAN countries with the expectation of building a free trade zone. As a result, trade has increased considerably among East Asian countries, the proportion growing from less than 20% in 1982 to 60% in 2008. In addition, the investment volume among East Asian countries has also reported rapid growth.

Even as East Asia showed signs of economic integration, the global financial crisis triggered by the subprime crisis in the United States broke out, which resulted in new difficulties for East Asia. Since the efforts of this region to offset the negative impacts of currency substitution were still ongoing, the US dollar continued to dominate the market. The US' subprime crisis caused financial institutions in that country to face difficulties with an acute shortage of liquidity. Massive quantities of the US dollar flowed back to the United States, causing the East Asian region to be suddenly faced with difficulties in international payment. Therefore, trade and investment shrank sharply. Even the countries with "double deficits" (international trade deficits and fiscal deficits) like Vietnam and India were likely to fall into the rut of the Asian financial crisis.

In order to relieve economic pressure and to prevent another crisis, given circumstances in which the liquidity of the US dollar experienced a shortage, East Asian countries turned their attention towards China. Because the RMB enjoyed a stable currency value and China was and is an important participant in intra-regional trade, the RMB has all the makings of a money of account and an appropriate means of settlement for international trade within East Asia. Considering China's continual economic growth and the RMB's trend towards strength and appreciation, the RMB can serve as a reliable foreign exchange reserve for East Asian countries. Because of this, East Asia began to evince strong demands for the RMB. The Philippines and other countries announced in short succession their intention to adopt the RMB as one of their reserve currencies. There was a trend towards applying the RMB to evaluate and settle trade in East Asia, especially trade with China. Faced with increased demand, the RMB began the process of internationalization for the purpose of meeting extant global needs even though the basic requirements for internationalization hadn't yet been met—requiring internationalization to start from and focus exclusively on trade.

In November 2008, the Chinese government decided to initiate pilot programs in the Pearl River Delta, Yangtze River Delta, Guangxi province, and Yunnan province for the purpose of cross-border trade settlement in yuan with ten ASEAN countries, Hong Kong, and Macao. On July 2, 2009, the *Detailed Rules for Applying the RMB in Cross-border Trade Settlement* was promulgated. The pilot programs were launched in 365 companies in Shanghai, Shenzhen, Guangzhou, Zhuhai, and Dongguan, mainly targeting Hong Kong and Macao. The means of settlement followed two separate models: via agencies of mainland China (the Shanghai model) and direct clearing (the Hong Kong model).

Under the agency model, offshore banks, via an agency in mainland China, are able to settle with the Shanghai branch of the Bank of China and/or the headquarters of the Bank of Communications (see Fig. 2.6). Under the Hong Kong model, offshore banks may settle with the Bank of China (Hong Kong) which will then directly settle with the People's Bank of China (see Fig. 4.2). In the business of cross-border trade settlement in RMB, particularly when dealing with the trade of goods, imports may be paid in foreign exchange currencies without mitigating restriction from the pilot list, while only the companies on the pilot list are allowed to collect foreign exchange for exports. Cross-border payment in RMB is allowed for trade-related issues without the circulation of goods such as the commission fee or discounts. This type of business is categorized under trade-related subordinate expenses. For the trade of services, both the payment and the collection thereof are not restricted to the pilot list (Figs. 2.7 and 2.8).

Subsequently, the volume of RMB-based cross-border trade settlement grew rapidly. As of the end of December 2014, the volume of cross-border trade settlement in RMB routed through banks reached RMB6550 bn. As estimated by international and domestic investment banking economists, RMB as a trade settlement currency maintains significant potential. At present, the trade volume of

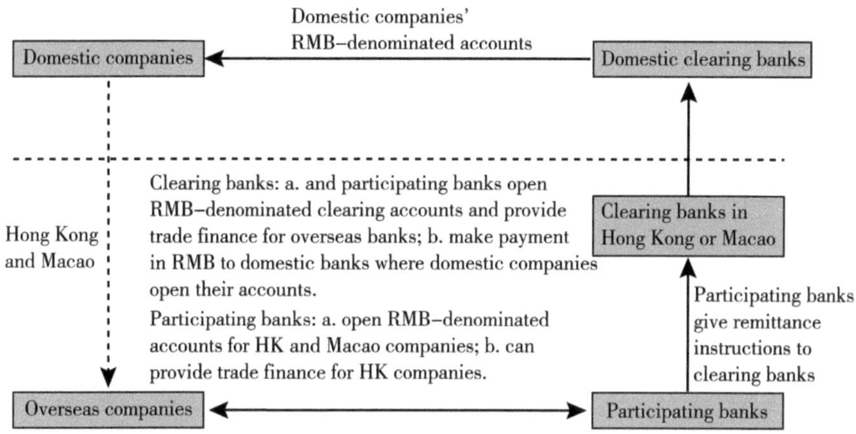

Fig. 2.6 RMB-denominated cross-border trade settlement—HK and Macao Model

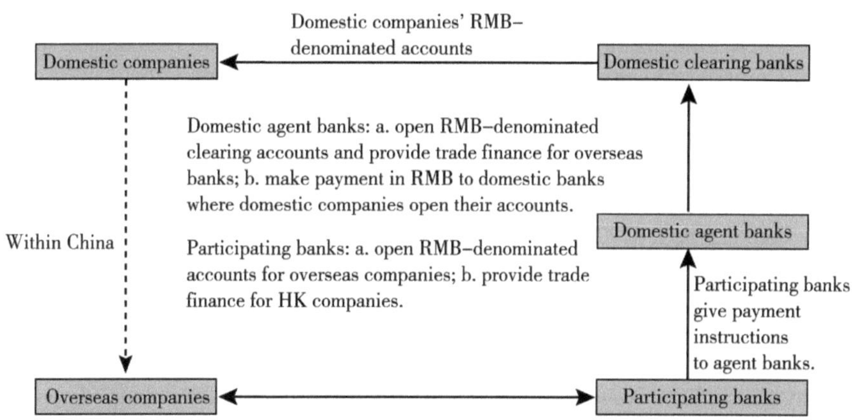

Fig. 2.7 RMB-denominated cross-border trade settlement—Shanghai Model

China that has been contributed by emerging markets accounts for 55% of total trade volume, as opposed to only 47% ten years ago. In the next three to five years, it is estimated that 50% of all trade between China and emerging countries can be settled in RMB, though this proportion is less than 3% right now. Every year, nearly USD2 tn in trade will be settled in RMB, and it is likely that the RMB will become one of the world's three major trade currencies.

There is no doubt that this initiation of cross-border trade settlements in RMB marks the beginning of China's comprehensive and official preparations for internationalizing the RMB. The RMB's internationalization meets both domestic and international needs. Once this arrangement is initiated, it will develop rapidly. To some extent, the pilot program of cross-border trade settlement in RMB has already been finalized. The RMB has already become an instrument for valuation and

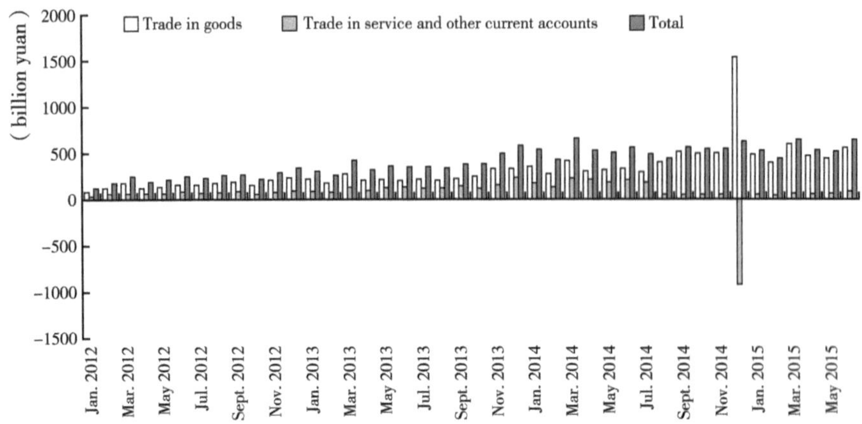

Fig. 2.8 Growth in RMB-denominated settlement for cross-border trade

settlement under the current account, thereby opening up new prospects for its further internationalization and facilitating the RMB's entry into the balance sheets of non-Chinese residents. All said, the RMB has started a journey that can be seen as fulfilling its international obligations.

The internationalization of the RMB has made significant progress within the financial market. There has been great success in the initiation of cross-border trade settlements in RMB. As of December 2010, the number of pilot companies using RMB had reached 67724, nearly 20 times those operating in 2009 (365 pilot companies); cross-border settlements using RBM reached RMB6550 bn, 1824 times that of 2009. Accordingly, the RMB has made great progress within the global financial market. China's offshore RMB market, centering on Hong Kong, has made remarkable developments. As of December 2014, the deposits in RMB held by the banks in Hong Kong had risen from RMB900 mn at the end of February 2004 to RMB1003.6 bn, reporting an increase 1114 times over. Compared to the RMB62.7 bn of 2009, the figure had increased around 15 times. The growing RMB deposits in Hong Kong hastened the development of the offshore RMB bond market. By the end of 2014, there had been 311 RMB-denominated bonds (dim sum bonds) issued in Hong Kong with a total scale of RMB338.4 bn. In 2014, the circulation of dim sum bonds reached RMB181.6 bn and the two issuances of treasury bonds in 2009 and 2010 by the Ministry of Finance of the People's Republic of China became the center of the attention.

As the dim sum bond develops, RMB-denominated derivatives and other offshore financial products have come into being. Now, in the offshore RMB market in Hong Kong, besides insurance (which went live in 2009), term deposits (which went live in July 2010), structured deposits (which went live in July 2010) and investment funds (which went live in August 2010), only the depository receipts for purchasing domestic shares from the mainland's A-share market and the ETF funds are yet to be actualized. On the basis of the already-considerable progress achieved by the global applicability of the RMB under the current account and by the RMB's offshore use in the financial market, China's central bank released its first document for 2011 on January 13, titled *Administrative Measures on the Pilot of Overseas Direct Investment Settlement in RMB*. According to the *Measures*, domestic companies which have obtained permission to deal in foreign direct investments are allowed to settle their businesses in RMB. On August 17, 2011, during his visit to Hong Kong, China's Premier Li Keqiang announced six preferential policies to boost Hong Kong's economy. Specifically, these policies included the development of the RMB market in Hong Kong; expanding the channel for the RMB's circulation in Hong Kong and mainland China; extending cross-border settlement in RMB throughout the country; supporting Hong Kong's push to settle domestic direct investment in RMB; allowing RMB Qualified Foreign Institutional Investors (RQFII) to make investments in the domestic securities market with a threshold of RMB20 bn; and setting up more domestic financial institutions to help domestic companies to issue RMB bonds in Hong Kong. The central government of China has long-term plans for issuing RMB-denominated treasury bonds in Hong Kong and will gradually expand the scope of its issuance. These measures indicate that the opening-up of the RMB under the financial account continues to progress. In order to coincide with the progress of the RMB's offshore financial market, it is expected that the opening-up of the RMB's onshore financial market will be expedited. Hong Kong and Shanghai, taking the opportunities offered by the RMB's internationalization, are no longer far off from their vision of becoming international financial centers.

On January 15, 2011, in the Joint Communiqué published during then-president Hu Jintao's state visit to the United States, the United States, for the first time, explicitly supported China's efforts in promoting the RMB in its efforts to join the IMF's SDR basket. The host of the G20 Summit at that time was France, and then French President Nicolas Sarkozy clearly stated that the central topic of this Summit was the reformation of the IMF—and this reform required the participation of the RMB. Sarkozy also convened a G20 Finance Ministers and Central Bank Governors Meeting in Nanjing, China, on March 31, 2011, focusing on reshaping the international monetary system. On April 14, 2011, at the BRICS Summit in Sanya, China, all member states released a joint document called the *Sanya Declaration*, deciding to expand the application of the local currency and deepen the corresponding financial market. Marked by the above-mentioned developments, the internationalization of the RMB is no longer a bilateral affair between China and another country/region; rather, it has become an international affair with global participation.

2.4 The Internationalization of the RMB Challenges the Financial System in China

The internationalization of the RMB is, in essence, the internationalization of a sovereign currency. Just as with the process of internationalization governing other sovereign currencies, concerns about costs and returns are foregrounded. The return is reflected in four aspects: earning revenue from seigniorage; reducing the exchange rate risk in foreign trade and investment; effectively improving the domestic financial market; and strengthening the country's capability for international payment. In terms of cost, during the RMB's internationalization process, China will inevitably face the "Triffin Dilemma" and meet many challenges—for instance, whether the independence of a country's monetary policy can be maintained. To explain more, the challenges are explored in four aspects:

2.4.1 The Full Convertibility of the RMB

Full convertibility is one of the basic requirements for the internationalization of a sovereign currency. As for the RMB, convertibility is a prerequisite for more widespread and extensive use for cross-border trade settlements, its inclusion in the SDR basket, and facilitating investment and trade. In recent years, as internationalization accelerates, different means of settlement using the RMB have been widely adopted and the scale of the RMB's outflow has expanded. On the overseas market, non-Chinese residents increasingly hold deposits valued in RMB, thus posing a significant challenge to the management of the international balance of payments, notably the regulations extant under the capital account.

After 1996, when the RMB became convertible under the current account, the focus of China's financial reform shifted to the RMB's convertibility under the capital account. According to the divisive criterion for transactions under the capital account that had been included in the IMF's 2011 *Annual Report on Exchange Arrangements and Exchange Restrictions* (AREAER), the RMB was considered partially convertible under the capital account in 75% of items and fully convertible in 12% of items. Worse, the RMB is not yet considered to be convertible at all in 25% of items. As the RMB seeks internationalization, its convertibility under the capital account should be pursued, especially considering that an international currency should have an interactive mechanism for controlling outflow-inflow. Under regulations established by the capital account, the offshore RMB lacks a stable and predictable inflow mechanism. Because of this perceived unpredictability, demand for the RMB among overseas financial markets is weak. But once the RMB becomes convertible under the capital account, it is very likely to face fierce competition from international capital after the country loosens or abandons regulations governing the balance of payments under the capital account. The consequences will be devastating. The difficulties that the Central and Eastern

European countries faced during the Asian financial crisis and during the global financial crisis have already extensively illustrated this point.

By contrast, both during the Asian financial crisis and throughout the global financial crisis, China's financial system remained relatively healthy. One of the most important reasons for this anomaly was China's regulation under the capital account. Considering that the current international financial system is still in turmoil, it is not advisable to loosen regulations completely under the capital account.

2.4.2 A Mechanism for Forming the RMB's Deficit

China is a developing country. Much like the history seen in the evolution of other developing countries, China is still in the process of industrialization. In this stage, most developing countries face a shortage of capital. Under the circumstances in which both the capital and the foreign exchange are in short supply, foreign capital should be introduced to make up for this shortage. Such a maneuver was inherent to China's policy of attracting foreign capital after the country's reform and opening-up in the 1980s.

During the process of internationalization of a given sovereign currency, the sovereign state should provide the international market with enough liquidity to meet the needs of economic development. In order to provide liquidity, the country should create either a trade deficit or capital account deficit. In the process of the RMB's internationalization, due to the typical industrial structure and the issue of employment in China, instead of creating a trade deficit, it is only feasible for China to create a capital account deficit in order to provide the world with liquidity. In fact, in the evolutionary history of previous global currencies—for example, when the pound sterling and the US dollar served as the world's reserve currencies—the UK and the United States both exhibited trade surpluses. The main method by which these two countries were able to export their currencies was through capital export. Credit loans were exported in the wake of the trade of goods.

Whether based on an opinion drawn from the historical precedent set in the internationalization of a sovereign currency or the industrialization of developing countries, or whether it is the means by which foreign exchange reserves are held of the capital gap is bridge, a trade surplus is required.

After China's entry into the WTO, the international trade of China has rapidly developed along with an expanding trade surplus. From this trade surplus, we can infer that foreign countries are forming a net currency payment against China. If the US dollar is the major currency for settlement, China will experience an increase in foreign exchange reserves and those RMB funds still outstanding for foreign exchange will report their own growth. In addition, there will be a passive injection of monetary base. If the RMB is the major currency for settlement, however, the circulation of the RMB in the overseas market should be adequate for foreign countries to pay their deficits against China. Only when China experiences a trade deficit and thus make external payments, however, can offshore RMB accumulate.

This assumption is in conflict with the previously-mentioned requirement. The only way to deal with this contradiction is to form a capital account deficit of the RMB. Regardless of if China is able to form a stable capital account mechanism in a short time or even if China is able to form a sustainable model, it seems that the "Triffin Dilemma" is unavoidable.

The "Triffin Dilemma" refers to the inner contradiction between a world currency issuer's goal of maintaining the stability of the exchange rate and providing the world with adequate liquidity. In order to maintain the stability of the currency's value, the global currency should be scarce, and the output volume should be controlled in order to guarantee its stability. In order to meet global demand for the application of this world currency to economic development, however, there must be sufficient output despite its scarcity. These two aspects reflect the contradiction between the requirement for the balance of payments surplus and that of the balance of payments deficit. The "Triffin Dilemma" reveals the inherent instability of a sovereign currency's internationalization. This Dilemma was, in fact, one of the key factors contributing to the collapse of the US dollar-centric Bretton Woods system.

The mechanism controlling the US dollar or the Japanese yen in providing the world with liquidity reveals the subtleties of the "Triffin Dilemma." The United States, for example, leverages the current account deficit to provide the world with liquidity while using the capital account deficit to enable the influx of the US dollar, thus mitigating and postponing the risks brought by the "Triffin Dilemma." Japan, which often experiences a current account surplus, utilizes the capital account deficit through external investment to provide the world with liquidity, thereby offering a solution to stabilizing the balance of payments and mitigating the "Triffin Dilemma."

China's method of providing the world with RMB will inevitably come at the cost of this country's current status in the international balance of payments. The internationalization of the RMB will unavoidably be tested by the "Triffin Dilemma."

The "Triffin Dilemma" additionally runs the risk of triggering another problem, namely, the risk of a bubble in the monetary market caused by financial innovation (Zhang Yuyan, Zhang Jingchun, 2008). If a reserve country uses its international currency reserves to purchase the currency issuer's physical assets (notably, the national strategic resources), the issuer might begin to worry about national security. To deal with this concern, the issuer must continue creating financial products with high rates of return—for instance, financial derivatives to absorb the reserve country's monetary assets. Excessive financial innovation might crowd the issuer's monetary market, however, enlarging the potential risk of separating finance from the real economy. The subprime crisis of the United States is a typical example of such a problem.

2.4.3 A Sophisticated Financial Market

When a sovereign currency is held by foreign countries' private institutions and official agencies as a store of value, the country must have a correspondingly sophisticated financial market. Otherwise, the shortage of financial instruments and products such as fixed-income products and derivatives will not meet investors' differing requirements for security, liquidity, and convenience. In other words, the investors' appetites for asset portfolios and risk management cannot be met. While the gap between developed countries and developing countries in the aspect of GDP is growingly increasingly narrow, the gap in the financial market and financial regulation capabilities remains great. For China, contemporary concepts of finance were born after the country's reform and opening-up, yet even after more than 30 years' development, the depth and the breadth of China's financial market remain inadequate, with relatively weak regulatory capabilities. Meanwhile, under a competitive and diversified international monetary system, the RMB, as an up-and-coming currency, should be further reformed and developed by China's financial policies for the purpose of gaining and keeping a competitive advantage. As China's real economy is experiencing disequilibrium and instability, the financial market will inevitably face a larger exposure to risk.

2.4.4 The Independence of the Monetary Policy

If an overly-loose monetary policy is adopted by a country when issuing a world currency, the interest rate of the domestic currency and the rate of return on assets will be lowered. As a result, the focus of foreign private institutions and official agencies is likely to shift from domestic currency-denominated assets to other monetary assets with higher rates of return. Asset outflow will partly offset the functions of a loose monetary policy, and will additionally exert pressure on the global status of the domestic currency; on the other hand, a tight monetary policy will enhance the interest rate of the domestic currency and the assets' rates of return. As a result, the domestic currency will be more globally appealing. The resulting influx of capital, to a certain extent, will offset the functions of a tight monetary policy. From the perspective of the "Impossible Trinity" of an open economy, since a currency's stable value and convertibility required to be considered a currency, any inner contraction in the independence of a monetary policy, the stability of the exchange rate, and the free movement of the capital will be more obvious against the background of globalization.

The monetary policy of an issuer, compared to that of an ordinary country, will either indicate externality or produce a spillover effect. From the perspective of the capital flow, if an issuer adopts a tight monetary policy, the interest rate of the domestic currency and the assets' rates of return will increase and a greater amount of foreign capital will be absorbed. This will result in a deflationary effect on the reserve country. If the issuer and the reserve country are in different economic cycles, a negative impact will be exerted on both the reserve country and the issuer. The monetary policy held by a given issuer will unequally shock the reserve country, while the monetary policy of the reserve country will also create a feedback loop for the issuer. The effect would not be large, but if several reserve countries simultaneously adopt an monetary policy opposite to that of the issuer, they are likely to create a significant reverse shock. Therefore, in order to safeguard its global reputation and to mitigate any unequal shocks, the issuer, when designing monetary policy, must consider other countries' interests. In other words, the potential independence of the monetary policy will be weakened.

The spillover effect and the feedback effect are themselves present in China's monetary policy as it moves to internationalize the RMB. But these two effects are produced in different stages and are not necessarily concurrent. In the preliminary stage of internationalization, the spillover effect might not be as strong as the feedback effect, while in the later stages of internationalization, the spillover effect would be stronger than the feedback effect.

In conclusion, during the internationalization process, the RMB will face challenges in realizing full convertibility, setting up a mechanism for forming the deficit, developing a sophisticated financial market, and fostering an independent monetary policy. The key to the internationalization of the RMB is to properly approach these challenges. In this sense, the internationalization of the RMB is not only a strategic opportunity in the pursuit of nationalism, but is also significant to the process of internationalism.

Chapter 3
Experiences of Internationalizing Sovereign Currencies and Lessons Learnt in the Process

When China has "double surpluses" in terms of the balance of payments while also facing challenges in enabling the opening and convertibility of the capital account, given the circumstances of a still-imperfect domestic financial market, the RMB has begun to embark on the journey of internationalization. Challenges, traditional or unorthodox, lie ahead. It is worth investigating methods by which to guarantee initiative and controllability in the process of internationalizing the RMB and to guarantee a smooth process. Using a historical lens, since the 1950s, both developed countries (ex: the Deutschmark and the Japanese yen) and developing countries (ex: the Thai baht, the Indonesian rupiah, and the Malaysian ringgit) have embarked on a similar journey. Some succeeded and some failed. The general trend is that developed countries tend to succeed and developing countries tend to fail. Why? What are the causes? What implications will this have on the internationalization of the RMB?

3.1 The Formation of the Balance of Payments Surplus and Deficit, as Well as the Issue of Circulation—Experiences of the Deutschmark and the Japanese Yen as Well as Lessons Learnt

According to the "Impossible Trinity" theory of Mundell, the very essence of the internationalization of a sovereign currency is one of providing the world with liquidity through the domestic currency's inflow and outflow mechanism, made available on the basis of the domestic currency's full convertibility and the total opening-up of the capital account. Due to this, we can approach this topic from the perspective of determining a current account, a capital account, and an exchange rate regime, as well as the independence of a given monetary policy. A world currency is derived from market competition among sovereign currencies.

© Social Sciences Academic Press and Springer Nature Singapore Pte Ltd. 2018

Y. Cao, *Strategies for Internationalizing the Renminbi*, Research Series on the Chinese Dream and China's Development Path,
https://doi.org/10.1007/978-981-13-0800-0_3

A sovereign currency's degree of internationalization is the external manifestation of the country's economic strength. Developed countries' sovereign currencies, typified by the Deutschmark and the Japanese yen, experienced a smooth process of internationalization. After WWII, the Deutschmark and the Japanese yen embarked on similar but divergent journeys of internationalization. Their ability to rise on the international market depended on the breakup of the Bretton Woods system. Due to various reasons, however, these two sovereign currencies ultimately evolved along different paths. The Deutschmark succeeded while the Japanese yen eventually stumbled in the process of internationalization. Both their experiences are enlightening.

According to the theory behind internationalizing a sovereign currency, the more competitive a country's exported products, the higher pricing power enterprises in this country will have. As a result, this country's currency will be more likely to be applied in valuation and settlement, thus further promoting the currency's internationalization. Because different countries have various arrangements for dealing with the deficit mechanism in the capital account, however, they will often choose different paths in the process of internationalizing their sovereign currencies. If both a country's trade and current account report persistent surpluses, the evolutionary path will be as follows: settlement in domestic currency, full convertibility of the domestic currency, opening-up of the capital account, and capital export. In other words, if a country's trade registers a current account surplus and capital account deficit, a circulation mechanism will gradually be established. This not only constitutes one common feature for the internationalization of both the Deutschmark and the Japanese yen, but also contributes to the subsequent divergent processes between the two countries.

3.1.1 The Internationalization of the Deutschmark

The process of internationalizing the Deutschmark underwent three stages—namely the initial stage, the developmental stage, and the successfully internationalized stage.

(1) 1950s—the initial stage

After going through the period of post-war economic recovery, Germany's continued to expand. In the 1950s, Germany began to loosen control of foreign exchange and made the Deutschmark convertible. In September 1954, West Germany abolished the "account" that once restricted the free convertibility of the Deutschmark and then set up an account without restrictions. Existing restrictions for non-German investment in West Germany were eased, which served as the first step in the process of internationalizing the Deutschmark. Soon afterwards, in order to expand the function of the Deutschmark in the international community and to create conditions for the free convertibility of the Deutschmark, in December 1954,

West Germany divided the external payment into one category that was settled in the US dollar and another category which was not settled in the US dollar. In January 1959, the Deutschmark became fully convertible under the current account. At the same time, the capital of residents and that of non-residents was able to flow without restrictions.

(2) 1960s—the rapid development stage

During the Cold War, Europe was trapped between powers in the Western Bloc and those of the Eastern Bloc. In order to seek political independence and economic development, West Germany, France, Italy, Luxembourg, Belgium, and the Netherlands signed the *Treaty of Rome* in 1957 to develop a free trade zone and to build the European Economic Community. In the 1960s, a customs union was created and a common agricultural policy was adopted. In 1965, the *Brussels Treaty*, which combined the executive bodies of the European Coal and Steel Community (ECSC), European Atomic Energy Community (Euratom), and the European Economic Community (EEC) into a single institutional structure known as the European Community, was signed. Leveraging the expanding market of the European Community, both the economy and trade of West Germany experienced newly-rapid growth. The growing trade scale and regional economic cooperation not only enhanced the economic strength of Germany, but also enabled the Deutschmark to play an increasingly important role in the regional economy, thus further laying a solid foundation for internationalizing the Deutschmark.

(3) 1970s–1990s—the successfully internationalized stage

Facing the collapse of the Bretton Woods system, the oil crisis, and the global economic crisis, in 1973, six member states of the European Community adopted "the snake in the tunnel" system and then established the "European monetary system" in 1979, in which, the Deutschmark always played a central role. With the help of the European monetary system, however, the Deutschmark also began to play an increasingly prominent role in the international monetary system. In 1984, the Deutschmark became convertible under the capital account. As economic integration in Europe accelerated, the *Report on the Economic and Monetary Union in the European Community* was published in 1989. In 1991, European countries signed the T*reaty on the European Union* (also known as the *Maastricht Treaty*). With the European Community as its basis, the European Union was established. As the European market integrated, the Deutschmark disappeared. The dissolution of the Deutschmark showed that Germany, following efforts lasting nearly half a century, had successfully leveraged regional economic and financial cooperation to enable its currency to evolve from the Deutschmark into the euro. In this sense, the Deutschmark's process of internationalization was successful.

3.1.2 The Internationalization of the Japanese Yen

Generally speaking, the internationalization of the Japanese yen has experienced three stages—namely, the initial stage, the stage of rapid development, and the period of decline.

(1) 1950s–1970s—the initial stage

Following the country's post-war economic reconstruction, Japan experienced rapid economic growth during the 1950s–1960s. Along with its rapid economic growth, Japan's external trade reported a persistent surplus. In July 1960, as stipulated by Japan's Ministry of Finance, the Japanese yen was applied towards foreign trade settlement. In addition, non-residents were allowed to open a "Japanese yen account" that was capable of holding the Japanese yen. Thereafter, the Japanese yen began to be internationalized, and, concurrently, Japan gradually loosened its control of foreign exchange. In 1964, Japan became one of the Article VIII members of the IMF. Article VIII promoted the free convertibility of the Japanese yen under the current account. In 1973, the Japanese yen adopted a floating exchange rate system; since 1977, non-residents were able to issue Euroyen bonds in Japan. During this period, however, instead of focusing on internationalizing the Japanese yen, the emphasis of the Japanese government was to prevent the appreciation of its currency and to expand the scale of its external trade.

(2) End of 1970s–1990s—the rapid development stage

At the end of the 1970s, the outbreak of the second oil crisis triggered corresponding economic crises among the United States, the UK, and other major western countries. Because Japan had previously adopted powerful preventive measures, this country successfully avoided being affected by the crises and emerged economically strengthened. Under such circumstances, the Japanese government accelerated the process of internationalizing the Japanese yen. In December 1980, the free convertibility of the Japanese yen under the capital account became a reality; in May 1984, Japan published two follow-up reports, namely, the *Report by the Japanese Yen-US Dollar Committee* and the *Status Quo and Outlook of Financial Liberalization and the Yen's Internationalization*, which allowed for individual foreign exchange futures trading premised on the lack of restrictions from physical trade. This allowed companies to freely convert foreign currencies into the Japanese yen so that those companies could bring funds raised in the yen market of Europe back to Japan. The reports also laid out three measures for promoting the financial liberalization and internationalization of the Japanese yen: liberalize the domestic financial market; improve market access for foreign financial institutions; and liberalize the yen market in Europe. In 1986, Japan set up the Tokyo offshore financial market, increased the quota for foreign capital inflow, and eliminated altogether existing restrictions on foreign capital outflow. These measures not only created conditions for the free circulation of the Japanese yen, but also steadily increased the proportion of the Japanese yen available for international reserves.

(3) The Southeast Asian financial crisis—present—the period of decline

During the 1990s, as the stock market and real estate market bubbles burst, Japan's economy found itself unable to recover. Particularly during the Asian financial crisis, the currency value of the Japanese yen fluctuated sharply, causing the status of the Japanese yen in the international monetary system to decline. After the birth of the euro in 1999, the Japanese government began to be aware of the potential risk which might be triggered by the immature development of the domestic financial market as a result of its the overly strict financial regulations. Japan had long been aware of the importance of building and enhancing a financial assets investment platform for its aging society. In addition, Japan was already aware of the danger of the internationalization of the yen lagging behind the process of financial globalization. Therefore, Japan began to carefully review and promote the internationalization of the Japanese yen by altering the originally independent route of internationalization, updated the financial services industry to a high value-added industry, focused on strengthening monetary and financial cooperative ties with other Asian countries and regions, and converted the function-based strategy of internationalizing the Japanese yen to a regionally-based one. Japan's Ministry of Finance proposed specific policies outlining the internationalization of the Japanese yen: that is, a series of policies and measures have been carried out to enhance the global status of the Japanese yen by encouraging Japan to cooperate monetarily and financially with other Asian countries (see Appendix 1). In May 2000, the Chiang Mai Initiative was signed and a consensus about monetary and financial cooperation in East Asia was reached, especially about the establishment of a bilateral monetary exchange mechanism under the 10 + 3 framework (10 ASEAN countries + China, Japan, and South Korea). Affected by the Plaza Accord and the collapse of Japan's bubble economy, Japan's economy lost more than 20 years of growth. If we look at the current status quo, we will find that the Japanese yen hasn't shown any obvious progress in the process of internationalization and has even shown signs of regression.

3.1.3 Common Points Between the Internationalization of the Deutschmark and the Japanese Yen

Following a comparison of the internationalization process of the Deutschmark to that of the Japanese yen, one common point emerges: theoretically, if a country's currency were to become an international reserve currency, there are usually two options: 1. to maintain a trade deficit and a capital account surplus; or 2. to maintain a trade surplus and a capital account deficit. Only with one of the above preconditions can the sovereign currency develop an inflow and outflow mechanism, a capacity for payment in the international community, and the necessary liquidity required for complete internationalization. But in point of fact, when aiming to internationalize a sovereign currency, a country usually adopts the second option (to keep a trade surplus and a capital deficit), a choice which creates increased circulation between the current account and capital account. When the pound sterling and the US dollar became major reserve currencies, both the UK and the United States reported a trade surplus instead of a trade deficit. The UK and the United States exported capital to enable the outflow of their sovereign currencies and to report a trade surplus and a capital account deficit. The same route was followed by the Deutschmark and the Japanese yen were in the process of internationalization, with the prerequisite for the internationalization of the Deutschmark and that of the Japanese yen being the maintenance of a persistent large-scale current account surplus.

Initially, both of these countries enjoyed great economic strength. The economy of West Germany grew rapidly after WWII and this country's products were increasingly competitive in the global marketplace. From 1952 on, West Germany began to replace the United States as the major exporter of capital goods (e.g. machinery, equipment, etc.). In the 1980s, West Germany became the strongest economic power in Europe, and—ranking only after the United States and Japan—it was the third-strongest economic power in the world at large. According to statistics, from 1950 to 2005—excepting 1986 and 1993, when the trade volume of West Germany reported negative growth—this country's trade kept a constant rate of growth. Data showed that, in 1950, the export volume of West Germany was EUR4.3bn and its import volume was EUR5.8bn. In 2005, the export volume reached EUR786.2bn, while its import volume was EUR625.6bn. Over a period of 56 years, exports increased 183 times over while imports enjoyed a growth of 108 times over; the ratio of dependence on goods trade (import and export volume of the trade of goods/GDP) increased from 15.6% in 1950 to 69.2% in 2005. From 1950 to 2005, the goods trade surplus of West Germany reached USD1909.8 bn, and a total of USD48.7 bn reserve assets were accumulated in the international balance of payments. The huge trade surplus increased the world's holding of the Deutschmark as one of the premiere foreign exchange reserves, further promoting the application and circulation of the Deutschmark. As a result, the world's demands for the Deutschmark increased, which guaranteed that it would keep a stable value.

Second, more amenable terms of trade created prime conditions for the internationalization of the Deutschmark. West Germany's exports accounted for 9.9% of the world's total in 1980, while this proportion increased to 11.4% in 1989. The proportion of goods in industrialized countries contributed by West Germany increased from 10.5 to 13.1%, reporting a net growth of 2.6% point over a period of ten years. Simultaneously, the United States' contribution of exports to the global market share increased from 11.3 to 12.1%, while the percentage of exports to other industrialized countries increased from 9.2 to 10.3%. The growth rates of the United States were lower than those of West Germany. The rising proportion of export being sent to industrialized countries showed that West Germany had both economic strength and globally competitive products. According to statistics, the nominal goods trade volume of West Germany between 1950 and 2005 had an average annual increase of 11.4%, which was far higher than 8.4%, the average annual increase of nominal GDP. To be more specific, the export of goods had an average annual increase of 11.9%, while the import of goods had an average annual increase of 10.9%. Over a period of 56 years, West Germany experienced 38 different current account surpluses. During the 40 years before German reunification, there had been 34 current account surpluses. Even after the Plaza Accord, when the Deutschmark kept appreciating, West Germany maintained a persistent trade surplus.

Table 3.1 shows that from 1972 to 1996, West Germany registered surpluses in both net imports and exports. Yet after signing the Plaza Accord in 1985, West Germany's exports continued to maintain a stable growth rate while its imports continuously dropped. From 1986 to 1989, at a point when German reunification had yet to occur, the trade surpluses of West Germany all reached over DEM100mn. West Germany had become one of the most important participants in global trade. The sheer quantity of its exports had greatly outstripped that of its imports. Table 3.2 indicates that, from the middle of the 1980s to the middle of the 1990s, West Germany maintained a high level of dependence on both imports and exports, but with a greater reliance on exports. This situation was in contrast to that of the United States and that of the UK. Trade surpluses were accompanied by the appreciation of the Deutschmark. The constant reporting of a trade surplus boosted the further appreciation of the Deutschmark, which created a sound external environment for its further internationalization.

The experience of the Deutschmark also held true in internationalizing the Japanese yen. The initial conditions that fostered this process were trade surpluses.

Table 3.1 Import and export volume of West Germany between 1972 and 1996

Year	Export	Import	Total	Surplus	Year	Export	Import	Total	Surplus
1972	148.92	128.14	277.06	20.78	1985	537.10	483.82	1020.92	53.28
1973	177.72	145.51	323.23	32.21	1986	526.37	414.21	940.58	112.16
1974	230.07	177.89	407.96	52.18	1987	527.37	409.47	936.84	117.90
1975	221.35	183.25	404.60	8.10	1988	567.74	439.76	1007.50	127.98
1976	256.65	222.17	478.82	34.48	1989	641.34	506.65	1147.99	134.69
1977	273.62	235.18	508.44	38.44	1990	642.66	550.57	1193.23	2.09
1978	284.57	243.87	528.44	40.70	1991	662.33	643.10	1305.43	19.23
1979	314.02	292.16	606.18	21.86	1992	658.48	628.20	1286.68	30.28
1980	350.33	341.38	691.71	8.95	1993	598.62	540.32	1138.94	58.3
1981	396.98	369.23	766.21	27.75	1994	694.68	622.92	1317.60	71.76
1982	427.74	376.47	804.48	51.27	1995	732.26	641.12	1373.38	91.14
1983	432.28	390.20	822.48	42.08	1996	777.70	667.10	1444.80	110.6
1984	488.20	343.21	922.41	53.99					

Unit billion Deutschmark
Source: *International Financial Statistics Yearbook (1972–1996)* [Z] published by IMF

Table 3.2 Ratio of dependence on trade of Germany, USA and UK (Unit: %)

Year	Germany		USA		UK	
	Export	Import	Export	Import	Export	Import
1985	29.3	25.3	5.5	8.9	22.1	24.0
1987	36.3	20.4	5.7	9.4	19.3	22.7
1989	28.4	22.4	7.0	9.5	18.2	23.6
1992	23.4	22.3	7.4	9.2	18.2	21.1
1994	23.1	20.7	7.4	9.9	19.9	22.1
1996	23.5	19.5	8.2	10.8	22.6	24.8

Source The International Financial Statistics Yearbook (1972–1996) [Z] published by IMF

At the time of internationalization, post-war Japan was in the initial stage of industrialization, yet its industries lagged far behind those of Europe and the United States. Among all industries, the textile industry experienced the smallest gap in experience and relative comparative advantages. Hence, Japan frontloaded the textile industry as one of its key industries and exported silk, cotton yarn, cotton cloth, and other consumer goods to industrial developed countries (notably those in Europe and the US). In 1946, the textile industry became central to the manufacturing industry as a whole, accounting for 23.9% of all manufacturing production. In 1950, the export volume of fiber and fiber products accounted for 48.2% of the country's total exports. Japan exported textiles and other light industrial goods in order to earn foreign exchange and spent this foreign exchange on the introduction of new technologies, renovating existing equipment, and purchasing raw materials for heavy and chemical industries. Starting in 1955, Japan's economy entered what can be considered the highest point of its development. During this period, Japan began to produce textile machineries as a substitute for previously-imported ones, thereby driving the development of its domestic machinery industry. Following this, Japan included its machinery, petro-chemistry, steel and iron, non-ferrous metals, synthetic fiber, and electronics industries into prioritized categories. During the postwar recovery period, Japan expanded its export of labor-intensive products to earn foreign exchange and funds with which the country was able to introduce foreign advanced production technologies. The development of the machinery industry would then drive the development of the steel and iron industry, as well as that of the electromechanical industry, which was slated to surpass that of European and American industries. From 1960 to 1965, Japan introduced over 5000 new technologies, among which, the technologies for the chemical industry, the steel and iron industry, and the machinery industry accounted for over 75% of the total. During the period from 1950 to 1973, Japan introduced 136 new steel- and iron-related technologies. Since 1973, the technologies associated with Japan's steel and iron industry have played a leading role in the world.

Starting in the 1960s but reaching its height in the 1970s and 80 s, Japan—as the only economically advanced country in East Asia, began to directly invest in East Asia at the same time that its own industrialization process accelerated. A division of the labor system based on the flying geese model with Japan as the center was established in East Asia. Based on this system, an "East Asian flying geese development model" was fostered.

Japan's process of investment followed a vertical path: Japan-NIES-ASEAN-China's coastal regions. During this industrial structural transition, Japan played a leading and central role in technology and the economy. Through funding and technology, market absorption and traditional industrial transition, Japan was able to mobilize the economic growth of East Asia. NIES members played the role of "wings." Specifically, NIES members proactively leveraged Japan's funds, technologies, and markets to develop capital- and technologically-intensive industries while transferring less competitive labor-intensive industries to the tail——that is, ASEAN countries and regions (including China's coastal regions). During this period, Japan, as the largest investor in East Asia, provided the necessary funds and technologies. When the economy of East Asia took off, Japan's labor-intensive industries (such as the textile industry and the heavy chemical industry) weakened, while its capital-intensive industries (e.g. the machinery industry and electronic industry) developed rapidly, with its industrial structure rushing towards modernization. As a result, Japan's investment in East Asian processing and assembly not only met the economic development needs of East Asia as a whole, but also firmly established a flying geese model for East Asia's economic development, with Japan playing the leading role. Ultimately, an tiered system for the division of industries in this region developed: technologically-intensive industries and high value-added industries at the top, followed by capital- and technologically-intensive industries, and labor-intensive industries forming the base.

As the flying geese pattern of development in East Asia was established, interdependence among East Asian economies deepened. Throughout East Asia, the proportion of exports from one East Asian member to another in this region increased from 30.2% in the late 1980s to 38.3% in the early 1990s. In terms of imports during the same period, the proportion increased from 28.2 to 34.5%. In 1994, interregional trade among East Asian members accounted for 43% of this region's total. Since economic interdependence among East Asian members deepened based on the traditional flying geese system and the fact that these members shared a close geographical location and similar cultures, a Japan-centric non-institutionalized economic circle grew in East Asia.

3.1.4 Divergences in the Process of Internationalizing the Deutschmark and the Japanese Yen

A difference in the arrangement of the capital account deficit was the prerequisite for a divergence between internationalizing the Deutschmark and internationalizing the Japanese yen. The difference in the capital account deficit arrangement was caused by difference variation in both the evolutionary process and model of monetary cooperation for regional and international trade settlement, as well as for international financial investment trading, which resulted in a measurable difference in the internationalization process. On the condition that a country holds an open policy, when this country maintains constant trade surpluses, in order to sustain the equilibrium of the balance of payments, this country has to leverage the capital account deficit. This solution is not only conducive to internationalizing the sovereign currency, but will also largely reduce difficulties associated with re-rating the sovereign currency in question.

The sound industrial foundation and the domestic market of Germany, following the economic upturn after the war, attracted significant investment. Meanwhile, as the branding "Made in Germany" began to garner a global reputation for quality, this country's manufacturing products soon became widely sought-after and available internationally. In 1973, before Germany adopted a free-floating exchange-rate regime, Germany's direct investment in the domestic market was nearly equal to that in the external market. During the years between 1950 and 1974, Germany's accumulated net investment reported a total surplus of USD2.7 bn. Later, as the Deutschmark appreciated and the domestic pay level rose, Germany began to gradually move its industrial production to other countries. From 1975 to 2005, under Germany's direct investment, surpluses existed in 2000 (due to the substantial depreciation of the euro, overseas investors swarmed into Germany through mergers and acquisitions. As a result, Germany's direct investment reported a net inflow of USD150 bn—a record high), 2002, and 2003, while deficits existed in the other 27 years. During the same years between 1975 and 2005, Germany's net direct investment showed an accumulative deficit of USD215.4 bn, indicating a general trend of significant net outflow.

Between 1950 and 2005, Germany maintained a current account surplus and a capital account deficit. In this time, only eight years witnessed surpluses for both the current account and the capital account and only one year witnessed deficits for both the current account and the capital account. Between1950 and 2005, due to Germany's current account surpluses, a total of USD390 bn foreign exchange revenue was earned. Through capital transfer, foreign direct investment, securities investment, and overseas debit and credit, the equivalent of USD500 bn Deutschmarks had been exported. By using overseas capital and utilizing a long-term assistance plan for the export of capital, deals using Germany's reserves reached only USD45 bn over the course of 56 years, realizing the fluctuating value of the Deutschmark. It is worth noting that when the Deutschmark leveraged its current account surpluses to form a loop with the capital account, it was done on the fundamental basis of the stability of its domestic currency.

Early in 1972, when the Deutschmark began to be internationalized, the European Community member states reached an agreement that the exchange rates of this region's sovereign currencies should fluctuate within ±2.25%. In 1979, the European monetary system was officially established and the exchange rate linkage mechanism was therefore inherited. Regional monetary cooperation was seen as being able to mitigate the effect of speculative capital on the strong powers in this region and would reduce the negative effect of exchange rate appreciation on trade units. Under the exchange rate linkage mechanism of the European Monetary Area,

Germany guided speculative capital towards weak sovereign currencies, which, to some extent, transferred the pressure of appreciation to other countries. At the same time, by leveraging the exchange rate linkage within this region, Germany was able to mitigate the appreciation of the Deutschmark and thus maintain the stability of trade and investment within this region. Other countries, whose sovereign currencies were pegged to the Deutschmark, were able to depend on its stability to maintain the constancy of their own domestic price levels. This, in turn, consolidated the status of the Deutschmark as the center of the Western European monetary system. With this powerful status, Germany did not have to suffer from the pain of the so-called "currency mismatch." which laid a foundation for forming a smooth loop between the current account and the capital account.

The situation in Japan differed from that of Germany, though the post-war Japanese economy also experienced rapid growth. Together with Japan's competitive advantage in manufacturing, a huge current account surplus had accumulated. Along with this surplus, Japan began to export capital, and gradually introduced the flying geese model to Asia. Among the key features of the internationalization of the Japanese yen were, on one hand, the developing economies of East Asia depended on developed countries within or outside the region (most notably Japan) to absorb industries through direct investment; while on the other hand, the developing economies of East Asia (except for the Chinese mainland), due to their own small domestic markets, had to depend on the demands of the external market. Theoretically, such a supply chain required financial support from a central sovereign currency. As mentioned previously, however, the supply chain of East Asia was led by Japan, while the region's monetary system was led by the US dollar—resulting in a serious currency mismatch. Under such circumstances, Japan held a huge current account deficit, but was not able to develop a corresponding capital account deficit. The only way of producing a capital account deficit would be to increase foreign direct investment, which further required that Japan not only undergo rapid technical progress to ensure the "flying geese"-modeled vertical division of labor in East Asia, but also that the country must continually increase its exports, particularly to developed countries in Europe or North America, due to increasing productivity. Japan found it difficult to bear the accumulative effects produced by the gradual openness of this system. This is primarily because, first of all, Japan was not the tech center of the world and its capacity for innovation was relatively weak; secondly, under pressure from developed countries in Europe and the US, it was difficult for Japan to continue expanding its exports. As a result, the "flying geese"-modeled traditional vertical division of labor was soon flattened. Countries with equal or similar levels of economic development (e.g. between China and ASEAN countries, or between the Four Asian Tigers and Japan) expressed varying degrees of homogeneity in their industrial and export structures, resulting in pressure and economic competition among countries. Take the competition between ASEAN countries and China, for example. Since both parties had rich labor resources, competition in the exportation of labor-intensive products (clothing, textile, footwear, etc.) and assembled electronic products intensified. Due to existing similarities and the competiveness of industrial and export structures among countries at similar levels, this region has leaned towards a common export destination and a global universal currency—as such, the significance of the US dollar increased and the existing currency mismatch became much more serious. Eventually, a vicious circle formed. That is, due to the currency mismatch, it was difficult for Japan to develop a capital account deficit by injecting financial investment funds or by utilizing other forms of international indirect investment. Instead, using direct investment to develop a capital account deficit relied on faster technical progress. Barring that, a vertical division of labor would become a horizontal one, and competition among export industries would further increase the currency mismatch.

In the late 1980s, Japan became aware of the problem's severity and, in response, initiated mitigating measures such as granting overseas assistance loans and allowing foreign institutions to issue samurai Bonds within Japan's financial market in order to establish and thoroughly implement the "Capital Recycling Program." This plan was terminated almost immediately, however, due to the collapse of Japan's bubble economy. Unlike Germany, Japan was not able to set up a solid system of circulation between the current account surplus and the capital account. The internationalization of the Japanese yen ultimately failed as a result, despite the country's best intentions. Before the birth of the euro, the Deutschmark was among the major global currencies, and the status of which was just second to that of the US dollar while higher than that of the Japanese yen. The change in the percentage of the Japanese yen and that of the Deutschmark applied in the international trade settlement, international financial exchange, and international reserve system more firmly cemented this configuration of international standings.

As far as the percentage of a country's import and export that was capable of being settled in this country's sovereign currency, Germany utilized the Deutschmark far more than Japan applied its yen. As far as the currency being applied on the international financial exchange—foreign exchange transactions and international bond transactions, mostly—the percentage of the Japanese yen was lower than that of the Deutschmark. The percentage of foreign exchange transactions settled in the Japanese yen dropped from 11.7% in 1992 to 8.3% in 2007. Early in 1998, however, the percentage of the global foreign exchange settled in the Deutschmark had already reached 15.1%. As to the percentage of the global bond issuance valued in one country's sovereign currency, according to BIS statistics, as of June 2009, the percentage of the Japanese yen was 3%, the percentage of the pound sterling was 9%, and the percentage of the euro was as high as 47.5% (Table 3.3).

Table 3.3 Proportion of domestic currency-settled export and import in Japan and in Germany

Nation	Export (%)				Import (%)			
	1980	1988	1996	2006	1980	1988	1996	2006
Japan	29	34	36	40	2	13	21	24
Germany	82	79	76	61	43	53	53	53

Source Ministry of Economy, Trade and Industry

3.2 Opening the Capital Account—A Traditional Difficulty Faced by Developing Countries

The experience of internationalizing the Deutschmark and internationalizing the Japanese yen demonstrates that when the current account registers persistent surpluses, it is necessary to develop capital account deficits in a timely and effective manner, thus fostering a connection between the two accounts. This is a requirement for internationalizing a sovereign currency, the prerequisite for which is the opening of the capital account. For developing countries, however, opening the capital account has traditionally been a difficult process

"Developing countries" is a description that exists only in comparison to "developed countries." Compared to developed countries, developing countries lag behind in economic and social development, especially in terms of industrialization. According to development economics, this lag has manifested in a dual economic structure. That is, developing countries possess a relatively weak industrial sector structured by modern enterprises and a widely self-sufficient agricultural sector, thus producing a dual economic structure covering both the traditional agricultural sector and the modern industrial sector. To overcome the problem of having a dual economic structure and in order to boost the economy, the only road is industrialization. After WWII, as global colonialism largely collapsed, many politically independent developing countries invariably embarked on this road and became emerging economic powerhouses.

Once developing countries embarked on the road of industrialization, the primary problem they faced was that of the formation of capital. In economics, capital is the material base of production, enlarging the capacity for production and enhancing productivity. Capital includes physical capital, human capital, and financial capital, among which, physical capital is the primary factor. Physical capital refers to durable goods (machines, equipment, factories, facilities, etc.) used to manufacture other consumer or capital goods. Capital is sourced from savings, namely, the balance after deducting the amount of consumption from the national revenue. If the balance (savings) is equivalent to the overall investment, then the process of investment is a process of forming or accumulating capital. As defined by development economics, the low savings ratio of resources is the reason behind why developing countries are less developed than their wealthier peers. The core task of economic development is to take a country whose ratio of savings and investment is no higher than 4–5% of the national revenue and develop it into a country whose savings ratio of resources accounts for over 12–15% of the national revenue. This is a central issue because the core tenant of economic development is to rapidly accumulate capital (including the knowledge and technologies for using capital). If the contribution of savings to the rapid growth of national revenue cannot be explained, any industrial revolution cannot itself be explained.

Total supply (total income) equals to total demand (total expenditure).

If Y represents total income (total supply), C represents consumption, S represents savings, T represents government income and M represents import, then

$$Y = C + S + T + M \tag{3.1}$$

If Y represents total expenditure (total demand), I represents investment, G represents government expenditure and X represents export, then

$$Y = C + I + G + X \tag{3.2}$$

If the government income equals to the government expenditure, then

$$S + M = I + X \tag{3.3}$$

After the merger of similar terms

$$I - S = M - X$$

The gap in savings equals to the gap in foreign exchange reserves.

In order to accelerate economic development, increasing savings and attracting foreign capital are generally agreed to be the best courses of action, especially related to a country's financial policies and systems, as well as a given series of supporting policies and systemic arrangements.

The logic behind this process is that, in terms of pricing, bringing down the costs of agricultural products and inflating the costs of industrial goods will help industrial investors turn a profit and attract surplus rural labor forces to work in the industrial sector, thereby narrowing the investment gap caused by a shortage of savings. In terms of the external economy, it is reasonable to adopt a series of trade policies that restrict imports while encouraging exports with the aim of fostering trade surpluses. Logic also dictates that adopting preferential investment measures will attract foreign capital to attract an influx of capital, thereby easing the foreign exchange gap by levering the current account surpluses and the capital account surpluses. In terms of the fiscal aspect, adopting industrial policies to encourage industrial development while leveraging tax deduction and exemptions as well as fiscal subsidies will accelerate the formation of capital.

It should be noted that in order to accelerate the formation of capital after the war, nearly all developing countries already undergoing rapid development adopted the following financial arrangement: in terms of domestic finance, the development of commercial banks tended to take place both earlier and more thoroughly than the developmental rate of the capital market. The business model of commercial banks was such that accepting deposits became central to their business, as a result of to which, commercial banks were uniquely capable of doing so. In other words, commercial banks would gather funds from all corners of society. What's more, insofar as indirect financing, deposits have been kept relatively separate from loans. As a result, it would be possible to control spreading interest rates—namely, bringing down the deposit interest rate and further driving down the loan interest rate. Such a measure for bringing down the price of capital would help accelerate its formation.

Another measure undertaken at this time was to further increase and define the separation between deposits and loans, thus allowing for differentiated loan interest and credit quotas. By adopting this measure, commercial banks were able to support the country's industrial policies so that the development of certain industries (e.g. export-oriented industries) could be prioritized. In contrast, leveraging the capital market served as a kind of direct financing between investors and financing parties. As opposed to the above-mentioned indirect financing, there was no condition under which market manipulation was feasible. In the capital market, it was difficult to bring the cost of financing down. As a result, it was similarly difficult to bring down the price and accelerate the formation of capital, causing the development of the capital market to lag. What's more, in order to further accelerate the formation of capital, a country would attempt to directly control available financial resources. This was the reason why so many commercial banks found in developing countries were state-owned. If a country was not able to nationalize all commercial banks, it would, at the very least, establish a development bank to facilitate the country's developmental policies. In terms of international finance, in order to stimulate exports and absorb foreign capital, a country's domestic currency would, of course, be undervalued. Undervaluing the exchange rate of the domestic currency in order to overvalue the exchange rates of foreign currencies and distorting international trade conditions in order to make export-oriented industries profitable and obtain greater foreign exchange earnings were the stated goals.

At the same time, since the exchange rates of foreign currencies were overvalued, foreign investors were able to purchase factors of production for cheaper, the purpose of which was to attract foreign investment. To distort the exchange rate, a country had to engage in capital control for the international balance of payments. In the initial stage of economic development, domestic currencies were not convertible. Even in the middle stage of economic development, domestic currencies were only convertible after meeting certain requirements and at most times were convertible only under the current account. Often, a domestic currency was convertible when the country imported capital goods. At that time, the capital account was strictly controlled. Usually, it was allowed to convert foreign currencies to the domestic currency, but was not vice versa.

When considering developing countries' financial arrangements, the most vital issue was being able to control foreign exchange, notably, the capital account. The exchange rate cannot be distorted for a long time without the corresponding condition that the capital account is also under control. Since the exchange rate is the price of capital in foreign currency, interest rate parity exists between the two. To distort the exchange rate, a country must first distort its interest rate. Similarly, to distort the interest rate, a country must distort the exchange rate. As such, the distortion of the exchange rate and the distortion of the interest rate are related to the degree of openness of the capital account. It should be noted that under the Bretton Woods system, developing countries' requirements for development systems and policies, especially for financial arrangements, could generally be met. After WWII, the Bretton Woods system and the corresponding GATT were arrangements made under the terms of multilateralism, namely, the rules and coordination arrived at without the basis of discrimination. As a result, "a subtle balance vitalized this system: The sufficient international control and trade openness guaranteed the global business prosperity. Meanwhile, governments had enough policy space to meet the needs of domestic social and economic development. International economic policies and domestic polices (full employment, economic growth, equitable distribution, social insurance and public welfare) took a back seat." (Rodrik 2011) In concrete terms, the following two points most prominently manifested this subtle balance: first, the IMF, as the central pillar of the international economic system, had duties and obligations to provide deficit countries and those member states without sufficient foreign exchange and difficulties paying foreign debts with short-term loans in order to address the international balance of payments. It facilitated the absorption by developing countries of foreign capital and dealt with difficulties caused by the outflow of foreign capital. Secondly, under the fixed exchange-rate regime wherein the US dollar was pegged to gold, member states, when facing a "liquidity disequilibrium," were allowed to adopt a "one-off depreciation" in order to adjust their exchange rates. The principle behind making such an adjustment was that a member state's obligation to repay foreign debts had badly affected the country's economic growth and employment while the short-term financing provided by the IMF was not able to eliminate these deleterious effects. In order to avoid economic loss, the country in question was allowed to adjust the exchange rate. It obviously provided a basis for developing countries to underestimate the exchange rates of their own domestic currencies and constituted a reason for the control of capital account.

The reason why the Bretton Woods system was able to achieve the above-mentioned balance was entirely due to the fact that the US dollar kept a fixed exchange rate against gold. The adjustment of one country's exchange rate would only affect the exchange rates of some countries, but would not harm the system as a whole. In addition, since the US dollar kept a fixed exchange rate against gold, the IMF was able to achieve a balance of payments equilibrium by granting loans in US dollars to deficit countries. As the Bretton Woods system collapsed, however, followed shortly thereafter by the Jamaica system, development-oriented policies aimed at developing countries were faced with great challenges.

First, the floating exchange-rate regime was challenged. Due to the demonetization of gold, the status of the US dollar as an anchored currency was greatly weakened. The world's currencies floated not only against the US dollar, but also against one another, a situation which challenged developing countries' long-term efforts towards undervaluing their sovereign currencies. As such, they could be shocked quite easily. Correspondingly, it was difficult for these countries to control the market interest rate. In order to stabilize the exchange and interest rates, the only solution was to cement the regulation and control of the international flow of capital and to forbid the convertibility of domestic currencies, especially the convertibility of the capital account (which can be considered to be the last defense).

Secondly, the mechanism for keeping the balance of payments equilibrium was challenged. The US dollar, after losing its restrictions from gold, was able to make monetary policies according to the specific macro-economic situation of the United States without the corresponding need to consider its obligations as a global central bank. Following this reversal, the US dollar's credit was considerably weakened. The IMF's expectation of using SDR to remedy existing issues was only a drop in the bucket. After all, the SDR did not possess the full array of functions inherent to an international currency (that is, it was without the function of valuation and settlement for trade). The balance of payments equilibrium in the United States depended more on the market mechanism (financing from the market or seeking assistance from exchange rate adjustment), the results of which would be extremely uncertain, with potentially large risks. The Asian financial crisis was the best illustration of such a situation. In order to prevent such a passive state of affairs, developing countries relied increasingly on trade surpluses. Therefore, it was necessary to regulate and control the international balance of payments related to the capital receipts, especially the capital account. By this token, the openness of the capital account became a recognizable bottleneck for developing countries.

History bore out the consistency of this logic. Following WWII, many developing countries embarked on the road of industrialization, foregrounding economic opening-up as a primary strategy supporting the process of industrialization and thus forming various models of industrialization, including the import substitution model (Latin America) and the export-oriented model (Asia). At that time, because the international economic order represented by the Bretton Woods system provided a relatively stable external environment for the aforementioned models of industrialization, developing economies reported rapid growth. The collapse of the Bretton Woods system brought instability to the international environment, however, causing many developing countries to simultaneously experienced what became known as a "lost decade."

During the 1980s, the economic growth of developing countries slowed substantially (see Table 3.4).

Sub-Saharan Africa, central Africa, and Latin America registered a negative growth in terms of per capita GDP. Latin America was beset with a debt crisis and its import-substitution-based industrialization model was seriously impeded. Even

Table 3.4 GDP growth (%) and per capita GDP growth (%) of developing countries

	GDP growth		Per capita GDP growth	
	1965–1980	1980–1989	1965–1980	1980–1989
Industrial country	3.7	3.0	2.8	2.5
Developing country	5.9	4.3	3.4	2.3
Sub-Saharan Africa	5.2	1.0	2.0	−2.2
East Asia	7.3	8.4	4.8	6.7
South Asia	3.6	5.5	1.2	3.2
Latin America & the Caribbean	6.0	1.6	3.4	−0.6

Source World Bank, Report on World Development for 1990, Table 3.1, p. 16

in East Asia, where the export-oriented model had been adopted, there was a decrease in the trade surplus and an economic bubble. Indonesia represents an ideal case study. In 1983, the total trade demands of the world declined, oil prices dropped, and exports decreased. The increasing trade deficit of non-oil products exceeded the decreasing trade surplus for oil. In 1983, the current account deficit of Indonesia surpassed USD7 bn, accounting for around 8% of the GDP for that year. Since it was unable to balance this high trade deficit with capital inflow, the country experienced a net capital outflow, causing foreign exchange reserves to drop by USD250 mn every month.

As described previously, under "an unsystematic system" such as the Jamaica system, the IMF lacked compulsory means by which to achieve an international balance of payments equilibrium. Instead, their only hope was to leverage a floating exchange rate. If a country's current account registered a serious deficit and showed a worsening trend unable to be eased by a floating exchange rate, however, the only option remaining was to open the capital account, expecting that the inflow of overseas capital would be able to offset the current account deficit. It is worth noting that this solution was the suggestion proposed by the IMF to its member states. In 1997, the IMF held its annual meeting in Hong Kong. Michel Camdessus, then Managing Director of the IMF, expected that this meeting would officially put the task of driving the free mobility of global capital within this institution's scope of authority and believed that the flows of capital would play an increasingly important role in the global economy, stating: "It has been proven that a more open and free capital flows system will greatly facilitate the global economic development. When the global capital flows, the savings in the world will be utilized in a most efficient way. And the target of increasing the investment, boosting the growth and prospering the society will be achieved. Of course, governments should allow the capital flows in order. Appropriate national and international policies should be adopted to ensure the smooth capital flows. In any case, the Committee's opinion is: we should firmly develop the global economy to achieve free capital flows...In this age of globalization, to efficiently run a country's monetary system, it is inevitable to liberalize the capital." (Rodrik 2011).

In fact, before this annual meeting, East Asian countries had already initiated their actions following the recommendations of the IMF. During the 1990s, the sovereign currencies of Indonesia, Malaysia, the Philippines, and Thailand were overvalued, causing that the growth of exports to slow, while rapid economic growth caused demands for imports to expand, thus resulting in the current account deficits. In 1996, Indonesia's current account deficit as a percentage of GDP reached 3.37%. This percentage for Malaysia, the Philippines, and Thailand was 4.43, 4.77, and 8.07%, respectively, surpassing the globally recognized warning line. In order to balance the current account deficit, these four countries had to depend on the capital account, in order to accelerate the process of opening the capital account. In the absence of financial regulations, much of the capital being absorbed was US dollar-denominated short-term foreign debt or "hot money" for arbitrage. Due to the expansion of bank loans and the aggregation of foreign currency-denominated debts at this time, these countries were easy victims to capital flight and infectious currency depreciation, thus developing what has become known as "excessive borrowing syndrome." Thailand was the most typical representative of this particular issue. Thailand leveraged The Bangkok International Banking Facilities and loans to meet domestic demands for investment. The country also set up a state-funded financial market with the purpose of fostering appropriate channels for financing, so as to better take in foreign currency-denominated deposits and grant domestic loans. In 1992, Thailand established BIBF with the purpose of developing Bangkok as the financial center of the Asia-Pacific region, as well as with an eye towards exploring Thailand's international loan business so as to reduce the cost of fundraising from the overseas market. Within this framework, the central bank of Thailand granted the license of BIBF to 15 domestic commercial banks and 35 branches of foreign commercial banks in Thailand. Licensed commercial banks were allowed to take in deposits and raise funds from the overseas market. Both domestic loans and overseas loans were foreign currency-denominated. In Thailand, non-residents were allowed to open Thai baht-based accounts in commercial banks for the use of depositing and borrowing. The Thai baht in these accounts was convertible. By 1996, Thailand had almost fully opened its capital account. For the purpose of closing its huge current account deficit, Thailand borrowed extensively from overseas. Under such circumstances, the scale of Thailand's overseas borrowing rapidly expanded, along with an imbalanced foreign debt structure. The scale of foreign debts increased to USD93 bn in 1996, equaling 50% of overall GDP. Of this 50%, around 45% was contributed by short-term foreign debts. Furthermore, many private institutions raised their funds from overseas markets; as to the asset-liability structures of enterprises and banking institutions, the problem of a currency mismatch was omnipresent and most debts were short-term foreign acquisitions for the sole use of long-term investment in domestic non-trade sectors, notably the real estate sector. When the Thai baht suffered from a forced depreciation and a rising interest rate, Thailand faced a heavier burden of debt, thus triggering liquidity problems. In February and May of 1997, the Thai government, in order to maintain its exchange rate relationship with the US dollar, was forced to intervene in the foreign exchange market by underselling substantial foreign currencies. Later, because the pegged exchange rate lacked flexibility, the monetary policies of the Thai central bank were incapable of flexibly and effectively regulating economic variables. As a result, the Thai baht faced frequent shocks from global hot money. In July 1997, when foreign exchange reserves were nearly exhausted, a financial crisis arose and soon spread to the whole of Asia. Facing what was increasingly obvious as an Asian-wide financial crisis, countries adopted different solutions, among which, Malaysia's solution was the most straightforward. In August 1998, Malaysia announced that it would control the foreign exchange. Because this move achieved measurable results, many other countries followed in its steps. After the Asian financial crisis was quelled, countries gradually began to regulate their capital accounts, which soon revealed itself as a more complicated issue than had been expected.

3.3 Monetary Policies—The Different Choices of Developed Countries and Developing Countries

As described previously, the underlying feature of the Bretton Woods system is as follows. Under this system, the Federal Reserve played the role of the world's central bank, while the central banks of all other countries actually served as executive arms of the Federal Reserve without the need for or necessity to carry out independent monetary policies. Furthermore, the interest rate was stable due to a fixed exchange rate, and it was not necessary to use financial derivatives to hedge the risks of either the exchange rate or that of the interest rate. All other countries' financial regulators simply followed the criteria established by the United States to maintain market order. As the Bretton Woods system collapsed, however, everything started to change. One immediate consequence was that the exchange rates and interest rates of all countries began to float. Liberalizing the interest rate, freeing the exchange rate, and opening the capital account became pressing domestic issues. To adequately address such concerns, countries needed to have the capability to independently make and implement monetary policies, and, most notably, should have the capability to regulate monetary prices. To cultivate these capabilities, a country must develop a comprehensive financial market, which posed significant challenges to both developed countries and developing countries alike. A historical difference in various countries' system and policy arrangements is apparent, however, and due to this difference, developed countries like Germany and Japan had different fates in internationalizing their sovereign currencies from developing countries, which experienced divergent economic growths.

To begin with, it may be prudent to look closely at the situations in Germany and Japan. If we examine the interest rate liberalization, exchange rate liberalization, the opening of the capital account, and domestic currency liberalization chronologically, we can clarify two features: firstly, it seemed that neither the exchange rate reform nor the capital account opening in Germany and Japan can claim precedent. Once a particular reform was initiated, other items changed accordingly, indicating some degree of linkage. Secondly, Germany's initiation to reform occurred earlier than that of Japan. A number of reforms were carried out in Germany before the collapse of the Bretton Woods system, while those in Japan took place only after the collapse of this system. This can be taken as demonstrating that the reforms in Germany, to a considerable extent, were active actions, while those in Japan were largely passive responses to external stimuli. These features are reflected in the two countries' respective attitudes towards their sovereign currencies' appreciation.

As the Cold War ended, the global economy began an extended process of in-depth globalization. In the "unsystematic system" discussed earlier—the Jamaica system—each country adopted an individualized economic plan with a frequently fluctuating exchange rate, causing the export-oriented economy of East Asia to face severe difficulties.

After 1995, the exchange rate of the US dollar against the Japanese yen skyrocketed. The Thai baht and the Malaysian ringgit, whose exchange rates were pegged to the US dollar also appreciated considerably against the Japanese yen and European currencies. The overvaluing of the Thai baht was detrimental to the country's exports, leading to substantial decreases and a huge current account deficit. After the 1990s, Thailand's current account deficits were outstanding (see Table 3.5). The average current account deficit of Thailand as a percentage of the country's GDP was 7%. In 1995, this percentage was 8.1%. The unprecedented advantage of Malaysia and Thailand—at least in terms of the exchange rate—eventually came to be seen as a disadvantage. Consequently, the exports of both Thailand and Malaysia were also at a disadvantage. The average export growth of the four ASEAN countries for 1996 decreased by 12.25% compared to that of 1995. Among these countries, the export growth of Thailand reported the largest decrease; the growth rate of Thailand's exports was 22.5% for 1995 but dropped to 3% in 1996. The immediate consequence brought about by weak exports was an increasingly frequent occurrence of current account deficits. Thailand's current account deficit as a percentage of GDP reached 8.2% at one point. After the exchange rate of the US dollar became strong at the beginning of the 1990s, ASEAN countries would have been well-served by the adjustment of their exchange rates—for instance, depreciating their domestic currencies to offset the negative impacts brought by the actual exchange rate increase, or rearranging their exchange-rate regimes to make their exchange rates more flexible so as to adapt to the new situation—but such a policy of regime adjustment was difficult to realize. In overseas markets, the exchange rate of the US dollar remained strong and greatly appreciated against other major currencies.

Because Thailand's current account reported deficits, it was difficult for the Thai baht to become one of the strong international reserves. Yet as the current accounts of most developing countries indicated higher deficits, the number of short-term debts and total debts became increasingly common and these countries were more likely to be attacked by hot money.

Indonesia shared a similar experience. When the Japanese yen depreciated, the export price of Indonesia rose against the Japanese yen. The result was that the competitiveness of export weakened, thus enlarging the current account deficit and worsening the international balance of payments. The exchange rate of the Japanese

Table 3.5 Thailand's balance of payments

Year	Current account's net amount	Capital account's net amount	Net export	Foreign exchange reserves
1990	−7281	9098	−6751	13,247
1991	−7571	11,759	−5989	17,287
1992	−6303	9475	−4161	20,012
1993	−6364	10,500	−4297	24,078
1994	−8085	12,167	−3726	28,884
1995	−13,554	21,909	−7968	35,463

Unit 1 million US dollar
Source International Financial Statistics, 1996

yen against the US dollar frequently and substantially fluctuated. Under such circumstances, the macro economy of Indonesia would experience sharp fluctuations (see Table 3.6).

Meanwhile, due to the fact that a typical export-oriented strategy was usually driven by increases in foreign capital, overdependence on the capital, technologies, and markets of foreign countries, along with widespread ignorance of domestic capital accumulation and developing domestic markets was the result. Since the economic growths of Thailand, Malaysia, and other Southeast Asian countries were driven by investment, the competitiveness of these countries' exports was predicated upon advantages in their low exchange rates and low labor force costs. As these countries' national incomes increased, their labor force costs became correspondingly higher. Furthermore, the rise of neighboring countries posed a new challenge to the previous countries' labor force costs. For instance, after China adopted its reform and opening-up policy in 1978, its economy stepped into a period of rapid growth starting in the 1980s and continuing until the present day. After saying goodbye to its domestic shortage China's products began to become increasingly available on the global market starting in the 1990s. China's exportable products were indiscernible from those of neighboring Southeast Asian countries. They even had the same export destinations. However, the labor force cost of China was much lower than that of Southeast Asian countries. Due to the low labor force cost and its wide market potential, China became the new ideal for international capital investment. After the 1990s, China was second only to the United States in terms of capital attraction. During the same period, however, Thailand and other Southeast Asian countries lost their advantage in labor force costs. Even more seriously for their economies, because their exchange rates were overvalued, their return on investments (ROIs) kept falling. As a result, overseas market began to withdraw their long-term investment capital from this region. Because these countries' advantages in export were no longer that competitive, their current account deficits continued to degrade.

Table 3.6 Current account performance of Indonesia's major trade countries

Year	1990	1991	1992	1993	1994	1995	1996
Export (Unit: 1mn US dollar)							
Japan	10,923.4	10,766.8	10,760.5	11,172.2	10,929	12,288.3	12,885.2
US	3364.59	3508.5	4419.11	5229.8	5828.56	6321.71	6794.66
Singapore	1902.14	2409.77	3313.54	3371.98	4149.67	3766.72	4564.61
Import (Unit: 1mn US dollar)							
Japan	5454.81	6326.89	6013.75	6248.43	7740.11	9216.82	8504
US	2519.52	3396.89	3822.44	3254.52	3587.85	4755.91	5059.81
Singapore	1283.47	1698.44	1670.69	1793.27	1877.05	2367.47	2875.27
Current account/ GDP (%)	−2.55	−3.13	−2.03	−1.32	−1.54	−3.04	−2.91

Source International Monetary Fund, Wang Haiquan (2009)

In the 1960s, both the current account and the capital account of Germany reported surpluses (Table 3.7), bringing about increased concerns over the country's macro-economic stability. At the same time, due to the United States' own double surplus, a crisis centered around the US dollar broke out and negatively affected the Deutschmark. According to its position within the global economic arrangement, Germany had to stay in the Bretton Woods system and the Deutschmark was forced to keep a fixed exchange rate against the US dollar. Germany's monetary authority once purchased excess supplies of the US dollar from the market in order to hold a large sum of foreign exchange reserves. To purchase the US dollar, a significant lump sum of the Deutschmark was injected into the market, resulting in too much liquidity within Germany and seriously threatening price stability. The price of real estate and that of other assets in Germany, along with workers' salaries, faced huge inflationary pressure. In the late 1960s, the Deutsche Bundesbank was forced to adopt a fixed exchange rate policy, and was unable to satisfy the demands for both maintaining the exchange rate and stabilizing the price of goods, thus triggering a typical macro-economic conflict between internal equilibrium and external equilibrium. In terms of this very issue, an argument flared up within Germany as to whether the country should appreciate the Deutschmark with the aim of achieving a new equilibrium. After weighing both advantages and disadvantages, Germany finally began to actively appreciate the Deutschmark. Between 1969 and 1973, the Deutschmark appreciated thrice.

As the Deutschmark appreciated, Germany initiated the reformation of its exchange-rate regime. On May 10, 1971, Germany actively adopted a floating exchange-rate regime and accordingly adjusted its capital account management.

Table 3.7 Overview of West Germany's balance of payments for 1968–1973

Period	Current account	Capital account[a]	Total balance[b]
1968–1969 Mark Crisis			
1968.01–1969.09	+16.9	−2.1	+14.9
1969.10–1969.12	+2.4	−20.5	−18.1
1968.01–1969.12	+19.4	−22.6	−3.3
1971 Mark Crisis			
1970.01–1971.05	+5.6	+35.3	+40.9
1971.06–1971.12	+0.7	−3.3	−2.6
1970.01–1971.12	+6.3	+32.0	+38.3
1972–1973 Mark Crisis			
1972.01–1972.07	−0.1	+19.0	+18.9
1972.08–1973.01	+2.7	−6.4	−3.7
1973.02–1973.03	+1.5	+18.8	+20.3
1972.01–1973.03	+4.2	+31.4	+35.6
From the floating of the exchange rate			
1973.04–1975.12	+44.3	−41.9	+2.4

Unit 1bn Deutsche Mark

The active reformation of the country's exchange-rate regime, along with the constant adjustment of its capital account management was adapted to changes ongoing in the domestic and foreign economic situation and that of West Germany's balance of payments. Under such circumstances, the exchange rate—as the price signal—would necessarily play a regulatory role. Meanwhile, Germany began to simultaneously develop the country's financial infrastructure and financial market. In terms of the aspect of opening-up, foreign institutions were allowed to issue Deutschmark-denominated bonds within Germany. The only requirement, however, was that funds raised in this manner must be utilized within other countries. The emergence of the fixed-income market in Germany followed global steps, speeding up this country's process of liberalizing the interest rate and providing support for the further opening-up of the capital account and liberalizing the exchange rate. In 1981, Germany achieved full openness of the capital account, and its exchange rate subsequently fully floated on the basis of such management.

The financial market of Germany, most notably its fixed income market, successfully linked the floating exchange rate to the liberalized interest rate. Furthermore, the central bank of Germany leveraged this market to autonomously manage and regulate the floating exchange rate and the interest rate. It not only guaranteed the smooth operation of the domestic micro-economy, but also mitigated potential external disequilibrium. What's more, it laid a foundation for internationalizing the Deutschmark after the 1980s.

Compared to the situation in Germany, the appreciation of the Japanese yen was passive. Starting from April 25, 1949, Japan began to adopt a fixed exchange rate against the US dollar (1 USD = 360 JPY). The overvaluing of the US dollar in this fixed exchange rate was conducive to Japan's exports. From the late 1950s on, as Japan's export rate reported an increasing surplus, trade conflicts between Japan and the United States began to increase both in rate and severity. In the initial period of monetary reformation, trade conflicts were mainly centered around cotton textiles and other light industrial goods. In the late 1960s, however, the conflicts extended to nearly all important industrial goods. In August 1971, after the collapse of the Bretton Woods system and during the first oil crisis, the exchange rate of the US dollar dropped sharply. In order to maintain price parity between the Japanese yen and the US dollar, the Bank of Japan absorbed around USD5 bn and injected JPY1.8tninto the overseas market in the space of two weeks. Under intense circumstantial pressure, however, this action had to ultimately be terminated. On August 29, Japan reluctantly announced that it would temporarily float the Japanese yen. As a result, the Japanese yen was forced to experience appreciation. Since this floating was a temporary action, however, it meant that it was not considered a long-term systemic arrangement. The central bank of Japan continued to intervene in the currency market by purchasing the US dollar. Consequently, Japan's foreign exchange reserves skyrocketed and injected an excess supply of monetary base into the country's economy. Furthermore, the Japanese government, aimed at preventing the appreciation of the Japanese yen, maintained a rapid economic growth and cut the official interest rate six consecutive times. The outcome was the rapid expansion of banks' credit quotas, serious inflation, and the rapid rise of commodity prices, further triggering the "panic purchasing" already prevalent within Japan. In order to stabilize commodity prices, the Japanese government had to adopt measures to control total demands. The rise of commodity prices had been controlled in a timely manner, but in an environment of global economic depression, the recession of Japan's economy lasted for five years. On the basis that the exchange-rate regime hadn't been reformed, the wrong macro-economic policy enabled Japan to be aware of the significance of the floating exchange-rate regime. Japan was forced to carry out economic reform.

In the preliminary stage, Japan shared the same challenge as Germany—appreciation. In its case, however, a different solution was adopted. Japan persisted in using the fixed exchange-rate regime and continued undervaluing the exchange rate of the domestic currency. In September 1973, when the second oil crisis broke out, Japan had to partially adopt a floating exchange-rate regime. On the one hand, the frequently-adopted solution of Japan's monetary authority was to control the capital account to intervene in the exchange rate of the Japanese yen. On the other hand, Japan loosened the regulation of capital inflow while simultaneously sustaining the regulation of capital outflow, thereby unilaterally restricting the flows of the Japanese yen. This measure effectively maintained the short-term stability of its exchange rate and prevented interest arbitrage in the domestic and overseas market of the Japanese yen, but also sharply increased Japan's balance of payments surplus.

Under such circumstances, it was objectively necessary for Japan to accelerate the process of opening its capital account. The Japanese government, however, assumed an ambiguous stance towards this move. In December 1980, Japan amended its *Foreign Exchange Law*, terminating the centralized management of foreign exchange and allowing domestic residents, companies, and foreign exchange banks to hold foreign exchange reserves. In this way, the positive connection between the balance of payments surplus and the increase in foreign exchange reserves was cut off. According to the amended *Foreign Exchange Law*, if the central bank was not willing to purchase foreign currencies and inject Japanese yen into the foreign exchange market, it could make the Japanese yen appreciate in a floating format. But the fact was that the Japanese government rarely let the Japanese yen appreciate in a floating way. Even when the Japanese yen was forced to appreciate under the 1985 Plaza Accord, in order to prevent the further appreciation, Japan had leveraged a dirty float to keep intervening in the foreign exchange market.

In summary, since Germany and Japan held different attitudes towards appreciating their own domestic currencies by adopting a floating exchange-rate regime and opening the capital account, these two countries' monetary policies embraced different operational targets and different degrees of independency.

After September 22, 1985, when the Plaza Accord was reached, the internationalization of the Deutschmark and that of the Japanese yen embarked on divergent roads. One significant reason for this was that the operational target of Japan's monetary policy was to stabilize the nominal exchange rate even while the locking of the exchange rate undermined the independence of Japan's monetary policy. Japan's monetary authority believed that the exchange rate was the decisive variable for restricting the relative price level of Japan against the United States, and for further guiding the future evolution of the country's monetary policy. While the exchange rate was causal to this, it was expected to fluctuate. The adopted monetary policy was the result of this assumption, with the purpose of weakening the fluctuations of the exchange rate. Therefore, when the Japanese yen was forced to appreciate, the monetary authority continued adopting a loose monetary policy to hedge its risks. The Japanese authority reduced the discount rate on multiple occasions and intervened in the foreign exchange market to ease the pressure of appreciation. From 1985 to February 1987, Japan lowered the discount rate five times, from 5% to 2.5%. Such a low level of interest rate was considered to be sustainable until April 1989. Meanwhile, the Japanese monetary authority intervened in the foreign exchange under the aegis of stabilizing the nominal exchange rate. Due to the country's long-term policy of keeping the interest rate low, the scale of bank loans expanded rapidly. Furthermore, the existence of the current account surpluses enhanced the expectation for appreciation, thus resulting in a significant influx of global hot money, enlarging growing balance of payments surplus, and an excess of liquidity in the domestic market.

Seeking profit, an excess of capital from credit loans and global currency flowed into the stock and real estate markets, which not only threatened the security of the banking system, but also fostered an asset bubble. In 1990, Japan's economic bubble broke down, the stock market collapsed after a singularly significant setback, and the banking institutions suffered heavy losses. Thereafter, Japan's economy entered a period of recession and deflation that lasted over a decade. At one point, Japan attempted to adopt expansionary monetary policies (e.g. reducing the discount rate) to boost its economy. Since Japan was in a "liquidity trap," however, its nominal interest rate had already dropped to zero without any sign of economic improvement during that period, the monetary policy no longer had any effect, and Japan entered what has become known as the "lost decade."

In contrast to Japan, Germany insisted on adopting an independent monetary policy, one which focused on the stability of the country's domestic prices and the development of its economy. After the Plaza Accord was signed, in order to mitigate the contractionary effect brought about by the appreciation of the domestic currency to the domestic economy, Germany put more currencies into circulation. The central bank of Germany repeatedly reduced the discount rate, from 4.5% in July 1985 to 2.5% in December 1987. As Germany's prices rebounded and its economic growth accelerated, the central bank of Germany adjusted its monetary policy and began to adopt a tighter monetary policy to stabilize the rate of inflation. In July 1988, the central bank of Germany began to raise the discount rate. Up to April 1989, the discount rate reached 4.5% and kept increasing until September 1992. The reunification of West and East Germany in the early 1990s decelerated the overall growth of the country as a whole. In order to boost the economy, at the end of 1992, Germany entered into a stage wherein a moderately expansionary monetary policy was adopted. Such a policy not only buoyed the economy, but also controlled the rate of inflation within an acceptable range. Under the pressure of the

Deutschmark's appreciation, Germany kept a close watch on its domestic prices, which not only alleviated the expectation for appreciation, but also steadily enhanced the real effective exchange rate. As the domestic economy and finances remained stable, the Deutschmark enjoyed a higher status as an international currency (see Table 3.8).

Also differently from Japan, the monetary policy of Germany foregrounded the equilibrium of the domestic economy as its primary goal. As such, the issue of the exchange rate took a backseat to the issue of inflation. With this monetary policy, the German economy was able to rid itself of the pressure of imported inflation and to achieve a rapid growth. For a long time, CPI had been regarded by the central bank of Germany as the foundation of the monetary issuance mechanism. Germany once strictly controlled the monetary credit loans as long as the monetary base did not register a large growth. For example, from the 1950s to the 1980s, the inflation rate of Germany held steady at around 37%. Even after the 1985 Plaza Accord, when Germany should have mitigated the contractionary effect brought by the domestic currency appreciation to the domestic economy, the country continued to expand its currency issuance. The central bank continuously cut the discount rate, from 45% in July 1985 to 25% in December 1987. As Germany's prices rebounded and its economic growth accelerated, however, the central bank of Germany adjusted its monetary policy and began to adopt a tight monetary policy to stabilize the rate of inflation. In July 1988, the central bank of Germany also raised the discount rate. By April 1989, the discount rate had reached a level of 4.5% and continued increasing until September 1992. The reunification of West and East Germany in the early 1990s decelerated the overall growth of the country; in order to boost the economy, at the end of 1992, Germany entered into a stage in which a moderately expansionary monetary policy was adopted. Such a policy not only buoyed the economy, but also controlled the rate of inflation within an acceptable range. From the above explanation, it can be seen that the monetary policy of Germany always put anti-inflation as its priority. The openness of the exchange rate and that of the capital account were always subject to the principle of maintaining the independence of this monetary policy. As a result, Germany's domestic economy was always stable, which laid a foundation for the internationalization of the Deutschmark.

Let us look, then, to the developing countries. As previously mentioned, after WWII, developing countries had a fundamental need to achieve rapid economic growth through industrialization, yet this required an as-yet unproposed series of policies and systemic arrangements (including finance) for accelerating the formation of capital. The central aim of these arrangements was to foster a distorted

Table 3.8 Inflation rate of Japan versus Germany

Time	1970–1974	1975–1979	1980–1984	1984–1989	1970–1989
Japan	10.7	7.5	3.9	1.2	5.8
Germany	5.6	4.2	4.5	1.3	3.9

Unit %

market. When this goal was reflected in the foreign exchange system, foreign currencies would be overvalued while domestic currency would be undervalued. Furthermore, the country pursuing such a goal would adopt various measures to consolidate the distorted exchange rate, which would then be developed into a stable and long-term situation. It should be pointed out that under the Bretton Woods system, due to restrictions from the inherent regulations of the international monetary system, any and all efforts put forward by developing countries had the potential to be effective. Consequently, a fixed exchange-rate regime was adopted by both Latin American countries and East Asian countries. As the Bretton Woods system collapsed, however, the running rules of the international monetary system underwent a significant change. As a result, the precondition for the fixed exchange-rate regime was lost, which greatly challenged Latin American countries with their import substitution industrialization strategy and East Asian countries with their export-oriented industrialization strategy. Each of these countries had to independently choose another exchange-rate regime. The results of their different choices varied significantly, however, they arrived at the same end by different means, all ultimately pegging their currencies to the US dollar.

For a long period while under colonial rule, Latin America exhibited a dependent economic model under which primary products were exported in exchange for light industrial goods. After these countries gained independence, to rid themselves of this core-periphery dependent economic model, Latin American countries adopted import substitution industrialization. Specifically, Latin American countries were encouraged to manufacture light industry goods to replace their original demands for import. Based on this industrialization strategy, six Latin American countries (Argentina, Brazil, Chile, Columbia, Mexico, and Uruguay), all of which had economies based on different industries and products, adopted multiple exchange rates that were facilitated with import quotas, licenses, and bans to consolidate this system. Because the domestic markets were small and the costs of enterprises in these countries were relatively high, however, it was difficult for domestic enterprises to realize an optimal scale of production, thus challenging the process of import substitution industrialization and worsening the international balance of payments.

In the 1970s, encouraged by the achievements of the export-oriented industrialization prevalent in East Asia and concurrently affected by the collapse of the Bretton Woods system, Latin American countries began to adjust their strategies for economic development. Central to this adjustment was acquiring foreign currency earnings. Following this, three models were formed in response. The first model was a strategy to comprehensively promote imports and exports. Countries adopting this model included Brazil, Colombia, Haiti, Mexico, and Dominica. The second model was the export-oriented strategy previously favored by East Asia. Countries adopting the second model included three MERCOSUR (Mercado Común del Sur, or the Southern Common Market) countries (i.e. Argentina, Chile, and Uruguay) and Peru. The third strategy was to export primary products. Countries adopting the third model were the remaining eleven Latin American countries, namely, Bolivia, Ecuador, Paraguay, Venezuela, Panama, Cuba, and five other Central American countries. Due to their weak industrial bases, these countries were not able to export industrialization-based manufactured goods. However, they grasped the opportunity to raise the prices on primary products in the late 1970s. As a result, these countries not only exported more primary products, but also created more types of primary products for export.

The problem with the above three strategies is that they achieved only negligible results for the countries utilizing them: the global trade volume of Latin American countries continued to decrease while the scale of its foreign debts continually increased. Excepting different national situations, the one common causal feature was one related to the paradox of opening the capital accounts of developing countries: if a developing country does not open its capital account, it is not able to absorb foreign capital on a large scale. As a result, the country in question will be unable to overcome its inadequate export capabilities due to a shortage of domestic capital. If a country does open its capital account, however, the exchange rate will float and the domestic currency will tend to appreciate, thus damaging the country's exports. Reflected in the exchange-rate regime, the only result of such a dilemma would be to adopt a periodically-adjusted pegged exchange rate. Adopting an adjustable pegged exchange-rate regime, however, was not synonymous with a liberalized floating exchange-rate regime. Due to irregular adjustments, market expectations were unstable and the opening-up of the capital account was unsustainable, resulting in a mismatched capital inflow structure and an excessive inflow of short-term capital. When short-term debts increased, domestic currency faced the pressure of appreciation. To prevent a situation in which the appreciation of domestic currency would exert a negative impact on the competitiveness of a given country's exports, the monetary authority in question had to purchase foreign currencies. At the same time, this monetary authority would be well-advised to sell government bonds in order to protect the increased money supply being produced from the monetary base injected for purchasing foreign currencies so as to alleviate inflation. The resulting short-term capital inflow was due to the difference in interest rates. One government's hedge policy of issuing bonds would only increase the difference, thereby causing more capital inflows. These excessive capital inflows resulted in an overblown macro economy, a rising rate of inflation, and an appreciation of the actual exchange rate, all of which further degraded the current account and expanded the liquidity of financial institutions. As a result, the financial system became more fragile. Under such circumstances, being afraid of the potential risks, large scale foreign capital would flow out. The consequences might be a financial or economic crisis. If such an occurrence were to come to pass, the domestic currency would be forced to depreciate greatly.

Latin America was the first to suffer from this disastrous phenomenon. After the collapse of the Bretton Woods system, Latin American countries remained undecided in their choice of exchange-rate regimes and policies: it was unclear whether they would be best served by adopting a competitive exchange rate to expand their exports or floating the exchange rate to contain inflation. A pegged exchange rate with small adjustments was the compromised result. This regime, however, triggered widespread speculation-based floating. Foreign capital on a large scale flowed in and the burden of foreign debts sharply increased (see Table 3.9).

In the 1970s, the foreign debts of Latin American countries grew rapidly while the debts' nominal interest rate was lower than the growth rate of their exports, though the situation was still largely under control. Entering into the 1980s, however, and with the commencement of the second global oil crisis, the terms of trade in Latin America rapidly worsened and export earnings dropped sharply. As a result, the debt service ratio—namely the ratio of debt service payments (principal + interest) to the country's export earnings—skyrocketed from 17.6% before the collapse of the Bretton Woods system to 59% in 1982. The unsustainability of such a ratio triggered a large degree of capital flight. Ironically, the first country to face disasters was an oil exporter—Mexico, whose exports were still quite promising. Although Mexico still had increasing oil exports, the country's total export volume dropped. Consequently, its export income was not able to cover the interest of foreign debts. In August 1982, Mexico announced its failure in fulfilling its obligations in debt contracts, which ignited the debt crisis in Latin America (see Table 3.10).

Table 3.9 Distribution of Latin America's foreign debts for 1960–1982

	Public, private and short-term foreign debts	Contribution of banks to public foreign debts	Contribution of loan and interest payment to export	Contribution of interest payment to export
1960	7.2[a]	16.4	17.7[a]	3.6[a]
1970	20.8[a]	19.5	17.6[a]	5.6[a]
1975	75.4	42.9	26.6	13
1980	229.1	56.6	38.3	21.2
1981	279.4	57.6	43.8	26.4
1982	314.4	57.6	59	34.3

Note [a]refers to public foreign debts
Source Bulmer-Thomas (2010)

Table 3.10 Mexico's international balance of payments (1990–1995)

	1990	1991	1992	1993	1994	1995
Current account	−7.4	−14.6	−24.4	−23.4	−29.7	−1.6
Net capital inflows	5.8	19.9	23.5	30.3	10.3	−13.3
FDI	2.6	4.8	4.4	4.4	11	9.5
Stock	2	6.3	4.8	10.7	4.1	0.5
Bond	1.1	1.3	3.6	6.3	2.8	−0.5
Banking loan	9.1	7.9	1.6	3.6	−0.3	−4.3
Official net capital inflows	5	2.4	2	−0.9	0.9	24.5
Net foreign exchange reserves change	3.4	7.7	1	5.9	−18.4	9.6

Unit 1 bn US dollar
Source IMF, international balance of payments and statistics

After the outset of the 1982 debt crisis, Latin America remained deeply troubled. Starting in 1985, however, with the launch of the "Baker Plan" (a rescue package proposed by former US Treasury Secretary James Baker), the situation in Latin America began to take a turn for the better, and most Latin American countries started to adopt a managed floating exchange-rate regime. The export rate for 1991 increased by 78% compared to that of 1981. But many countries forgot the cause of the previously-existing pain after the wound was healed, still believing that the floating exchange-rate regime could solve their developmental problems while having ignored the fact that their export product mix was still insufficient and their focus was still on primary products. As a result, these countries did not foster a consolidated trade surplus, and as a result fell into a rut. As the income of the current account further deteriorated, another debt crisis took place once again in 1994, again in Mexico. In 2001, Argentina was unable to repay the over USD100 bn foreign debts it had accrued, thus triggering another debt crisis. In 2012, a similar situation occurred, focusing on a huge current account deficit and capital flight. Furthermore, the highest rate of depreciation of the domestic currency for 2012 reached over 36%. Hence, Latin American countries still had troubles in selecting an exchange-rate regime and opening a capital account.

Unlike Latin American countries, East Asian countries soon shifted from a model of industrialization centered on import substitution to one that is export-oriented, and achieved great success, reporting persistent current account surpluses. As the Bretton Woods system collapsed, the US dollar depreciated, while the currencies of East Asian countries appreciated, a fact on which East Asian countries predicated their abandonment of the fixed exchange-rate regime and started to adopt the floating exchange-rate regime. This was not thoroughly pursued, however. For instance, according to the criteria of the IMF, the exchange-rate regimes adopted by many ASEAN countries are categorized as flexible arrangements. Thailand's exchange rate was pegged to a basket of currencies; Indonesia adopted a managed floating exchange-rate regime; the Philippines adopted a separate floating exchange-rate regime, etc. Despite this, these countries' domestic currencies were directly or indirectly pegged to the US dollar. The weight of the US dollar in pricing the nominal exchange rates of domestic currencies was too large, such that domestic currencies were actually pegged to the US dollar. Take Thailand and Indonesia, for example: the exchange rate of the Thai baht was pegged to a basket of currencies. Although any type of detailed composition of this basket was unknown to the public, insiders estimated that the basket was composed primarily of the US dollar (78%), the Japanese yen (12%), the Deutschmark (8%), and the Singapore dollar (negligible). The central bank of Thailand published the central rate every day, and required that the exchange rate to float within ± THB 0.02 based on the central rate.

With this measure, the exchange rate of the Thai baht fluctuated only slightly or was essentially fixed against foreign currencies. Nominally, the Indonesian rupiah adopted a floating exchange-rate regime. But since the Indonesian rupiah was almost pegged to the US dollar, and, furthermore, capital could rapidly flow across countries due to innovations within the fields of IT and financial instruments, potential shocks could come on fast and strong (Tables 3.11 and 3.12).

As previously mentioned, a pegged exchange-rate regime is easily shocked by the influx of overseas capital resulting from the opening-up of a country's capital account. Seen from a certain perspective, the mechanisms of the Asian financial crisis are different from those of the Latin American debt crisis. In Asia, the crisis was not totally caused by the current account deficit. Instead, the crisis was related to the "currency mismatch" and "maturity mismatch" of East Asian countries. According to research by Ronald I. Mckinnon, the "Asian financial crisis" was mainly caused by the short-term US dollar-denominated debts accrued between 1994 and1996 and the drastic depreciation of the Japanese yen during 1997–1998 (external factors).

East Asian countries applied the US dollar towards valuing and settling their trade and capital, and pegged their currencies to the US dollar. Since both their trade destination and investment sources lay with Japan, however, these countries were easily affected by fluctuation in the exchange rate of the Japanese yen against the US dollar. Between 1997 and 1998, the Japanese yen depreciated upon the collapse of the Japanese economic bubble, and the issue of a "currency mismatch" was exposed. The financial market of East Asia, especially the fixed-income market, was not mature. East Asian countries were not able to apply their domestic currencies in international loans. Instead, all loans were denominated in the US dollar and most loans were borrowed via banks in the form of short-term debts. The problem of "currency mismatch" and "maturity mismatch" in the capital supply triggered the "dilemma of high savings" mentioned by Mckinnon: at first, as these countries had higher current account surpluses, the rights of the US dollar increased, forcing these countries' domestic currencies to appreciate; at the same time, however, these countries noted that the reason for their current account

Table 3.11 Weight of USD, JPY and EUR in Indonesia rupiah's nominal value

Researcher	Frankel	Kwan Chi Hung	Mckinnon
Duration	Weekly data (Jan. 1979–May 1992)	Monthly data (Jan. 1991–Dec. 1995)	Daily data (Feb. 1 of 1994–May 30 of 1997)
USD	0.95	0.99	1.00
JPY	0.16	−0.01	−0.01
EUR			0.01

Source Honghui and Shen (2007)

Table 3.12 Inflation rate of Japan versus Germany

Year	1970–1974	1975–1979	1980–1984	1984–1989	1970–1989
Japan	10.7	7.5	3.9	1.2	5.8
Germany	5.6	4.2	4.5	1.3	3.9

Unit %
Source Bloomberg

surpluses was the depreciation of their own domestic currencies. Therefore, the need to appreciate their domestic currencies arose. Secondly, once the expectation of appreciation was broached, the US dollar-denominated assets would be converted to assets denominated in domestic currencies. Therefore, these countries' domestic currencies rapidly appreciated. The appreciation of these countries' domestic currencies would trigger deflation and hit the economy hard. Faced with this dilemma, the only path for East Asian countries was to undersell their domestic currencies in order to maintain a pegged exchange rate. Following past experiences, once speculation developed, a pegged exchange-rate regime would further degrade the situation, because under a pegged exchange-rate regime, governments of East Asian countries were to provide an implicit guarantee for the potential exchange rate risks faced by domestic companies, financial institutions, investors, and international creditors. Since the exchange rate risks had been prevented under a pegged exchange rate regime, speculated capital would naturally flow in and out on a large scale. Take the Thai baht as an example: in 1989, the overseas private capital which flowed into and out of Thailand was around THB 100bn. In 1994, the overseas private capital which flowed into and out of Thailand reached THB 1500bn, or an increase of over ten times within just four years. Among shares of overseas private capital, short-term capital had a large share coupled with rapid growth. During 1995–1996, the Thai baht-denominated deposits of non-residents, the US dollar-denominated short-term loans to firms, and foreign capital's investment in the stock market all sharply increased. Just seeing the balance of debts against the banks, we can find that of the USD70.1 bn debts recorded at the end of 1996, 65.2% was in the form of short-term debts.

Shocked by Thailand's financial crisis and the world's speculation, the Indonesian rupiah started to depreciate at the end of June 1997 (at that point, 1 USD = 2650 IDR). This exchange rate was very nearly the same as the upper limit previously stipulated by the central bank of Indonesia (which was 1 USD = 2682 IDR). The initial response by the Indonesian government was to protect the pegged exchange-rate regime for the purpose of maintaining its stability. The central bank intervened in this issue by selling foreign exchange reserves and raising the interest rate. Due to these interventionist behaviors, Indonesia's foreign exchange reserves were almost completely exhausted and the country's interest rate skyrocketed—for example, the interest rate of short-term securities issued by the central bank alone increased to 28%. After carrying out these measures, the Indonesian government was still not able to stop the depreciation of the Indonesian rupiah. Indonesia was not economically strong enough to deal with the impact wrought by speculative capital and to protect its pegged exchange-rate regime. Consequently, the Indonesian government gave up providing this protection. The exchange rate of the Malaysian ringgit against the US dollar had once decreased by 46%, with the composite index of the stock market dropping by 50% in Malaysia. In 1998, however, Malaysia reported a negative growth of 7.5% for the first time during the past 13 years. In addition, both the unemployment rate and the inflation rate went up.

Facing enormous shocks from overseas hot money, on July 2, 1997, the central bank of Thailand had almost exhausted its disposable foreign exchange reserves. As a result, much like Indonesia, the Thai government was forced to abandon the pegged exchange-rate regime and announced that it would subsequently adopt a floating exchange-rate regime. On that day, the Thai baht depreciated by 20% and the first domino of the Asian financial crisis fell. After successfully attacking the Thai baht, speculative capital then initiated attacks upon other three ASEAN countries (Malaysia, Indonesia, and Philippines), South Korea, Singapore, Hong Kong, and other countries and regions in the area. The attack was ineffective in Singapore and Hong Kong, but fundamentally shocked the four ASEAN countries and South Korea, which all adopted a pegged exchange-rate regime in response, causing their exchange rates to fluctuate acutely. It was not until the next half year of 1998 that the exchange rates of the five East Asian countries trapped in the crisis began to stabilize.

3.4 Exchange Rate or Interest Rate—Lessons Learnt from the Monetary Policies of Developed and Developing Countries

Following to the previous description and analysis, we can more or less establish that in order to internationalize the Deutschmark and the Japanese yen, some sort of currency circulation needed be fostered by developing a capital account deficit based on the current account surplus. The precondition for which, of course, was the opening of a capital account. To facilitate this, a floating exchange-rate regime was adopted. The success of the internationalization of the Deutschmark was closely related to this arrangement; the failure in internationalizing the Japanese yen was also due to the hysteresis and lack of coordination surrounding the facilitation of this arrangement. In order to continue expanding the current account surplus, Japan slowed it steps to opening a capital account and adopted a dirty float regime.

The top priority of developing countries was to accelerate their economic development through industrialization. Objectively, developing countries demanded the distortion of the exchange rate and then the unchanging maintenance of the distorted exchange rate. To achieve this goal, the best solution was to strictly control the capital account. Experience showed, however, that the cost of such a practice could be quite high. For instance, before its reform and opening up, China strictly controlled both the capital account and the current account. Consequently, China was isolated from the rest of the world, and was unable to foreground its opening up as an important component of the country's economic development strategy, like other East Asian countries had done. Therefore, China not only was not able to utilize foreign capital to accelerate its technical progress and industrial growth, but was also unable to depend on the global market to expand its exports and accelerate economic growth. Currently, North Korea and Iran are now also in such a situation.

We can draw two conclusions from the above. First, in a market-oriented economy, a country should maintain a balance of payments equilibrium; especially when its capital account is open, this country should adopt a floating exchange-rate regime, and vice versa. Under this condition, if a country wants to adopt a macro-economic policy to control its inflation, the country in question can control an independent monetary policy. It worked well in Germany after the collapse of the Bretton Woods system. Secondly, when the balance of payments—most notably the capital account—is under strict control, a country should adopt a fixed exchange-rate regime, and vice versa. Under this condition, it is possible for a country to keep the independence of its macro-economic policy (including its monetary policy) with a high price. To a great extent, this country's national administrative power should be leveraged to curb the functions of the market. As a result, a controlled economy or a planned economy will develop easily in countries such as those during the war and the former East European countries.

As has been stated previously, most countries—especially developing countries—have no need for controlling the economy in peacetime. What's more, it is unnecessary for these countries to abandon a market-oriented economy in the pursuit of an ambiguous goal. In terms of economic and social development, it is important to meet prior needs first. For instance, during the process of economic modernization, the initial goal was industrialization. To achieve this, it is necessary for a country to fully leverage its domestic and overseas resources and open up as part of its strategy towards industrialization. Once a country adopts an opening-up policy, however, it inevitably follows that this country will open its balance of payments, most notably the country's capital account. To facilitate this process, the choice of an appropriate exchange-rate regime is also central. Looking at the experiences of Latin America, East Asia, and other developing regions, we can see that many times a strategy of gradually opening the capital account based on the openness of the current account was attempted. To coordinate this strategy from the aspect of arranging an exchange-rate regime, most of the countries in question chose to adopt a pegged exchange-rate regime. Experience has shown, however, that such a strategy has been repeatedly unsuccessful or unstable. In a sense, a pegged exchange-rate regime is a measure to be adopted only during the transitional period of opening the country's capital account. Foregrounding the openness of the capital account as the ultimate goal may potentially result in the severe instability of the domestic objective economy. Vivid case examples include the debt crisis in Latin America and the financial crisis in Asia, the macro-economic policies of which, with the purpose of promoting economic development, gave rise to the financial economic crisis.

What's wrong with these economic policies, especially the monetary policies? After the collapse of the Bretton Woods system—especially following the Asian financial crisis—economists did an in-depth analysis of this issue. Based on Mundell's theory of "Optimum Currency Area" and the "Impossible Trinity" in 1963, economists performed many empirical analyses on the international economic activities, optimizing and furthering Mundell's theory of "Impossible Trinity." In doing so, they discovered a trilemma at the heart of international economics—it was impossible to have all three of the following at the same time: free capital movement, a fixed foreign exchange rate, and an independent monetary policy. This means that if a central bank chooses the option of free capital movement, it cannot simultaneously choose an independent monetary policy and a fixed exchange rate. If the exchange rate is fixed at a certain level, the money supply and the interest rate must be allowed to automatically float; if the money supply is fixed at a certain level or grows at a fixed ratio, the interest rate and exchange rate must be allowed to automatically float; if the interest rate is fixed at a certain level, the authority should give up controlling the money supply and the exchange rate simultaneously. In other words, a country's central bank and foreign exchange control board can only pursue two of the above-mentioned three policies simultaneously, what is aptly known as "selecting two from the three options."

After WWII, the monetary policies adopted by Germany, Japan, and the developing countries of Latin America and East Asia were just the results of the aforementioned trilemma. Under the Bretton Woods system, market economic countries controlled the capital account and adopted a fixed exchange-rate regime. The situation differed in Europe, however. In 1958, when the European Community was established, Western European countries abandoned the control their foreign exchanges one after another and enabled the convertibility of their currencies within the free capital movement. Among these countries, there were no reserve requirements for foreign exchange deposits and there was no upper or lower limit for the deposit rate. The liberalization of the interest rate and the lax environment created favorable conditions for the development of Europe's burgeoning financial market, where banks running the business of the US dollar-denominated deposits and loans emerged without restrictions or sanctions. Europe thus came to occupy an important role for the Soviet Union, the Eastern European countries, and other developing countries in the process of raising funds. After the 1960s, facing the crisis of the US dollar, people rushed to purchase hard currencies such as gold, the Deutschmark, the pound sterling, and the French Franc. Outside European borders, the US dollar market, the Deutschmark market, the pound sterling market, and the French Franc market all continued to exist concurrently in Europe. As a result, one contradiction emerged: under the Bretton Woods system, capital accounts were usually under control. However, European countries opened their capital accounts while followed the principle of the Bretton Woods system. They had fixed exchange rates, especially against the US dollar.

The contradiction between the free capital movement and the fixed exchange rate embarrassed those Western European countries adopting a monetary policy. Looking at it from an economic perspective, the primary target of a monetary policy is to deal with inflation or deflation by controlling the money supply. Trapped in the above contradiction, however, an independent monetary policy is unable to satisfy this requirement. For instance, from 1951 to 1970, the monetary base issued by the central bank of Germany increased from DEM 11.4bn to DEM 67.8bn, or a growth of DEM 56.4bn, among which, DEM 50.6bn (around 90%) came from the growth of foreign exchange reserves and other foreign assets contributed by state banks and the central bank. During this period, the growth of the liquidity and money supply of banks was not due to monetary injections by the central bank of Germany. Rather, growth came from the inflow of the overseas foreign exchange, which served as a "substitute for the central bank." Due to the rising money supply, Germany constantly faced inflationary pressures despite the fact that inflation itself was quite mild. In fact, in 1955, the central bank of Germany began to adopt a traditional monetary policy in order to stabilize price levels. Solutions included increasing the discount rate and the required reserves ratio as well as underselling the Deutschmark in an open market. All these solutions, however, were unable to curb Germany's rising inflation. Particularly in the 1960s, when ten US dollar crises occurred, for the purpose of fulfilling its obligations within the international monetary system and maintaining price parity between the US dollar and gold, the central bank of Germany continued to undersell the Deutschmark for the purpose of purchasing the US dollar. As a result, the monetary base increased from the end of 1958 to the end of 1969 by DEM 27.9bn, accounting for around 50% of the monetary base increase seen during the years between 1950 and 1970. At the same time, however, the foreign exchange reserves of the central bank increased only negligibly. This meant that nearly all the gains on foreign exchange during this period had been spent by domestic credit agencies and German companies in exporting currencies and capital. In other words, they invested overseas assets with these funds. From this perspective, the trilemma was verified: under a fixed exchange-rate regime, any change in the monetary policy can only adjust the international balance of payments to achieve an external macro-economic equilibrium instead of internal equilibrium. In other words, monetary policies' independence will be affected and restricted by external factors. To achieve any stability in the exchange rate, a country has to sacrifice the independence of its monetary policy.

The monetary policy of Japan after the 1985 Plaza Accord verified the trilemma from another perspective. In December 1980, facing new phenomena in the transactions of its ordinary financial institutions, Japan revised the *Foreign Exchange Law*, recognizing (in principle) that foreign capital transactions would be unrestricted and the capital account would be essentially open. But for a variety of reasons, Japan worried that the appreciation of the Japanese yen would exert a negative impact on the export industry. Therefore, Japan "was afraid of adopting a floating exchange-rate regime." In 1972, upon the collapse of the Bretton Woods system, the exchange rate of the Japanese yen reached 260 JPY to USD. Due to the first oil crisis, between 1974 and 1975, the government deliberately depreciated the Japanese yen to 300 JPY to USD. Even in 1976, when Japan reported a current account surplus again, the Japanese yen did not indicate a trend of appreciation. Japan's manipulation under the "dirty float system" was criticized by the international community. In 1985, facing international pressure, Japan was forced to sign the Plaza Accord. Thereafter, the Japanese yen started to appreciate and its exchange rate increased from 260 JPY/USD in June 1985 to 120 JPY/USD in November 1988.

In consideration of the rapid appreciation of the Japanese yen, the economic competitiveness of Japan in the international community became a question of some concern. Between 1986 and 1988, 1993 and 1995, and 1999 and 2001, Japan's monetary authority regularly intervened in the foreign exchange market. In addition, the monetary authority believed that the exchange rate would be the decisive variable in controlling the relative price level of Japan against the United States and for the future evolution of the country's monetary policy. In terms of this relation, the exchange rate was the causal agent and would necessarily change first; while monetary policy was the result and its purpose was to mitigate the change of the exchange rate. When the Japanese yen appreciated rapidly, Japan adopted a loose monetary policy. On multiple occasions, the Japanese government lowered the country's discount rate and intervened in the foreign exchange market in order to alleviate the pressure of appreciation. The discount rate was lowered five consecutive times between 1985 and 1987, from 5% in 1985 to 2.5% in February 1987. Yet a low level interest rate was kept unchanged until April 1989 for the purpose of maintaining the stability of the nominal exchange rate. Under the long-term policy of keeping a low level of interest rates, the credit loans of banks rapidly expanded. Furthermore, since the Japanese government kept intervening in the foreign exchange market, there was a higher expectation for the appreciation of the Japanese yen. As a result, international hot money flowed into the country on a large scale, which aggravated the excess liquidity within Japan. Therefore, the inflation rate of Japan consistently remained higher than that of Germany.

When seeking profit, an excessive number of funds from credit loans and international hot money saturated the stock and real estate markets, threatening not only the security of the banking system, but also fostering the conditions necessary to create an asset bubble. In 1990, Japan's economic bubble finally burst. For over a decade thereafter, Japan experienced slow economic growth. The lesson to take from Japan's economic performance after the Plaza Accord can be summarized as: a country's capital account has been basically open, efforts to blindly maintain the nominal exchange rate at a certain level will be ineffective. In other words, in the long run, adopting a monetary policy is ineffective in terms of stabilizing the exchange rate. In turn, the effects of the monetary policy will be lost. The independence of a monetary policy ought to be primarily reflected in the stability of the domestic economy.

In fact, much like the situation seen in Japan, both the Latin American debt crisis and the 20th century Asian financial registered a "Meade Conflict," or, rather, a "binary conflict" between the fixed exchange rate and the free capital movement. The fixed exchange rate and the free capital movement cannot coexist. The free capital movement will consequently shatter the fixed exchange rate. Under the condition of the free capital movement, if any of the developing countries in Latin America or East Asia adopts a pegged exchange-rate regime, the country is, in effect, giving up the independence of its monetary policy. In order to maintain the stability of a country's domestic exchange rate against the US dollar, the country's central bank must frequently engage in foreign exchange trades, which will, of course, result in changes to the country's monetary base. If an economic crisis occurs, a dependent monetary policy in which the domestic currency is pegged to the US dollar will reveal its shortcomings, such as decreased ability for the government to leverage any type of monetary policy aimed at boosting the economy.

It is worth noting that, aside from the "Meade Conflict", the effectiveness of developing countries' independent monetary policies is also restricted by the immature financial market and the weak financial infrastructure.

The free capital movement is the precondition for Mundell's theory of the "Impossible Trinity." Under a specific set of circumstances, the interest rate will totally align with the international interest rate. This requires that all bonds in the economic system can be totally substituted. In other words, the spot exchange rate is totally consistent with the forward exchange rate. The operation of the monetary policy is manifested by trading securities on an open market. Specifically, when a central bank purchases foreign exchange reserves, it ought to also sell bonds. Through hedging, this operation will stabilize the exchange rate. The real-world economy is not necessarily as extreme as that found in theory, but the financial market—especially the fixed income market—-really plays an important role in the monetary policy. As explained previously, one explanation for why a developing country might be considered under development is due to an immature financial market. What's more, in order to accelerate economic growth, a developing country needs to distort the financial market—namely, to develop indirect financing (represented by commercial banks) that is capable of restraining direct financing (represented by the capital market). This underdeveloped situation is often caused by a poor financial infrastructure and a shortage of financial products in the capital market, especially on the fixed income market. Even if a central bank's speed in purchasing foreign exchange reserves is rapid enough to stabilize the exchange rate, its speed in selling bonds won't be fast enough to ensure that the monetary supply is unchanging. The result will be either an appreciation of the domestic currency or an increase the money supply, or vice versa. Both the Latin American debt crisis and the Asian financial crisis are due to this situation. In the initial stages of the crises, all central banks sold foreign currencies to purchase domestic currencies and purchased bonds to provide the market with liquidity. Consequently, the foreign exchange reserves were always exhausted and domestic currencies depreciated. The money supply, however, did not report any significant growth. Together with a monetary crisis represented by depreciation, both deflation and an economic recession occurred.

In the process of internationalization, the differing fates of the Deutschmark and the Japanese yen demonstrated the importance of the capital market and particularly the fixed income market. As the pace of European integration quickened, a European monetary market with multiple currencies was set up. After the collapse of the Bretton Woods system, the European monetary market enjoyed a higher status, and gradually became a well-structured and fixed-income financial market with plentiful products. Since multiple currencies coexisted in this market, it enjoyed a lower risk of "currency mismatch." In addition, since the market was well-structured, the risk of "maturity mismatches" decreased. Thanks to the market's abundantly-available products, it was relatively easy for European countries to operate within their own monetary policies. Overall, this market was vital to the internationalization of the Deutschmark—a markedly different situation from that of Latin America or East Asia.

Following the collapse of the Bretton Woods system, various European Communities signed an agreement initiating the so-called "snake in the tunnel" system. This agreement set bands of ±2.25% for currencies among member states. In 1979, the establishment of the European Monetary System (EMS), consolidated this linked exchange rate mechanism. Following this mechanism, the central banks of all member states formed an alliance by leveraging the open financial market operations, thus weakening the impact of investment on the Deutschmark and mitigating the negative impacts of the large fluctuations of foreign exchange on the economy of Germany. Meanwhile, relying on the stability of its currency value, the Deutschmark played the role of anchor currency for other European communities. Other member states pegged their currencies to the Deutschmark for the purpose of maintaining the stability of their own domestic price levels. The following three aspects reflect the relation between the Deutschmark and those currencies of other member states:

At first, as a result of the economic strength of Germany, the Deutschmark held premier place in terms of the European Currency Unit (ECU). The ECU functioned as the core of the European Monetary System for the use of valuation and settlement within European communities. The initial currency value of the ECU was constituted through the currencies of nine member states. Each sovereign currency's weight in the ECU was determined according to the proportion of each member state's GDP to overall trade within the European Communities between 1969 and 1973, as well as each member state's share in the mechanism of short-term financial support. It was also stipulated that the economic development status of member states should be reviewed every five years and that the shares of their currencies would be adjusted accordingly. Predicated upon its large economic scale and strong trade capacity of Germany, the Deutschmark accounted for 27.3% of the ECU's initial value. Following later adjustment, shares of the Deutschmark in the ECU peaked at 30.1% in 1989. After the Greek Drachma, the Spanish Peseta, the Portuguese Escudo, and other currencies were introduced into the ECU, the Deutschmark accounted for an even higher percentage of the ECU. This situation not only reflected the strength of the Deutschmark, but also demonstrated the confidence of the EMS in it. These factors combined in such a way that the Deutschmark enjoyed a unique central status in the ECU.

Secondly, the Deutschmark gradually became an interventionist currency within the EMS. The cooperative exchange rate system of the EMS—"a network of par exchange rates"—was such that the currency of each member state had a central exchange rate against the ECU, which would then determine a fixed bilateral exchange rate for currencies. In order to maintain the stability of the exchange-rate regime under this system, if any two sovereign currencies reported deviation, the two countries' central banks were to adopt measures intervening in the foreign exchange market. In principle, two sovereign currencies with large deviation would depend on each other to implement intervention. Since the trading of currencies between most member states was insufficient for such a task, however, the US dollar developed as the currency of choice.

Since the middle of the 1980s, excepting the Deutschmark, the currencies of EMS member states depreciated significantly, increasingly deviating from the Deutschmark. When the US dollar reported a persistent downward trend, the central banks of other member states sold their US dollars and purchased domestic currencies, which further brought down the exchange rate of the US dollar and damaged the stability of the exchange rate market. In recognition of this issue, all member countries chose to adopt a measure of intervention by selling the Deutschmark and purchasing domestic currencies. In taking such a measure, the Deutschmark served as a currency of intervention, eventually exceeding the amount of US dollars held by member states.

Due to the aforementioned policies, the economic strength of Germany, and the stable value of its currency, the Deutschmark gradually grew to be the central currency of the EMS. From 1983 on, the member states of the EMS abandoned the idea of pegging their currencies to the ECU, but father affixed them to the Deutschmark instead. As a result, the EMS gradually evolved into something that can be considered a "Deutschmark Zone." At the center of the EMS, Germany assumed responsibility for stabilizing the exchange rate of the Deutschmark against the US dollar so that other member states were able to peg their currencies to the Deutschmark. When the bilateral exchange rate fluctuated beyond acceptable limits, other member states could adjust the exchange rates on their currencies. Under such circumstances, the Deutschmark did not need to undertake its interventionist obligations and thus became established as the "anchor currency" of the European communities in question.

After German reunification in 1990, the Deutschmark went into circulation country-wide. Germany, with its global gold and foreign exchange reserves, had a GNP equaling to the sum total of the GNP of the UK and Italy combined. Nearly 30% of the budget revenue of the European Communities (comprising twelve member states) was contributed by Germany. The role of the Deutschmark was therefore not limited to serving as an anchor currency. It had developed into the de facto basic currency of Europe by widely entering into the balance sheets of member states.

In contrast, Japan at this time possessed an immature financial market, a fact which was reflected in its interest rate liberalization process. Not until the late 1970s did Japan begin to slowly liberalize its interest rate. In 1983, under the pressure of the United States, Japan, together with the United States, established a Japanese yen & US Dollar Committee for negotiation. The core of the negotiation focused on developing and opening the financial market of Japan, a process encompassing four issues: namely, liberalizing the financial capital market, optimizing the threshold for foreign capital, expanding the Japanese yen market in Europe, and facilitating direct investment. In March 1985, the Japanese yen & US Dollar Committee submitted a report proposing that in the aspect of liberalizing the financial capital market, Japan should keep a flexible interest rate for the bearer of fixed deposits, set up a commodity market linked to market interest rate, establish a promissory note market in yen, forego the control of the interest rate on inter-bank lending, build a short-term T-bond market, introduce futures trading, develop a foreign bond market in yen, and more. Such a list highlights the weaknesses of Japan's financial market. One can image that in such a weak financial market, the monetary policies adopted by Japan unlikely to see effective or timely implementation. As Japan lagged behind in developing its global financial market, the Japanese yen was not able to play a significant role. In the flying-geese model of East Asia led by Japan, issues of "currency mismatch" and "maturity mismatch" have always existed, and have, in turn, hindered the progress of internationalizing the Japanese yen.

Chapter 4
Selecting a Path for RMB's Internationalization

Even a cursory review of the monetary policies, the exchange rate systems and the experience of developed countries and developing countries in opening the capital account during the economic and opening-up process, clearly reveals Mundell's "Impossible Trinity." This theory reflects the central conflict plaguing the economic system under an open economy and indicates the extent of policy limitations when selecting from among multiple options. It signifies that the process of internationalizing the RMB may face multiple contradictions, conflicts, and risks—yet the time for selecting a path towards the internationalization of the RMB is now. At the same time, a review of various choices adopted by developed and developing countries in terms of Mundell's "Impossible Trinity" indicate that choices made among countries are determined by their status and structures at various stages of economic development. As their given economic development evolves, we find that there is actually no unique corner solution, and the question becomes whether there are any non-corner solutions. If there are, what's the significance of the non-corner solutions for internationalizing the RMB?

4.1 Corner Solutions to the "Impossible Trinity"

In *A Treatise on Money* (*Volume II*), published in 1930, Keynes argued that a given monetary policy can't work effectively in an economy that has both a fixed exchange rate and capital mobility. In *The Balance of Payments* (1951), James Meade discussed the internal and external balance of payments in an open economy. He argued that a policy mix should be applied if an open economy is to achieve both internal and external equilibrium; a system of fixed exchange rate prevents the government from adopting this type of exchange rate policy, such that when the government attempts to maintain an internal and external balance by merely relying on expenditure policy (adjustment to total social demands via fiscal policy and monetary policy), the goal of achieving an internal balance and the goal

© Social Sciences Academic Press and Springer Nature Singapore Pte Ltd. 2018
Y. Cao, *Strategies for Internationalizing the Renminbi*, Research Series on the Chinese Dream and China's Development Path,
https://doi.org/10.1007/978-981-13-0800-0_4

of achieving an external balance will necessarily conflict. This is known as "Meade Conflict." The conflict becomes most conspicuous in terms of monetary policy. Increasing trends in capital outflows occur as a result of cutting the interest rate by monetary methods, a move that will negatively impede the achievement of the balance of payments.

Tinbergen addressed the relationship between policy objectives and policy instruments in what has come to be known as the "Tinbergen Rule." According to the Rule, for each policy target, at least one policy instrument is needed; there should be at least the same number of instruments as targets. The Rule is instructive when making macroeconomic decisions. For example, the "Meade Conflict" is a special case of the "Tinbergen Rule," i.e. an increase or a decrease in spending is the only policy instrument used to achieve an internal and external balance, so it's impossible to have both internal and external equilibrium. In 1962, Fleming presented his model as an extension of Hicks-Hansen's closed IS-LM model based on Meade's framework. He argued that the monetary policy was more effective under the floating exchange rate. In 1963, Mundell developed the "Fleming-Mundell Model," based on the study of a small open economy. According to Mundell's analysis, if there were a system of fixed exchange rate with perfect capital mobility, an expansionary monetary policy and an increase in the money supply would result in downward pressure on the exchange rate as well as the capital outflow, preventing the interest rate from declining as the balance of payments deteriorated. The central bank would intervene by selling foreign money in exchange for domestic funds in order to maintain the exchange rate. It would continue until the foreign money being sold offset the rise in the domestic money supply, at which point the money supply would return to its original level. Yet, on the contrary, a tightening monetary policy would result in arising interest rate and capital inflow, impeding any increase in the interest rate; the balance of payments would be in surplus and there would be pressure on the appreciation of the exchange rate; the central bank would sell domestic currency and buy foreign money until the money supply returned to where it was in the first place. In this regard, the monetary policy would not have continuous effects on a country's income under a fixed exchange rate system.

An expansionary monetary policy under a floating exchange rate system would result in a decrease in the interest rate and the capital outflow; the balance of payments would be in deficit and the exchange rate would depreciate. The depreciated exchange rate would improve the balance of trade as well as have a multiplier effect on enhancing income and employment. The economic system would be in equilibrium if increased income drove people to hold money newly supplied by the bank. A tightening monetary policy, on the other hand, appreciates the exchange rate, resulting in a declining balance of trade and decreased income. Therefore, the monetary policy under a floating exchange rate system has substantial impacts at the level of income. In short, the "Fleming-Mundell Model" argues that an economy can't simultaneously maintain a fixed exchange rate, free capital movement, and an independent monetary policy, so that the "Impossible Trinity" establishes an important theoretical foundation for "the Trilemma."

Following the Asian Financial Crisis, Paul Krugman—in his text, *What Happened to Asia*—posited that a fixed exchange rate regime under capital movement was the main cause for the crisis. This was also the point at which he first introduced the concept of "the Trilemma." According to this theory, it is impossible to concurrently have all three of the following: an independent monetary policy, a stable foreign exchange rate, and free capital movement. A country can choose only two out of the three factors. Krugman believed that macroeconomic policymakers are generally trying to pursue three goals, considering that: a flexible monetary policy is needed to deal with the threats from the economic recession and the inflation; a stable exchange rate is needed to avoid too many uncertainties in business activities; and free international business activities, particularly the free trade of foreign monies, are needed to maintain the essence of a private economy. Despite this desire to accomplish all three goals, however, Krugman believed that a country can only choose two out of the three factors. If the stabilized exchange rate is abandoned, then a country may follow the US and Australia in adopting a floating exchange rate regime; a flexible monetary policy can be discarded, so as to adopt a fixed exchange rate as Argentina did or even abolish home currency as some European countries did; or the free market principle can be abolished and replaced by capital controls, as most nations did in the decades between the 1940s and 1960s.

The "Impossible Trinity" and "the Trilemma" reveal how capital mobility influences an effective (or independent) monetary policy under a fixed or floating exchange rate regime. Please see Fig. 4.1:

In Fig. 4.1, the three edges represent the free capital movement, an independent monetary policy, and exchange rate stability. The free capital movement refers to capital allocation around the world and improved capacity utilization; an independent monetary policy indicates positive adjustments made to domestic output and price fluctuations without interference from external factors; and the stable exchange rate helps stabilize prices of domestic and foreign currencies, benefiting activities related to global trade and investment. The three corners of the triangle

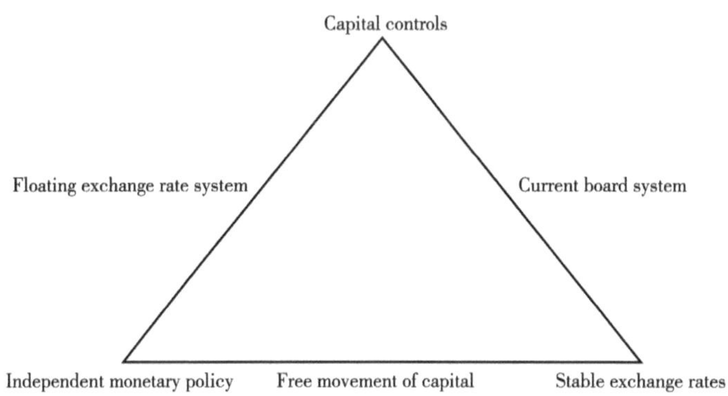

Fig. 4.1 Mundell's impossible trinity

represent regimes such as capital controls, floating exchange rates, and fixed exchange rates. According to "the Trilemma," however, it is impossible for an open economy to simultaneously have free capital mobility, a fixed exchange rate, and an independent monetary policy; it must choose two of them, while giving up the third. This is known as the "Corner Solution" to "the Trilemma".

According to the Mundell-Fleming Model, in a small open economy, an equilibrium condition needs equilibrium in the product market, money market, and balance of payments. In Fig. 4.2, *Y* is the national income, and *i* is the domestic interest rate; IS, LM, and BP curves stand for the equilibrium present in the product market, the equilibrium in the money market, and the equilibrium in the balance of payments, respectively. According to Keynesian macroeconomics theory, *IS* is a downward-sloping curve, *LM* is an upward-sloping curve, and *BP* changes based on the flow of capital.

1. Under a system of fixed exchange rate with no movement of capital, an open economy reaches equilibrium at Point E (Fig. 4.2). Assuming complete capital immobility, the BP Curve is vertical and the capital flow is unrelated to the exchange rate. The points on the BP Curve refer to the balance of payments; the points on the right-hand side refer to the balance of payments deficit; and the points on the left-hand side refer to the balance of payments surplus.

Assuming the central bank adopts an expansionary monetary policy and increases the money supply, the LM Curve shifts to the right to LM_1, the exchange rate falls, investment increases, and the national income rises. LM_1 meets IS at the intersection of E_1, where equilibrium is temporary and the balance of payments is in deficit.

In the long run, however, as the balance of payments is in deficit, the existing reserves of foreign currency fall and the money supply decreases, resulting in arising exchange rate and decreased investment and national income. With the help of rational expectations, the adjustment will continue until the balance of payments is in a state of equilibrium. Given no change in the exchange rate, this adjustment will continue until the national income returns to where it originally began. Other variables remain unchanged, but the central bank's foreign currency reserves fall.

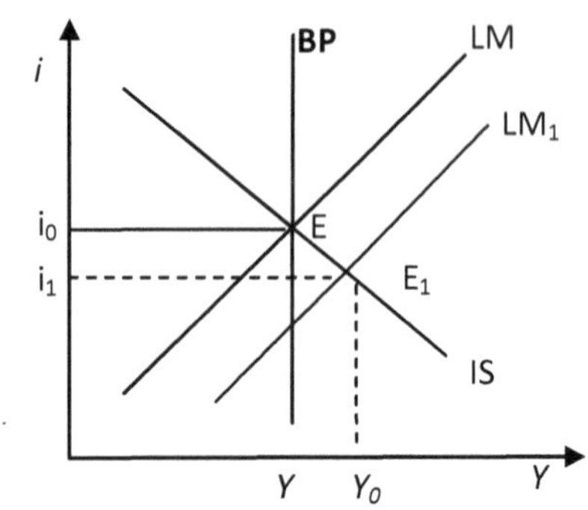

Fig. 4.2 The relationship between GDP and interest rate under capital immobility

In the long run, a given monetary policy does not affect the economy under a fixed exchange rate system with complete capital immobility.

2. Under a fixed exchange rate system with partial capital mobility, BP is an upward-sloping curve (Fig. 4.3). As the exchange rate rises, both capital inflow and the surplus increase, and as a result, it is necessary to improve the national income in order to offset demands for increased imports. The points on the right-hand side of the BP Curve refer to the balance of payments deficit, while the points on the left-hand side of the BP Curve refer to the balance of payments surplus.

If an expansionary monetary policy is adopted, the LM Curve shifts to the right to LM′. LM′ meets IS at Point E′, reaching a temporary equilibrium at that point. The national income increases and the interest rate falls, but the balance of payments remains in deficit. Income, however, rises, causing the growth of imports and deterioration in the current account. At the same time, as the interest rate falls there is a capital outflow, negatively impacting the capital account.

In the long run, the central bank will sell foreign money reserves to make up for the balance of payments deficit. LM′ shifts left until it coincides with LM. At this moment, the money supply, the interest rate, the national income, and other economic variables return back to their original levels except for some changes in the internal structure of the base money. Ultimately, such a monetary policy is ineffective in the long run.

3. Under a system of fixed exchange rate with full mobility, capital flows can correct any form of disequilibrium in the balance of payments for the current account. In this regard, the BP Curve is horizontal, being exempt from arising or falling interest rate (Fig. 4.4).

When an expansionary monetary policy is adopted, LM shifts to LM′, resulting in a falling interest rate. When capital is perfectly mobile, even a slight drop in the domestic interest rate is enough to result in the rapid outflow of capital and reduction in the foreign currency reserves, offsetting the effects of monetary expansion. That is to say, a monetary policy is even ineffective in the short run, nor is it fully independent. Such monetary policy effects can also be had under different forms of capital mobility with a floating exchange rate system.

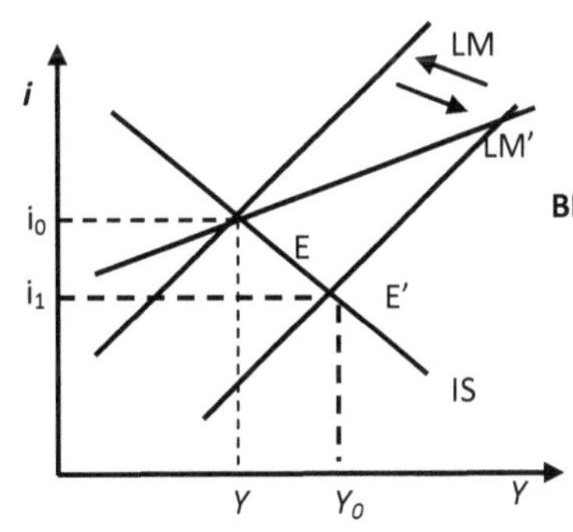

Fig. 4.3 The relationship between GDP and interest rate under partial capital mobility

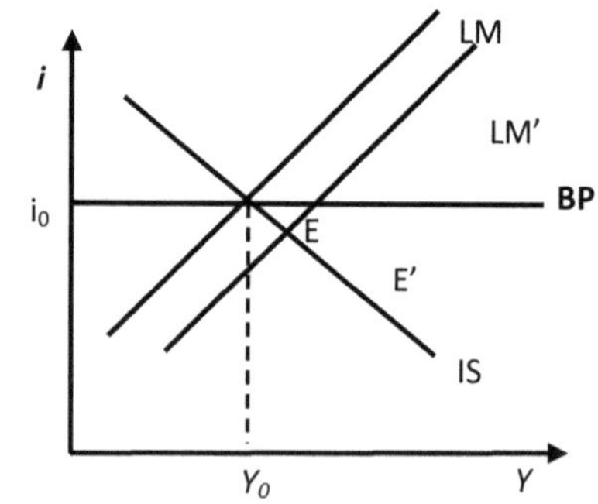

Fig. 4.4 The relationship between GDP and interest rate under full capital mobility

As the "Impossible Trinity" suggests, a country can either choose to have a fixed exchange rate regime (like the dollarization, the monetary union, or the Currency Board), or choose to have a full floating exchange rate regime (as represented by the USD). Intermediate rate arrangements are not sustainable and will eventually disappear. That is, extreme solutions are the only way out of the "Impossible Trinity;" i.e. only the "Corner Solution" works.

If K represents capital, M is monetary policy, and E represents the exchange rate, we can suppose:

K = 0, indicating minimal control and full mobility of capital;

K = 1, indicating the maximum control and no mobility of capital;

M = 0, indicating the minimum dependence on the monetary policy and the full independence of the monetary policy;

M = 1, indicating the maximum dependence on the monetary policy and the full ineffectiveness of the monetary policy;

E = 0, indicating the least likelihood of any change in the exchange rate while the exchange rate is fully-fixed;

E = 1, indicating the most likelihood of any change in the exchange rate while the exchange rate is fully floating; then:

Please refer to Table 4.1 for the conclusions.

We see that conflicts exist between the fixed exchange rate and the monetary policy, so the "Corner Solutions" to the "Impossible Trinity" are:

1. $E = 0 \cap K = 0 \cap M = 1$ (for example, Hong Kong's currency board regime, stabilizing the exchange rate between the Hong Kong dollar (HKD) and the United States dollar (USD), but losing monetary policy independence).

Table 4.1 Effects of monetary policy under the M-F model

Exchange rate regime E	E = 0	E = 1
Cash flow K	0 0 < K < 1	1 0 0 < K < 1
Monetary policy M	1 1	1 0 0 0

2. $E = 1 \cap K = 0 \cap M = 0$ (for example, the floating exchange rate for US dollar due to its pursuit of perfect capital mobility and an independent monetary policy).

The Mundell-Fleming Model tells us that under a fixed exchange rate regime, stability of the fixed exchange rate and independence may not coexist in spite of full controls on capital mobility. What's more, at best, the monetary policy is only effective in the short term. It implies that for a given open economy under a fixed exchange rate regime, its money supply is subject to changes in the global reserves and that the money supply is not fully controlled by the central bank. China's monetary policy practice conclusively indicates the validity of the Mundell-Fleming Model.

4.2 Limitations of Corner Solutions to the "Impossible Trinity," as Well as Non-corner Solutions in the Trilemma

The "Impossible Trinity" is important in its applicability to theoretical mathematics, while its only realistic significance is that under the condition of perfect capital mobility, an open economy either adopts a fixed exchange rate regime without the associated independence of monetary policy, or it adopts an independency monetary policy with a floating exchange rate regime. The various "Corner Solutions" appeared in the 1990s, materializing in the wake of the economic collapse in Southeast Asia in 1997. Some emerging economies adopting either "free floating" or "hard pegging" exchange rate regimes; for example, the currency board regime adopted by Argentina and Hong Kong—two countries that have, at least in the short run, avoided the worst of the financial crisis—while countries without pegged rates —South Africa, Mexico, and Turkey, for example—have been able to avoid such crises altogether. As economic globalization has increased, however, problems in the underlying economic structure of some emerging countries and regions are becoming conspicuous. Countries (or regions) that have adopted either pegged or unpegged rates have been falling into crises. For example, the Mexican peso crisis erupted in 1994; Taiwan, South Korea, and Indonesia were mostly affected by the Asian Financial Crisis in 1997; the Russian financial crisis occurred in 1998; the Brazilian financial crisis in 1999, and so on. In particular, Argentina's 2001 economic and financial crisis ran up against the concept of the corner solution. Argentina experienced one of the worst economic crises in the years between 1999 and 2002, almost completely offsetting the country's previous strong economic performance under the currency board between 1991 and 1998. Given the occurrence and reoccurrence of numerous financial crises, the floating/fixed exchange rate regime has unsurprisingly been questioned. The desire for a singular, certain exchange rate that will be either fixed or floating has led to a discussion of potential "Non-Corner Solutions" to the "Impossible Trinity."

Given the financial crises taking place in the 1990s, some economists advanced the theory of the "hollowing-out of intermediate exchange rate regimes," arguing that intermediate regimes are intrinsically less viable than both hard pegs and flexible regimes. Several studies, however, showed that the "hollowing-out of intermediate regimes" hypothesis was not supported by sample data, indicating that intermediate exchange rate regimes still play important roles in determining the final choice of "real" exchange regimes. Frankel, who advanced the "Impossible Trinity," commented in 1999 that certain types of intermediate regimes would be better than corner regimes for some countries. Based on this hypothesis, some researchers developed a more general theory of the "expanded triangle." They argued that, while it elaborated relationships between three policy objectives, the "Impossible Trinity" didn't adequately explain the potential effects of intermediate exchange rate regimes. They developed an indicator system and expanded upon the original "Impossible Trinity," formalizing Mundell's trilemma in an open economy. The expanded triangle acts as a formalized tool for Frankel's concept of "half-independence and half-stability."

In an equilateral triangle (see Fig. 4.5), the three edges represent objectives desired by the government or central bank: an independent monetary policy, free capital flow, or a stable exchange rate.

In the above equilateral triangle, edge M is a fully independent monetary policy, edge K is the free capital flow, and edge E represents a stable exchange rate. Three angles represent three types of exchange rate arrangements (Fig. 4.5). We should note that the sum of the perpendicular distances from an arbitrary point inside the equilateral triangle to the three sides of the triangle is a constant. Supposing an arbitrary point, O, inside the equilateral triangle, draw lines from O to each of the vertices of the triangle, and let those perpendicular distances be Ms, Kc, and Ev, where Ms is dependence on the monetary policy, Kc is the level of capital control, and Ev is changes in the exchange rates.

In the equilateral triangle, if the height Mh = 1, we get $0 \leq$ Ms, Kc, Ev ≤ 1.

Fig. 4.5 The impossible trinity

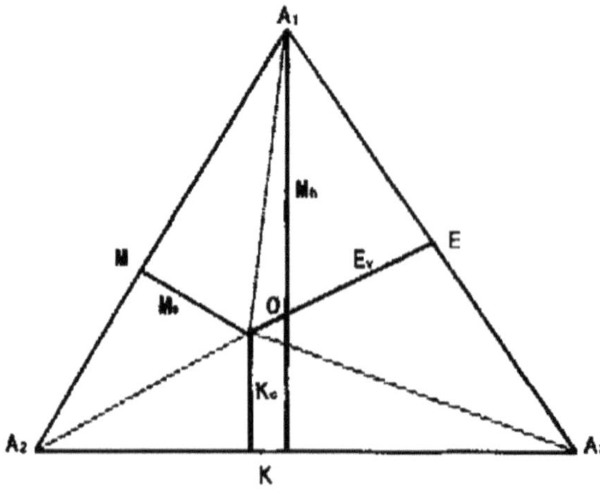

We can get the minimum level of capital control (full capital mobility) if Kc = 0; and we get the maximum level of capital control (capital controls) if Kc = 1. Once Ms = 0, it is least likely to depend on monetary policy (the full independence of monetary policy); once Ms = 1, we get the most likelihood of dependence on the monetary policy (loss of monetary policy independence). If Ev = 0, it is least likely to change in the exchange rate (fully-fixed exchange rate); if Ev = 1, it is most likely to change in the exchange rate (fully-floating exchange rate). The sum of the perpendicular distances from an arbitrary point inside the equilateral triangle to the three sides of the triangle equals the height. At that point, we have Ms + Kc + Ev = Mh. Because Mh = 1, we get Ms + Kc + Ev = 1.

If Ms = 0, Ms = 1, and 0 < Ms < 1, we may have the following solution sets (Fig. 4.2).

Among the solutions in Table 4.2, the 4th and 5th are solutions to the 3rd solution; the following eight solutions coincided with the IMF's classification of exchange rate regimes:

1. Exchange Arrangements with No Separate Legal Tender (NS): The currency of another country circulates as the sole legal tender (formal dollarization), or the member belongs to a monetary or currency union in which the same legal tender is shared by all members of the union.
2. Currency Board Arrangements (CBA): A monetary regime based on an explicit legislative commitment to exchanging domestic currency for a specified foreign currency at a fixed exchange rate, combined with restrictions on the issuing authority to ensure the fulfillment of its legal obligation. An example of this is the linked exchange rate system in Hong Kong.
3. Other Conventional Fixed Peg Arrangements (FP): The exchange rate may fluctuate within narrow margins of less than ±1% around a central rate; the country pegs its currency at a fixed rate to another currency or a basket of currencies; the currency composites can also be standardized, as in the case of SDR.
4. Pegged Exchange Rates within Horizontal Bands (HB): The value of the currency is maintained within certain margins of fluctuation of at least ±1% around a fixed central rate, or the margin between the maximum and minimum value of the exchange rate exceeds 2%. An example of this is the exchange rate mechanism (ERM) of the European Monetary System (EMS).
5. Crawling Pegs (CP): The currency is adjusted periodically in small amounts at a fixed rate or in response to changes in selective quantitative indicators.
6. Exchange Rates within Crawling Bands (CB): The currency is maintained within certain fluctuation margins; the central rate or margins are adjusted periodically at a fixed and publicly-announced rate or in response to changes in selective quantitative indicators.
7. Managed Floating with No Predetermined Path for the Exchange Rate (MF): The monetary authority attempts to influence the exchange rate without having a specific exchange rate path or target. Indicators for managing the rate include the

Table 4.2 Impossible trinity solutions

Type	Degree of dependence on the monetary policy		
	MS = 0	MS = 1	0 < MS < 1
Capital control and exchange rate change			
Kc = 0 Ev = 1	Solution 1: full capital mobility ∩ full independence of monetary policy ∩ fully-floating exchange rate (IF)	–	–
Kc = 1 Ev = 0	Solution 2: full independence of monetary policy ∩ full capital mobility ∩ fixed exchange rate (FP)	–	–
0 < Kc < 1 0 < Ev < 1	Solution 3: full independence of monetary policy ∩ limited capital mobility ∩ limited floating exchange rate	–	–
Kc → 0 Ev → 1	Solution 4: full independence of monetary policy ∩ close to full capital mobility ∩ close to fully- floating exchange rate (close to IF)	–	–
Kc → 1 Ev → 0	Solution 5: full independence of monetary policy ∩ close to full capital control ∩ close to fixed exchange rate (close to MF)	–	–
Kc = 0 Ev = 0	–	Solution 6: full capital mobility ∩ loss of monetary policy independence ∩ fixed exchange rate (NS, CBA)	–
Kc = 0, 0 < Ev < 1	–	–	Solution 7: loss of monetary policy independence ∩ full capital mobility ∩ limited floating exchange rate (HB, CP)
0 < Kc < 1 0 < Ev < 1	–	–	Solution 8: limited capital mobility ∩ limited independence of monetary policy ∩ limited floating exchange rate (CB)
0 < Kc < 1 Ev = 0	–	–	Solution 9: limited capital mobility ∩ limited independence of monetary policy ∩ fixed exchange rate (FP)

balance of payments position, international reserves, parallel market developments, and automatic adjustment.
8. Independently Floating (IF): The exchange rate is market-determined, with any official foreign exchange market intervention aimed at moderating the rate of change and preventing undue fluctuations in the exchange rate, rather than at establishing a level for it. An example of this is the exchange rate regime adopted by the US and Japan.

The non-corner solution to the "Impossible Trinity" refers to the "Intermediate Regimes" as mentioned above (i.e. Classes 3, 4, 5, 7, and 8). It makes no difference which, as they are all government-controlled and fluctuate within a certain range. The corner solution, on the other hand, refers to the "corner exchange rate regimes" as mentioned above (i.e. Classes 1, 2, and 6), which are either "free floating" or "hard pegging;" the exchange rate of Class 1 is absolutely fixed internally while floating externally; the exchange rate of Class 2 is completely fixed; and the exchange rate of Class 6 is fully floating.

To overcome the problem of the "Trilemma," a Chinese scholar conducted a spatial analysis. Li designed a 3-D coordinate system in which the x-coordinate is the exchange rate regime, the y-coordinate is the effectiveness of the monetary policy, and the z-coordinate represents capital flow. In the 3-D coordinate system, the X-axis represents exchange rate stability, and the fully-floating exchange rate will be found at the center; the Y-axis indicates the effectiveness of monetary policy, with the loss of effectiveness at the center; and the Z-axis represents the level of capital mobility, where the origin represents full capital controls. These three coordinates represent the projected goals of the government.

We set units for the three variants—namely, monetary policy effectiveness, exchange rate stability, and capital mobility—so as to simplify the following analysis. The value range of each of these variants is from 0 to 1. The value of 1 on the x, y, and z-axes represents absolutely fixed exchange rates, a completely independent monetary policy, and perfect capital mobility, respectively.

If the exchange rate is fixed and the capital is mobile at Point F (1, 0, 1), then Point F stands for the currency board system. Accordingly, if the exchange rate is fixed with an independent monetary policy at Point G (1, 1, 0), then Point G represents complete capital control. And if the capital is mobile with an independent monetary policy at Point D (0, 1, 1), then Point D represents the floating exchange rate regime. If all this is a given, then ΔFGD is the equivalent expression for the "Trilemma" in an open economy. The plane of FGD makes up the boundary when a country determines its policy goals. In other words, a country's goals should fall below this plane, while a country is able to make the choice inside or at the boundary of cube AOCDBGF (see Fig. 4.6).

Point W is taken either within the cube or on its boundary. Through W passes a cross section, HLKJI, parallel to the plane XY. This cross section meets line FG at Point I, while the cross section and line GD intersect at Point J. This is a model based on the CFEF Research Report—*Mathematical Analysis of Optimum Exchange Rate Regime*.

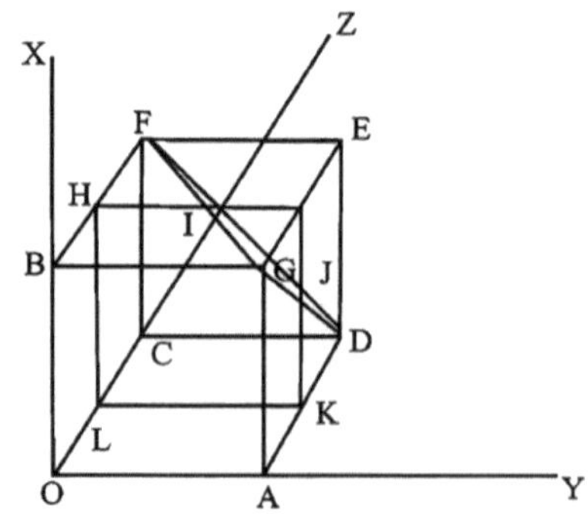

Fig. 4.6 Trilemma in three dimensions

BH = z because the cross section HLKJI is parallel to the plane XY. Additionally, ΔBFG is an isosceles right triangle, so IG = 2z. Considering that ΔIGJ is an equilateral triangle, we get IJ = 2z. On the plane HLKJI, we have Fig. 4.7.

Then Line MN: $x + y = 2 - z$. So $x + y \leq 2 - z$ when it is below Line MN.

Assumption 1: When capital mobility is given, Z becomes the external variable in the model that will be determined by the government's management ability for capital mobility.

Assumption 2: The exchange rate regime of an economy is controlled by the government.

We may assume that the loss function $M = A - \ln(1 + \alpha y)$ stands for the loss of monetary policy independence. In the loss function, A is the damage coefficient of the monetary policy, representing losses resulting from the total failure of the monetary policy. Since the monetary policy may not be completely effective, the value range of α would be $0 < \alpha < 1$. The actual value of α is determined by the level of development of the financial system and independence of the central bank. The higher the level of development of the financial system, the more independent the central bank will be, resulting in a more secure transmission mechanism of the monetary policy and a greater ability to intervene in the economy. The loss function for the exchange rate instability is shown as:

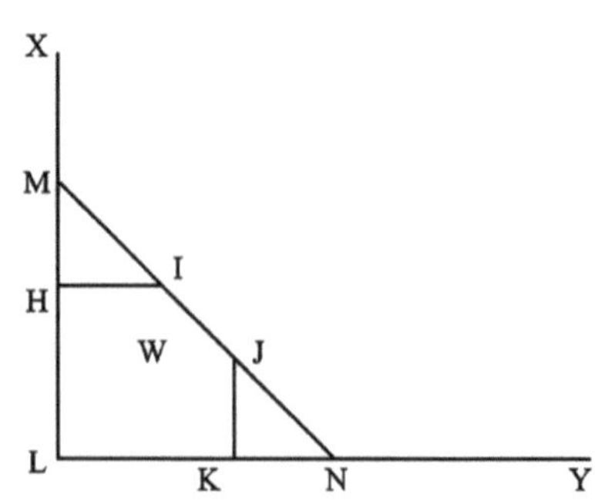

Fig. 4.7 Trilemma in two dimensions

$$N = s\ln[1 + \beta(1 + x)]$$

where $1 - x$ = exchange rate instability and β = damage coefficient for exchange rate fluctuations ($0 < \beta<1$). Hence, the integrated loss function can be shown as:

$$t[A - \ln(1 + ay)] + 1(1 - t)s\ln[1 + \beta(1 - x)]$$

therefore

$$\mathrm{MIN}\, C = t[A - \ln(1 + ay)] + 1(1 - t)s\ln[1 + \beta(1 - x)]$$
$$\mathrm{s.t.}\, x + y \le 2 - z$$
$$0 \le x, \quad y \le 1, \quad 0 \le \alpha, \quad \beta \le 1, \quad 0 \le t \le 1$$

where t is the weight for making a choice between monetary policy independence and exchange rate stability. Generally speaking, large countries prefer dependent monetary policies, while countries with abundant foreign exchange reserves or that have once experienced high inflation tend to have stable exchange rates. If S is the government's comprehensive ability to resist risks arising from the fluctuating exchange rate, p is the level of economic dependence on foreign countries, q is the trade concentration of a country, and f is the development level of the country's financial system, then:

$$S = pqf$$

whereas p and q increase, the economic operation costs due to exchange rate risks will be higher. The higher the value of f, however, the lower the economic operation costs will be. The country that is weak to resisting floating exchange rate risks always prefers the fixed exchange rate regime, while the country that is capable of resisting floating exchange rate risks always prefers the floating exchange rate regime.

In this way we can prove that a non-corner solution with minimum loss at the equilibrium point does exist in this model, assuming:

MIN $C = t[A - \ln(1+ay)] + 1(1 - t)s\ln[1+\beta(1 - x)]$

Line IJ: $x + y \le 2 - z$

Point I: $(1, 1 - z)$; Point J: $(1 - z, 1)$; Point K: $(0, 1)$; Point H: $(1, 0)$

(1) In the plane KLHIJ,
 $C \cdot x = -\beta(1 - t)s1 + \beta(1 - x) \cdot y \cdot C \cdot y = -t\alpha 1 + ay$
 Since $s > 0$, $0 \le x$, $y \le 1$, $0 \le \alpha$ and $\beta \le 1$, $0 \le \iota \le 1$, we see that $\alpha\beta = 0$, yx, $yx \ge 0$.
 Besides, C does not have an extreme value, so the only possible extremum point is located on the boundary.
(2) On the line KL ($X = 0$, $\le y \le 1$)
 $C = t[A - \ln(1+ay)] + (1 - t)s\ln(1 + \beta)$
 since $dcdy{-}ta1 + ay \le 0$, we see that C is a decreasing function.
 $\max = \iota A + (1 - \iota)s\ln(1 + \beta)$ if $y = 0$.
 $\min = \iota[A - \ln(1 + \alpha)] + (1 - \iota)s\ln(1 + \beta)$ if $y = 1$.

(3) On the Line KJ ($y = 1, 0 \leq x \leq 1 - z$),
$C = t[A - \ln(1 + a)] + (1 - t)s\ln[1 + \beta(1 - x)]$
dCdx = $-\beta(1 - t)s1 + \beta(1 - x) \leq 0$
We see that C is a decreasing function.
$\max = \iota[A - \ln(1 + \alpha)] + (1 - \iota)s\ln(1 + \beta)$ if $x = 0$
$\min = \iota[A - \ln(1 + \alpha)] + (1 - \iota)s\ln(1 + \beta z)$ if $x = 1 - z$.
(4) On the Line LH($y = 0, 0 \leq x \leq 1$),
$C = tA + (1 - t)s\ln[1 + \beta(1 - x)]$
Since dCdx = $-\beta(1 - t)s1 + \beta(1 - x) \leq 0$, we see that C is a decreasing function.
$\max = \iota A + (1 - \iota)s\ln(1 + \beta)$ if $x = 0$
$\min = \iota A + (1 - \iota)s\ln(1 + \beta)$ if $x = 1$.
(5) On the Line HI ($x = 1{,}0 \leq y \leq 1$),
$C = t[A - \ln(1 + ay)]$
Since dCdx-−ta1 + ay ≤ 0, we see that C is decreasing.
$\max = \iota A$ if $y = 0$.
$\min = \iota\{A - \ln[1 + \alpha(1 + z)]\}$ if $y = 1 - z$.

To summarize, along Line LKJ, it is clear that the loss function C reaches a minimum value only at Point J through referring to (2) and (3). On the other hand, along Line LHI, we find that the loss function reaches the minimum value at Point I by referring to (4) and (5). Hence, the minimum value of C should be along the boundary line IJ.

It can be extrapolated from the above model that when the external variable of capital flow Z is between 0 and 1, the minimum value for the loss function due to exchange rate instability and inefficiency of monetary policy always lies inside the "Impossible Triangle." That is to say, when the capital flow is external, the loss arising out of the conflict between the exchange-rate policy and monetary policy will, at this point, be minimum, although the profit generated by the combination of both might not be the most significant. Thus, a country can locate the equilibrium point of minimum loss due to exchange rate instability and monetary policy ineffectiveness inside the "Impossible Trinity" according to its capital mobility—that is, a country can trade partial exchange rate stability for a certain degree of monetary policy efficiency.

4.3 The Significance of Non-corner Solutions to the RMB Internationalization Process

Intermediate regimes still play an important role in the current international monetary system. Since the collapse of the Bretton Woods System in 1973, all countries have chosen their own exchange rate regimes according to their subjective economic situations and internal and external system environments. Contrary to what was expected, replacement of the fixed exchange rate regime by a fluctuating exchange rate regime did not take place. While most developed countries chose floating regimes, many developing countries chose to follow pegged exchange rate regimes. The international exchange rate system under the Jamaica exchange rate system actually represented the coexistence of multiple exchange rate arrangements. In 1999, the IMF adopted a classification system of exchange rate arrangements according to the actual conditions in each country. This new classification system differentiated multiple types of pegged exchange rate regimes in order to better reflect the autonomy and responsibility of each country's monetary authority.

According to studies undertaken by Yi Gang and Tang Xian, and Li Cheng, a significant number of countries chose intermediate regimes, seeing that it would enable them to employ fixed exchange rate regimes the majority of the time without losing the right to intervene in their exchange rates under extreme conditions. Frankel indicated that this is not the same thing as a pegged exchange rate, however, saying that one cannot give up both complete stability and complete independence for half-stability and half-independence in monetary policy. In this regard, intermediate regimes were more appropriate than the bipolar—or two-corner—regimes taken up by most countries, especially for developing countries incapable of mustering threaten large-scale capital mobility.

Hernandez and Motty studied post-crisis exchange rates in Asian countries and did not find any signs of shifting to a bipolar regime. Even Obstfeld, who opposed the use of intermediate regimes (1999), admitted that the fixed exchange rate is not absolute, and further pointed out that choice of a fixed exchange rate and a floating exchange rate is not an either-or situation. Since any given country would, by necessity, consider the impact on its exchange rate while making monetary policies, the so-called free floating exchange rate is, in practice, just an abstract concept without any practical meaning. Despite this, the more greater the impact a country's monetary policy is perceived to have on the exchange rate, the more extensive the restrictions it will enact are.

In the light of this theory and Mundell's "Impossible Triangle," the three sides of the triangle in Fig. 4.5 represent three macroeconomic objectives, while the vertex signifies the system arrangement necessary to achieve two related objectives. As shown in Fig. 4.8, the arrows x, y, and m represent exchange rate stability, monetary policy independence, and the direction of increasing capital mobility, respectively. Although this triangle shows the relationship among the three policies, it fails to reflect the impacts brought to bear by intermediate regimes. As such, a new indicator system that further expands this triangle needs to be established in order to solve this problem using all available data. For example, we set x, y, and m, standing for exchange rate stability, monetary policy independence, and capital mobility, respectively, which all belong to [0, 1] after standardization. When $x = 0$, the exchange rate can float freely; the exchange rate is totally fixed when $x = 1$; $y = 0$ signifies currency union, whereas $y = 1$ represents complete independence of monetary policy; $m = 0$ refers to full capital controls, and $m = 1$ means perfect

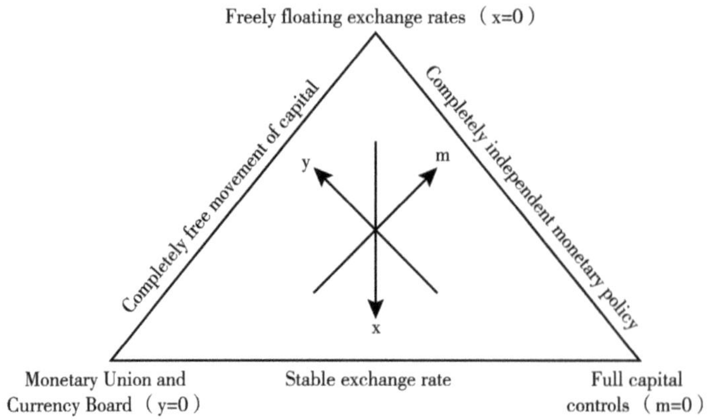

Fig. 4.8 Mundell's impossible trinity

capital mobility. All other values between 0 and 1 are medians. Every possible exchange rate system (x) and its combination (y, m) can be described using one matching point (x, y, m). For instance, (1, 0, 1) can be labeled as a Class 1 arrangement, and (0, 1, 1) as a Class 8 arrangement, to name just a few.

Thus, we have established an extended triangle. The distance from each point (x, y, m) to each of the three sides (stable exchange rate, full monetary policy independence, perfect capital mobility) is shown as $(1 - x, 1 - y, 1 - m)$. The number implies the approximate location of the exchange rate regime according to the above classification. Following comparison with Fig. 4.5, it is clear that $Ms = 1 - m$; $Kc = 1 - y$; $Ev=1 - x$.

Therefore, the non-corner solution to Mundell's "Impossible Triangle" can be shown as $x + y + m = 2$. The sum of the three variables will always be 2. Thus, the capital flow, exchange rate stability, and monetary policy are in equilibrium. This equation can take several typical forms depending on the variables involved:

$$x + y + m = 2$$

$$1 + 0 + 1 = 2 \tag{4.1}$$

$$1 + 1 + 0 = 2 \tag{4.2}$$

$$0 + 1 + 1 = 2 \tag{4.3}$$

$$1/2 + 1 + 1/2 = 2 \tag{4.4}$$

$$2/3 + 2/3 + 2/3 = 2 \tag{4.5}$$

Certainly, combination (4.1) is close to the current state of the United States, in which we can observe a monetary policy with full independence, a free floating exchange rate, and unrestricted capital mobility. As for combination (4.2), the monetary policy is totally independent and the rate of exchange is stable, though capital mobility is zero. This is very similar to the current state in North Korea. Combination (4.3) is very close to the actual condition of Hong Kong, where the monetary policy is not independent, the exchange rate is stable, and capital is freely flowing.

Combination (4.4) is an interpretation of China's current macro policy. When m = 1/2, there are still certain limitations on the monetary policy in spite of a high degree of autonomy. If y = 1/2, the current accounts are completely open, with some capital accounts open but without the free flow of capital due to a certain degree of restriction. If x = 1, the exchange rate of the RMB is quite stable, although this does not guarantee a fixed exchange rate system.

Combination (4.4) indicates that regardless of monetary policy, capital flow, and/or exchange rate systems, it is appropriate to maintain the equation under the framework of a normal equilibrium. In other words, it's necessary to consider coordination when formulating these three policies. Especially in the short- or medium-term, coordination becomes critical. We assume that it is possible to steadily shift to combination (4.5) from combination (4.4) via certain policy arrangements, which is predicated on the ability to meet requirements for capital liberalization and a pegged exchange rate in developing countries while also removing the impacts on China's macro economy in the process of the RMB's internationalization. Figure 4.9 illustrates this. In this schematic diagram, side M indicates that the monetary policy is totally independent; side K represents the complete freedom of capital flow; and side E represents a stable exchange rate. The three corners of the triangle indicate three different exchange rate arrangements. In China, the exchange rate system is still the traditional fixed system, which embraces an actual pegging system with managed floating (the exchange rate may fluctuate within narrow margins of less than ±1% around a central rate; the country pegs its currency at a fixed rate to another currency or a basket of currencies; the currency

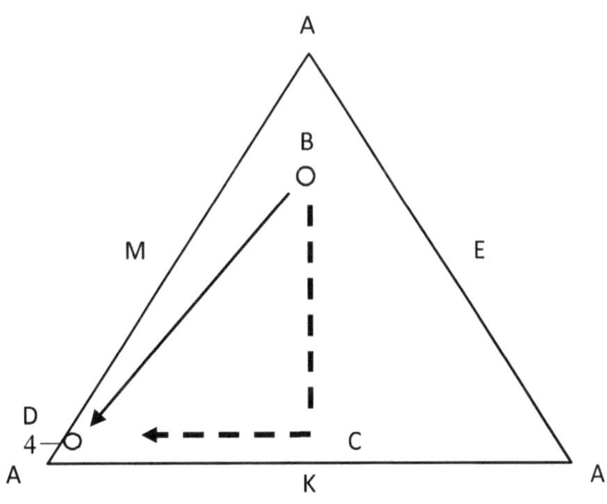

Fig. 4.9 RMB international process

composites can also be standardized, as in the case of the SDR). This system is located at point B1 in the "Impossible Triangle." If $0 < Kc < 1$, $0 < Ev < 1$ and $MS = 0$, the exchange rate regime and the monetary policy can be shown as an intermediate regime with full independence of monetary policy ∩ limited capital mobility ∩ limited exchange rate floating. This is the starting point of the RMB's internationalization.

Given a background of economic globalization, however, intermediate regimes are not stable while the corner exchange rate regimes are. In this regard, an exchange rate regime that is independently floating will be adopted as a result of the RMB's internationalization, in which the level of the exchange rate will be determined by the market. Occasional foreign exchange intervention aims at decreasing changes in the exchange rate and avoiding excessive volatility instead of setting a benchmark for the exchange rate, per se. When $MS = 0$, $Kc \rightarrow 0$ and $Ev \rightarrow 1$, the relation of the monetary policy and exchange rate policy follows a fully independent monetary policy ∩ of perfect capital mobility ∩ and a free-floating exchange rate (i.e. Point D in the triangle).

We are witness to this process in China's own economy, where exchange rate arrangements are particularly conspicuous. Ever since the country's initial reform and opening-up, China has been adopting a progressive approach to reform that takes into consideration its own national characteristics, as opposed to merely imitating others. China's rapid growth in foreign trade over the past 30 years is unprecedented. The total volume of foreign trade has grown to USD4.303 bn in 2014 from USD20.6 bn in 1978, or an increase of nearly 210 times over only 36 years. China has now become the largest exporter and the second largest importer in the world. Its degree of dependence on foreign trade has been steadily approaching 50%, making China a truly export-oriented economy. At the beginning of this process, a relatively fixed exchange rate regime was an essential prerequisite. On one hand, it's true that Chinese enterprises, as microeconomic entities, lack awareness and the ability to cope with potential exchange rate fluctuations. In order to guarantee the success of international trade and investment, the government has to lower transaction costs and provide a stable financial environment for these enterprises by adopting a relatively fixed exchange rate regime. On the other hand, the development of China's financial market is not well-rounded. There are very few financial instruments available that can be utilized to avoid foreign exchange risks. Thus, it's impossible to hedge against exchange rate risks within the capital market.

The exchange rate system began to change along with the development of an export-oriented economy, with China establishing its foreign exchange center in 1994. By following article No. 8 of the *Agreement of the International Monetary Fund,* the country was able to open up the current account for the RMB. Liberalization of the capital account has also been achieved to some degree through encouraging foreign direct investment, restricting foreign indirect investment, supporting the influx of capital, and limiting capital outflows, on the basis of which the RMB's exchange rate has begun to present features indicative of crawling pegs and crawling bands.

From July 2005 on, China has been in the process of adopting a managed floating exchange rate regime based on market supply and demand with reference to a basket of currencies. Beginning in May 2007, the PBOC began to allow as much as 0.5% in daily fluctuation of the value of the RMB. While the RMB was not allowed to fluctuate in the wake of the 2008 financial crisis, fluctuations in value were allowed to resume from June 2010 on. In June 2012, China allowed as much as 1% in daily fluctuation of the value of the RMB, a significant increase over the previous 0.5% limit. The exchange rate was allowed to rise or fall by 2% from a daily midpoint rate of1 percent in March 2014 so as to increase the flexibility of the RMB's exchange rate.

It is worth noting that previous statistical analysis indicates that an effective exchange rate will not be subject to much change when the RMB adopts a floating exchange rate regime. On the contrary, the effective exchange rate of the RMB always experiences changes when the system is dollar-pegged. Thus, in this sense, a fixed exchange rate does not result in guaranteed monetary stability. Instead, only a system allowing for a floating exchange rate or a more flexible monetary regime can really maintain a stable and effective exchange rate.

After the international financial crisis, there has been increasing voice for large-scale system reform of the international monetary system, predicated on the recognition that China has been playing an increasingly essential role in rebalancing the world economy. The strong economic performance and expanded international use of the RMB implies that it is the right time for opening the country's capital account.

What this means is that the opportunity to make a significant leap forward in the development of the RMB's internationalization only emerges under conditions of significant international economic crisis. As a result, changing demands for international currencies require the internationalization of the RMB. What's more, the theory of a non-corner solution to internationalization suggests that the internationalization of the RMB at a level that is adequate to meet global demand is feasible. In the future, the next goal of the RMB will be to open up the capital account in order to become fully convertible. China established this goal in 1994 and, by1996, had already successfully liberalized the current account, indicating solid progress in the process of full convertibility of the RMB.

As a matter of fact, the evolutionary path of the RMB's internationalization avoids the problem of the "Impossible Trinity" altogether. In Fig. 4.10, the "Impossible Trinity" refers to the gray triangle (IV) in the center, i.e. under the condition of the completely free flow of capital and the adoption of a fixed exchange rate without a corresponding fully independent monetary policy; in order to maintain full independence of the monetary policy, the fixed exchange rate system has to be given up. Capital controls must be implemented when choosing both a fixed rate system and independent monetary policy at the same time. That is to say, only two corner points can be chosen at one time in the triangle IV. The other policy combinations (I, II or III) are mutually compatible triangles with each of the three corners concurrently coexisting. Hence, when considering the process of currency internationalization for a given sovereign state, particularly a

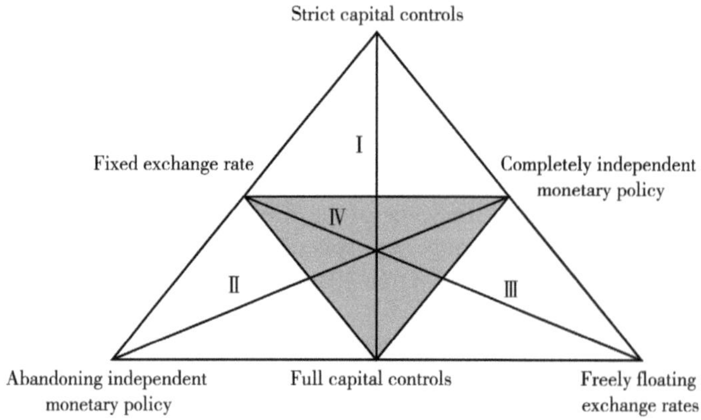

Fig. 4.10 Sketch map of the impossible trinity

developing country, it is extremely difficult, if not impossible, to navigate regimes that fall in the gray area. Nevertheless, the traditional path towards internationalization of many developing countries—i.e. the process of looking for a corner solution—must go through this central area at some point, at which they become trapped by the "Impossible Triangle." We should learn from the previous lessons and experience of many developing countries.

The internationalization of the RMB, however, seeks to bypass this intersection altogether. The path to development advances close to the boundary of this triangle while trying to avoid what is represented by the gray area, as shown in Fig. 4.9. The fundamental reason that the RMB alone—as opposed to the currencies of other developing countries—is able to follow take this developmental path is that mainland China is supported by Hong Kong's CNH and financial markets. The CNH market optimizes the RMB's internationalization, which would otherwise be subjected to instability and risks. Therefore, in next chapter, we will focus on the unique position and role of Hong Kong's financial market.

Chapter 5
The Role of the Hong Kong Financial Market in the Process of Internationalizing the RMB

The RMB's process of internationalization began to accelerate when the global financial crisis broke out, which resulted in a radical shift within the international monetary system and a necessity for the rebalancing of the global economy. Because the financial market in China has yet to be fully developed, interest and exchange rates are yet to be liberalized, and it is difficult to open the capital account within a short time, the process of internationalizing the RMB will be different from that of other sovereign currencies. For this reason, the internationalization of the RMB has encountered the following special circumstances: the internationalization of the RMB "began with trade, but is not able to end with trade;" and while the internationalization of the RMB requires the full convertibility of the RMB, China is not able to immediately open the capital account to do so.

By this token, the RMB must be internationalized under the condition that it is not convertible under the capital account. As the region's cross-border trade settlement progresses rapidly, one pressing task is how to develop an inflow mechanism for the RMB, which requires that China properly separate the openness of the capital account from the full convertibility of the RMB. For this task, it is necessary to leverage the Hong Kong financial market and to establish an RMB offshore market there. As such, the Hong Kong financial market will play an important role in the process of internationalizing the RMB.

5.1 The Evolution of the Hong Kong Financial Market and Its Arrangements Regarding the Exchange-Rate Regime

The Hong Kong financial market has evolved alongside the economic development and upgrading of the industrial structure of Hong Kong, itself. After WWII, as the economy of Hong Kong recovered and developed, its banking industry roared back

© Social Sciences Academic Press and Springer Nature Singapore Pte Ltd. 2018
Y. Cao, *Strategies for Internationalizing the Renminbi*, Research Series on the Chinese Dream and China's Development Path,
https://doi.org/10.1007/978-981-13-0800-0_5

to life after years of suppression. Before the war, the credit loan business was used purely for trade financing, but afterwards gradually extended to the emerging manufacturing and real estate industry. Due to the technological progress and the global industrial transfer taking place in the 1950s, Hong Kong leveraged its geographical advantage and rich labor forces to accelerate the process of industrialization, thereby transferring its economic structure from what could be considered a trade economy to a processing trade economy. The increasing demands for funds leveraged by industrialization boosted the banking industry in Hong Kong. From the 1950s to the 1960s, the number of commercial banks in Hong Kong increased from 29 to 73. What's more, in the early 1960s, the Hong Kong stock market developed rapidly. In this sense, the period from the earlier years after WWII to the 1960s represented a climax of sorts for the Hong Kong financial market.

In the 1970s, several favorable external and internal factors facilitated internationalization of the Hong Kong financial market internationalization. Externally, in the late 1960s, the US dollar market in Europe had achieved rapid progress and the US dollar market in Asia, with Singapore as the center, was initially established. In the early 1970s, due to the collapse of the Bretton Woods system, countries abandoned the control of foreign exchange, thus facilitating the global flow of capital across countries, which provided global opportunities for the Hong Kong financial market. Internally, from the 1970s on, Hong Kong began to be included with other emerging industrialized countries and regions. The new diversification of the economic structure of Hong Kong demanded diversified capital and financial services. To meet these demands, the Hong Kong government adopted measures to liberalize the market's finances in order to boost its own financial industry. During this period, Hong Kong abandoned the control of foreign exchange just as other developing countries had done, deregulated the import and export of gold, adopted a floating system for the Hong Kong dollar, resumed granting banking licenses, and abolished the interest tax on foreign currency deposits and other interest taxes. Through these measures, the Hong Kong government successfully promoted the rapid development of its foreign exchange market, gold market, and banking industry, and consolidated the status of Hong Kong as a free economy and an international financial center. Up until the end of 1984, there had been 140 banks (101 foreign banks), 1407 bank branches, 122 representative offices of foreign banks, and 343 finance companies in Hong Kong. In the same year, the main board of the securities market achieved a trade volume of HKD48.8 bn, accounting for 18.7% of the nation's GDP. The financial and insurance industries created HKD15.52 bn between them, accounting for 6.4% of Hong Kong's GDP. Hong Kong's status as an international financial center took shape initially thereafter.

In 1983, as Hong Kong's status as an international financial center began to take shape, Hong Kong adopted a linked exchange rate system (see Table 5.1).

The Currency Board system is another name used for the linked exchange rate system, which is a fixed exchange rate regime used to link the exchange rate of the domestic currency to another foreign currency. Here, the fixed exchange rate and the free capital movement coexist. According to the theory of the "Impossible

Table 5.1 History of HKD exchange rate

HKD exchange rate regime		
Year	Exchange rate regime	Reference rate
1863–1935	Silver standard	Legal tender: Silver
Dec. 1935–1972	Pegged to the pound sterling	1 GBP = 16 HKD (Dec. 1935–Nov. 1967) 1 GBP = 14.55 HKD (Nov. 1967–Jun. 1972)
1972–1974	Pegged to the US dollar with an intervene of ±2.25% based on the core interest rate	1 USD = 5.65 HKD (Jul. 1972–Feb. 1973) 1 USD = 5.085 HKD (Feb. 1973–Nov. 1974)
1974–1983	Free float	Nov. 25 of 1974 1 USD = 4.96:5 HKD Sept. 24 of 1983 1 USD = 9.600 HKD
Oct. 17, 1983	Pegged to the US dollar, linked exchange rate	1 USD = 7.80 HKD

Source Modern Economic Information, 2011 (12): 355

Trinity," this type of arrangement only comes at the cost of giving up an independent monetary policy. For this reason, Hong Kong does not have a central bank, and instead utilizes financial regulators.

A certain degree of historical background is necessary to explain why Hong Kong has adopted this particular exchange rate system. In October 1982, negotiations between the Chinese and UK governments over the exercise of Hong Kong's sovereignty triggered a "crisis of confidence," which resulted in aggravated capital outflow. Consequently, the financial market became destabilized and the HKD fluctuated extensively, at one point depreciating to an exchange rate of 9.60 HKD per USD. In order to stabilize the exchange rate of the HKD and to recover popular confidence, on October 15, 1983, the Hong Kong government announced a new policy pegging the HKD to the USD at a fixed exchange rate of 7.80 HKD per 1 USD.

The core of Hong Kong's linked exchange rate system is predicated on pegging the Hong Kong dollar to the US dollar at a fixed exchange rate. This fixed exchange rate is applicable to all HKD-denominated cash transactions (those between the note-issuing bank and the Exchange Fund, as well as those between the note-issuing bank and other banks with licenses). A liberalized exchange rate is applicable to all non-cash transactions (between the note-issuing bank and other banks), however, and all wholesale/retail transactions (among banks or between banks and customers). In this sense, the fixed exchange rate is an exchange rate specifically for the issuing of notes. A note-issuing bank would spend 1 USD to purchase a "liability certificate" from the Exchange Fund, which serves as a source of reserve funds for the issuance of 1 HKD. In turn, when withdrawing HKD-denominated currencies from the market, the note-issuing bank would be required to apply the same rate to exchange the HKD for the USD and return the "liability certificate." If other licensed banks would like to purchase HKD-denominated currencies from the note-issuing bank, they have to pay in US dollars. Under this framework, the Hong Kong dollar's issuance is based on the prospect of having sufficient reserves.

Thanks to the coexistence of the linked exchange rate, the liberalized exchange rate, the fixed exchange rate, and the floating exchange rate, the Hong Kong government is able to leverage the note-issuing bank in order to maintain a stable exchange rate between the HKD and the USD. What's more, because it is influenced by market behaviors and the arbitrage activities of both banks and citizens, the liberalized exchange rate is able to reflect the actual supply of and demand for funds. The Hong Kong government is able to maintain the liberalized exchange rate of around 7.8 HKD per 1 USD without a drastic fluctuation thanks to the automatic stabilization mechanism of Hong Kong's linked exchange rate system.

Hong Kong's linked exchange rate system took shape against a very special historical background, but such a system came about inevitably and out of necessity. According to both the Economic Theory and the Dependence Theory, the selection of an exchange rate system by a given country or region should be based on the country or region's particular economic development status, such as the degree of economic scale, economic openness, import and export structure, geographical location, degree of the maturity of the domestic financial market, and the degree of its integration into the global financial market as a whole.

The island economy of Hong Kong is equipped with characteristics typical of a small open economy: containing few natural resources, the region has historically had to depend on imports in order to gain the means of production and daily necessities. Additionally, due to the large proportion of foreign capital circulating in the economy, the economic growth of this region is restricted by many uncontrollable external factors. As a result, it would be difficult for the monetary authority to control the effect on currency performance caused by changes in foreign capital or foreign trade, or to put the interest rate or money supply as a target of domestic monetary policy. For example, the US dollar is the main trade settlement currency in Hong Kong. In order to minimize the foreign exchange risk posed by international trade, to conclude long-term trade contracts, and to pool overseas capital, Hong Kong's system pegs the domestic currency to the US dollar.

Though the performance of the US dollar is volatile, its status as the global reserve currency and international currency is well-established and, what's more, the United States itself has a strong domestic economy. As opposed to the UK economy of the 1960s, the US economy does not depend completely on the overseas market, and the status of the US dollar as an international currency is not likely to be shaken in the foreseeable future. In addition, Hong Kong, with its sound economic base, is equipped with abundant foreign exchange reserves. This deters international speculators from crowding Hong Kong's market, thus laying a solid foundation for the stability of its currency.

The linked exchange rate system initially has an internal mechanism for automatic adjustment, under which, the liberalized exchange rate will automatically draw close to the note-issuing rate, thus maintaining the long-term stability of the exchange rate of the Hong Kong dollar against the US dollar. The initial goal of the linked exchange rate system is thus achieved. According to data drawn from October 1983 to the end of 1997, the liberalized exchange rate of the Hong Kong dollar against the US dollar varied only slightly from the official exchange rate. The maximum deviation was ±2%. If we adopt the exchange rate index of the new HKD, the maximum fluctuation range will reach 31.4%, being between 99.6 and 131.0. This range is much narrower than the 50% that was seen when the floating system was first adopted (1974–1983).

In addition to this, the linked exchange rate system has greatly facilitated Hong Kong's development as an international trade center. Hong Kong, as an open economy, is highly dependent upon trade, especially trade with the United States. The United States is Hong Kong's fourth largest supplier of imported goods, the top destination of Hong Kong's own exported goods, and the fourth largest source of and second most significant destination of Hong Kong's re-export trade. To secure the smooth operation of Hong Kong's economic and trade activities, it is extremely important to maintain the stability of the exchange rate of the Hong Kong dollar against the US dollar. This will help alleviate any potential fluctuation caused by speculation, reduce uncertainties in future economic activities, and provide a stable valuation basis for foreign trade and other economic activities. In the meantime, a stable exchange rate will facilitate the estimation for costs and profits as well as for settlements, thus reducing the risks and the costs associated with international trade and further creating a stable environment for Hong Kong's trade in particular. Over a long period of time, the exchange rate of the Hong Kong dollar will stabilize against the US dollar. As the US dollar depreciates, the Hong Kong dollar will also depreciate against other trade partners' currencies, which is favorable for Hong Kong in terms of enhancing the competitiveness of its products on the global market.

Third, a stable exchange-rate regime will accelerate the internationalization of the Hong Kong dollar and Hong Kong's status as an international financial center. The stability of the exchange-rate regime and the free convertibility of the Hong Kong dollar, in turn, facilitate the internationalization of the Hong Kong dollar. Additionally, the linked exchange rate system can help lower associated risks and better attract overseas funds. As more capital begins to enter this international financial center's market, it has the effect of boosting industries such as banking, securities, and insurance, vitalizing the financial market, and driving forward Hong Kong's international standing as a financial center.

Fourth, the linked exchange rate system promotes the secondary economic transformation of Hong Kong from a manufacturing-oriented structural system to a service-oriented one. The linked exchange rate system not only boosts Hong Kong's finances and trade, but also creates a stable monetary environment to encourage the investment of foreign capital across all of Hong Kong's industries. Since nearly all service-related areas have been covered by the system, the service industry continues to develop alongside the evolution of the region's economic structure.

Fifth, the government is able to carry out prudent fiscal management under the linked exchange rate system. The very basis for sustaining this system is to keep and maintain huge foreign exchange reserves, which requires the government avoid carrying any significant fiscal deficit, thus urging the government to pay heightened attention to matters of fiscal management.

Sixth, since a reserve system that requires 100% of funds to be physically held and secured has been adopted for note-issuing, the linked exchange rate system is equipped with adequate functions for curbing inflation. On the one hand, the central bank is not able to issue excessive banknotes, while on the other hand, it is also not able to issue additional currencies in order to finance the fiscal deficit. As a result, any man-made factors which might trigger inflation have been largely evaded. The inflation rate of Hong Kong was 9.9% in 1983 and dropped to −4.8% in 1984. During the four years before the adoption of this linked system (1979–1983), this rate was once as high as 12.6%; however, during the 19 years after its adoption (1984–2002), the average rate of inflation was −0.41%.

It has been shown time and time again that the linked exchange rate system has the capacity for countering the political attacks and fluctuations of the international financial market. During the years 1982–1983, due to difficulties in predicting the political outlook of Hong Kong, many funds flowed out, and the Hong Kong dollar faced the possibility of being dumped. From July 1, 1982 to June 30, 1983, the exchange rate of the Hong Kong dollar against the US dollar depreciated by 18% from 5.913 to 7.2. At the height of the crisis, the Hong Kong dollar depreciated by 12.9% within the 48 h from September 23 to September 24. Against the average value of 15 major currencies, the Hong Kong dollar depreciated by 11.6%. In addition, the exchange rate of the Hong Kong dollar against the US dollar closed at 9.6. Merchants refused to accept the Hong Kong dollar and some banks closed the window for converting the Hong Kong dollar to the US dollar at all. A banking crisis was simmering. After the linked exchange rate system was adopted, the exchange rate of the US dollar against the Hong Kong dollar soon appreciated, and went back to the level of the official exchange rate within one week. From the second week on, the linked system ran smoothly under the competition mechanism. That is—put very simply—the linked system brought Hong Kong back from the brink of financial and economic collapse. Another example was in July 1984, when negotiations between the Chinese government and the UK government encountered difficulties, the European market began to undersell the Hong Kong dollar. While the HKD's exchange rate against the US dollar threatened to rise to 7.95, it ultimately maintained a stable level due to the existence of the linked system. Facing the Persian Gulf War in 1990, the bankruptcy of the world's commercial banks in May 1991, the storm overtaking the exchange rate market in autumn 1992, the conflict between the Chinese government and the UK government over the political development of Hong Kong in October 1992, the Mexican financial crisis in 1995, and the Asian financial crises in 1997 and in 1998, the securities and real estate market of Hong Kong were, understandably, volatile. Yet the exchange rate of the Hong Kong dollar against the US dollar remained rock-steady, however, which, to a large extent, raised the confidence of Hong Kong citizens in the linked system and stabilized the financial market and economy in Hong Kong overall.

The 1997 Asian financial crisis helped Hong Kong's financial industry mature. In September 2007, entrusted by the London municipal government, an assessment of the comprehensive competitiveness of the financial centers was implemented. In the "index of global financial centers" rankings, Hong Kong ranked No.3, just behind London and New York. In Asia, Hong Kong was the unquestionable leading financial center. In 2008, upon the outbreak of the global financial crisis, Hong Kong had HKD1678.5 bn GDP, HKD238.4 bn current account balance, USD182.5 foreign exchange reserves, and HKD10298.7 bn shares in the capital market, raising HKD427.2 bn funds. Hong Kong had the 7th largest stock market by market value, the 6th largest foreign exchange market, and the 4th largest gold market by transaction volume; by Asset under Management, Hong Kong was the second largest fund management center in Asia. Hong Kong was also one of only three global banking centers. As of December 2008, Hong Kong had over 200 banking institutions, 175 insurance companies, over 7000 securities companies, and 2100 unit trust/mutual trust companies.

As an international financial center, Hong Kong has a mature financial regulatory system, which is composed of the Hong Kong Monetary Authority (HKMA), Securities and Futures Commission (SFC), Office of the Commissioner of Insurance (OCI), Mandatory Provident Fund Schemes Authority (MPFA), and other relevant industry associations. These regulators are, respectively, in charge of the banking market, the securities and futures markets the insurance market, and retirement plans. The HKMA was founded in April 1994. Authorized by the *Banking Ordinance*, the HKMA prudentially supervises licensed banks, restricted license banks, and deposit-taking companies. In addition to the function of regulating the banking market, other responsibilities of the HKMA include maintaining the stability of the Hong Kong dollar, and enhancing the efficiency of, promoting the development of, and protecting the impartiality of the financial system. These functions and goals are more or less consistent with those of other central banks in the world. For its part, the SFC was set up in 1989 to prudentially regulate Hong Kong's securities, financial investment, and futures markets. According to the *Securities and Futures Ordinance,* which came into effect on April 1, 2003, the SFC has always been committed to maintaining and promoting the fairness, efficiency, competitiveness, transparency, and orderliness of the securities and futures industry and providing a guarantee for investors. The scope of the SFC's work includes exercising oversight of the regulations governing takeovers and mergers of public companies and of The Stock Exchange of Hong Kong Limited's regulation of listing matters; authorizing investment products, unit trusts, mutual funds, and other investment products; establishing and enforcing market regulations, including investigating breaches of rules and market misconduct; and more. Similarly, the OCI was founded in June 1990 and carries out prudential regulation of the insurance market of Hong Kong following the 1983 *Insurance Companies Ordinance*. Insurance companies are allowed to run insurance business in Hong Kong only when they are authorized by the OCI. The MPFA is an independent statutory body established in September 1998 under the *Mandatory Provident Fund Schemes Ordinance* (*MPFSO*). The main role of the MPFA is to regulate and supervise the running of the MPF system and to be responsible for ensuring compliance with MPFSO.

The banking industry, the securities industry, and the insurance industry in Hong Kong operate under a dual-level system of regulation, namely government regulation and self-regulation. The self-regulatory organizations for the banking industry, the securities industry, and the insurance industry are the Hong Kong Association of Banks (HKAB), Hong Kong Exchanges and Clearing Limited (HKEX), and the Hong Kong Federation of Insurers (HKFI), respectively. The government plays the role of both "administrator" and "coordinator" while self-regulatory associations focus on internal risk control and review. They separately perform their duties and have thus formed the multiform and multilevel financial regulatory system of Hong Kong. Of course, as the impacts of the 2008 global financial crisis continue to leave their mark, Hong Kong's financial regulatory system continues to evolve and will better develop.

5.2 The Hong Kong Offshore Financial Market and Its Significance for the Internationalization of the RMB

The background against which the RMB's internationalization began has ensured that its circumstances and approach will be markedly different from those of other sovereign currencies, the basis of which has historically been full convertibility, either spontaneous (e.g. pound sterling) or acquired (e.g. the Deutschemark or the Japanese yen). By contrast, the RMB's process of internationalization begins without full convertibility and with the capital account still under de facto regulation. This presents a paradox: on the one hand, as the RMB's application in cross-border trade settlements increases, the RMB-denominated long position will grow and be deposited in the overseas market as trade surplus. If this overseas long position cannot be arranged properly by the financial market, the international community will become discouraged or, at the very least, not be motivated to apply the RMB in cross-border trade settlement. If so, the internationalization of the RMB will prove unsustainable in both the long and the short run. On the other hand, if the long position is arranged by the financial market, the capital account should be open. Due to developing countries' weak financial infrastructures, underdeveloped capital markets, and unsound macro-economic control systems and tools, the risk of deregulating the capital account without careful consideration is significant. The lessons of the Asian financial crisis are clear and, at present, the aftermath of the global financial crisis remains visible. In addition, the appropriate external environment for China to fully open its economy does not exist. Premised on the idea that the RMB is not convertible under the capital account, it is relatively simple to predict a growing conflict between the RMB's convertibility under the current account and the country's considerable capital outflow. As to the RMB flowing out to other countries under the capital account, some degree will flow back under the capital account while the remainder will stay in foreign countries and pile up. The RMB held by non-residents will flow back in every possible way, thus impacting those regulations under the capital account. When there are no official channels under the capital account, that is when "private channels" will take their place and develop into a "black market."

The above conflict reflects the inner contradiction between the RMB's current account convertibility and capital account convertibility. On the one hand, opening the RMB's current account dooms the opening of China's capital account before it ever gets started; on the other hand, China's current situation indicates that a time interval between opening the current account and opening the capital account would be prudent. Previous global experience shows that as the economy of a given country develops, the domestic currency will become fully convertible. In addition, since all internationalized currencies are fully convertible, the RMB will also follow this trend. In order to achieve this, however, besides adjusting the economic structure, stabilizing the macro economy, and realizing the predictability of the economic policies, China must also improve the RMB's capital market, notably, the fixed income market. Great economic powers are likely to develop a flexible fixed income market aimed at mitigating or absorbing the instant shock brought about by the international capital. This, however, is a specific weakness of the Chinese mainland, and to adequately face such a dilemma requires the leverage of the Hong Kong financial market. As previously mentioned, in order to facilitate the prosperity of the Hong Kong economy and make arrangements for the acquisition of Hong Kong travel permits by mainland residents, people have been allowed to use the RMB in Hong Kong since November 2003. At first, only a few stores accepted the RMB. As its applicability expands, however, the RMB has begun to flow back into the country, developing into a sound economic mechanism for development in the process.

Both before and after the 2008 global financial crisis, the RMB flowed back via three channels—namely, currency swaps among countries, via non-governmental vendor banks, and CEPA (Closer Economic Partnership Arrangement). The former two models do not involve regulation under the capital account, but the RMB's flowing back from Hong Kong and Macao under SEPA does. Under the aegis of the third mechanism, the RMB flowed back from Hong Kong under the capital account via three channels: Financial institutions(designated RMB clearing banks in Hong Kong, according to the clearing arrangement that exists with the PBOC, can do business directly with the PBOC's Shenzhen branch, which itself serves as a channel for offshore RMB to be deposited in the PBOC),individuals(every Hong Kong resident is allowed to transfer a maximum of RMB80 K capital per day to a Chinese mainland account with the same name, and is allowed to open a RMB-denominated checking account in Guangdong province with an upper limit of RMB80 K per day. In addition, credit and debit cards issued by Hong Kong's banks are also valid in the Chinese mainland) capital market (Hong Kong investors are allowed to purchase the RMB-denominated bonds issued by financial institutions of the Chinese mainland in Hong Kong without any limitation regarding the amount).

The above three channels work smoothly both as separate institutions and cooperatively, demonstrating the feasibility of these types of special arrangements for the RMB's flowing back under the capital account. This led to a singular question: can China leverage the Hong Kong financial market, especially the nascent RMB bond market in Hong Kong, to meet the demands of non-residents for holding RMB on the one hand, while also postponing the process of opening the capital account? Success in doing so would win more time to develop the capital market in the Chinese mainland.

In fact, arrangements regulating the use of the RMB in Hong Kong have already been in place since 2003. From 2009 on, the RMB began to be applied in cross-border trade settlement. In July 2010, the HKMA and the PBOC, for the purpose of expanding the pilot areas, revised their existing settlement agreement, stipulating that both the inflow and the outflow of the RMB should be approved by the PBOC. The RMB's flowing back to the Chinese mainland was to be consistent with the regulations and laws of the Chinese mainland, and should further, be reviewed and approved by the authorities and banks of the Chinese mainland. If the destination were not the Chinese mainland, the business was to be handled by the Hong Kong authority according to all regulatory requirements and market factors, as well as the rules applicable to other currencies. This has actually defined Hong Kong's position as an offshore RMB market, as well as the arrangements for the RMB's flowing back. In other words, the RMB is able to flow in and out without restrictions under the current account. Under the capital account, however, the RMB's flowing back has to go through Hong Kong.

The significance of what can be termed as a "capital dam" for the RMB's internationalization is to achieve the following four goals:

The first goal is to enable the full convertibility of the offshore RMB in Hong Kong and separate the RMB's convertibility from the opening of the capital account. The key to this separation is to establish the Hong Kong market as a "capital dam" and to leverage both the onshore and offshore market to regulate the RMB's capital flow, so as to more effectively control the RMB's process of internationalization. That is to say, the RMB is, at first, convertible in the offshore market before it is convertible in the onshore market; additionally, before realizing the full convertibility of the RMB to foreign currencies, the capability to fully convert the onshore RMB to offshore RMB should be well-established.

At present, over half of the 43 items defined by the IMF as prerequisites under the capital account are not under regulation or are only under very loose regulation. Three items, however—namely, foreign direct investment, external debt management, and the restrictions set by the domestic capital market on foreign capital—are currently the focus of regulation. According to both theoretical and experiential precedent, China would be best served by gradually opening these three fields (for details, please refer to Chap. 8). In the future, Hong Kong is likely to become the largest offshore RMB financial center in the world, and by serving as a "capital dam," enough time and space for this process could be won.

The second goal is to leverage the "capital dam" to be able to stand up to the pressure of capital inflow, thus gradually accumulating the available supply of RMB in Hong Kong and fostering a large capital pool. In August 2012, the scale of Hong Kong's offshore RMB market exceeded RMB550 bn with no sign of slowing. One research institution estimates that, around 2013, the scale of Hong Kong's offshore RMB market will potentially reach over RMB1 tn. At the same time, China is able to make use of this "capital dam" to stop possible attacks from international capital on the liquidity of the domestic market.

The third goal is to facilitate the settlement, trading, investment, and the reserve of the RMB in a third country, outside of the Chinese mainland and Hong Kong. With the help of the "capital dam," the threshold for capital inflow will be much higher than it might otherwise be at the initial stages of the RMB's internationalization. In addition, the expectation that the RMB's will unilaterally appreciate is likely to encourage the financial institutions of all countries to apply the RMB towards their own international business. As the trading volume increases, the RMB will be applied in greater numbers of offshore dealings instead of flowing back. The start of the RMB's application in a third country represents the point of real internationalization for the RMB.

The fourth goal is the consolidation of the offshore RMB market. Along with the process of the RMB's internationalization and changes in the global environment, Asia's economic status is becoming increasingly important. The offshore RMB bond market in Hong Kong is likely to serve as the central core of the Asian bond market going forward. Particularly when China applies the RMB towards Europe's debt restructuring, RMB-denominated bonds are likely to be issued in Hong Kong or in the Chinese mainland. As a result, an offshore market similar to Europe's US dollar bond market will be established. In this way, Hong Kong's status as an international financial center is likely to be further reinforced.

There is one assumption being made in all this, which is that Hong Kong's financial market is a critical link and necessary component of the RMB's internationalization. By relying on the offshore RMB market, China has been able to develop a buffer zone that contributes to its economic stability. Judging present situation, Hong Kong's offshore RMB market is still far from being an adequate "capital dam" in terms of scale and depth, such that a special policy arrangement between the Chinese mainland and Hong Kong is required to bridge the existing gap. To be specific: the RMB has multiple channels through which to flow out and back under the current account. If the RMB needs to flow back under the capital account, however, it has to go through Hong Kong. This is similar to the concept between the difference between runoff and impoundment in hydraulic engineering. We can compare the movement under the current account to runoff, because it follows the principle of cash on delivery. During this process, the most vital task is to ensure free movement. The RMB cash position held by non-residents is similar to the surplus in- and outflow and needs to be impounded. The key to impoundment is making appropriate adjustments. While runoff has multiple channels, impoundment has only one gate. Following this rule, the regulation of the international balance of payments under the capital account is like the regulation of a reservoir dam. The Hong Kong financial market plays the role of reservoir, while the PBOC and the HKMA play the role of gatekeeper. These two authorities control the dam from two sides of the gate and monitor and regulate the RMB's inflow under the capital account. In other words, the authorities do not regulate the outflow; rather, they regulate the inflow under the capital account; there are multiple channels for outflow while there is only one single channel for inflow under the capital account. This principle can help ease regulatory difficulties and improve regulatory quality.

Historical precedent indicates that the Hong Kong financial market has almost met all the requirements for serving as a central component of the RMB's internationalization, such as: (1) the "reservoir" has been built and the RMB bond market has taken shape, thus attracting more investors, (2) the "gatekeeper" has accumulated adequate experience, and the cooperative relationship between the PBOC and the HKMA is fruitful, and (3) the "reservoir" has been broadly recognized by the market at large. The RMB market in HK has been regarded by global investors as an offshore RMB market just starting out at the initial stages. Following this line of reasoning, it is well within the bounds of imagination that as the RMB strengthens its position in trade finance, non-residents will hold more RMB-denominated currencies and the RMB capital market in Hong Kong will have a larger capacity and more active transactions. Hong Kong is likely to become the focal point of the RMB market in Asia. The development of the RMB market in Hong Kong, particularly the development of the bond market, will provide an opportunity for the RMB to take up a larger share in the Asian bond market as a whole, thus further facilitating the RMB's internationalization. The RMB's penetration into the Asian bond market will not only facilitate the economic development of the Chinese mainland and Hong Kong, but will also serve as a contribution to Asia's economic development.

Based on the above assumptions, we can easily come up with corresponding proposals. Both the Chinese mainland and Hong Kong should further enhance and adjust the already-successful RMB market in the following ways:

Hong Kong should further expand the RMB business through the following means: (1) gradually expand the scope of qualified RMB depositors, including individuals (Hong Kong residents) and institutions ("designated merchants" such as retailors, restaurants, stores, etc.). After that, overseas non-residents and institutions can be considered. (2) Gradually expand the application scope of RMB-denominated loans issued by financial institutions in Hong Kong. Currently, financial institutions are not allowed to use the RMB to issue loans towards enterprises or to do inter-bank lending. Following that, restrictions can be gradually loosened. During this process, inter-bank lending among Hong Kong financial institutions should be considered, thereby fostering an RMB interbank market. With the advantage of global banks in client resources, traders who do not come from the Chinese mainland or Hong Kong will also enjoy the convenience of applying the RMB in valuation and settlements. (3) Accelerate the formation of an RMB monetary market, which will further facilitate the formation of an RMB bond market. As the RMB bond market develops, overseas institutions other than those from the Chinese Mainland and Hong Kong (primarily governmental agencies of

ASEAN countries) will be encouraged to issue RMB-denominated bonds in Hong Kong. Accordingly, overseas individuals other than those from the Chinese mainland and Hong Kong will be encouraged to invest RMB-denominated bonds in Hong Kong. (4) Gradually render the Hong Kong stock market accessible to individual RMB holders outside of those from the Chinese mainland and Hong Kong.

As the RMB market in Hong Kong develops, the Chinese mainland should gradually adjust its regulation under the capital account and systematically promote the RMB's full convertibility under the capital account through the followings steps: (1) Further encourage overseas traders to apply the RMB in settlement and payment, as well as facilitate the ability of Hong Kong financial institutions to issue RMB-denominated loans towards traders other those from the Chinese mainland and Hong Kong. (2) Gradually allow, encourage, and facilitate institutions in the Chinese mainland, especially foreign-funded companies in China, to issue RMB-denominated bonds in Hong Kong. (3) Further regulate the individual channels by which Hong Kong residents are able to convert their currencies to RMB and transfer their currencies to the Chinese mainland. On this basis, gradually lift the controls over and standardize the channels for overseas individuals other than those from the Chinese mainland and Hong Kong to be able to transfer their RMB currencies into the Chinese mainland via Hong Kong. (4) When all this has been accomplished, then the Hong Kong financial market—most notably, the RMB bond market—can be connected to the Chinese mainland.

In fact, since July 2009, when the Chinese government announced the use of RMB to settle cross-border trade, the development of the offshore RMB market in Hong Kong and the process of opening the capital account in the Chinese mainland have proceeded along the above path. At the end of 2008, the RMB deposits in Hong Kong reported a balance of RMB56 bn, over four times that which was available at the end of 2004 (RMB12.2 bn), when the RMB first started to be circulated in Hong Kong. It should be noted, however, that the scale at that time was still limited. As the RMB cross-border trade settlement developed, the HKMA relaxed the restrictions on the RMB's application in Hong Kong accordingly. Thereafter, RMB deposits in Hong Kong mushroomed in growth. As of March 2015, the balance of the RMB deposits in Hong Kong had reached RMB952 bn (see Fig. 5.1).

The trend towards rapid growth began after July 2010, and was largely related to the increasingly-frequent interactions between Hong Kong and the Chinese mainland. One of the most iconic events of this process occurred in 2010, when the HKMA issued Circular Letter No. 2 and the corresponding supplementary agreement on RMB settlement signed by both the PBOC and the Bank of China (Hong Kong) in July 2010.

The Circular Letter No. 2 delivers two messages: (1) the RMB's application in Hong Kong or its flowing back to the Chinese Mainland should conform to and abide in accordance with the relevant laws and regulations of the Chinese mainland, specifically those under the purview of the PBOC, and (2) the RMB's application within the Hong Kong financial market needs to meet the relevant requirements for

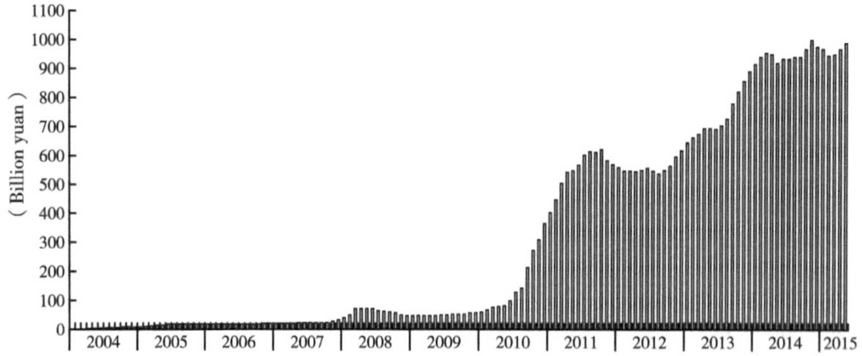

Fig. 5.1 Change in RMB deposits in Hong Kong (Jan. 2014–Jun. 2015)

foreign currencies. In other words, the rules for foreign currencies also apply to the RMB, such that, besides the PBOC's regulation on the RMB's inflow and outflow, the application of the RMB in Hong Kong does not face any other legal restrictions. This opens up great prospects for the RMB's entrance into the Hong Kong global financial market. As of June 2015, Hong Kong's RMB financial instruments had already covered deposits, loans, bonds, stocks, and financial derivatives. As a result, Hong Kong has become the largest and most important market for the RMB's offshore financing (see Fig. 5.2).

As the offshore RMB market in Hong Kong develops, the prospect of opening the capital account gradually becomes more feasible. Due to the RMB's application in Hong Kong, as well as its tendency towards flowing back into financial circulation, it is likely to jump-start the opening of the capital account. Inspired by this prospect, in July 2011, the Chinese government loosened its regulation of RMB under the capital account. The RMB can now be applied in investment in China by foreign merchants (RMB-denominated FDI); additionally, companies of the Chinese mainland are allowed to issue RMB-denominated bonds in Hong Kong. That is to say, Chinese individuals and institutions are not allowed to hold debts in foreign currencies but are allowed to hold RMB-denominated debts, the initial stage of which could reach as much as RMB70 bn. The capital market in China does not accept foreign currencies but can accept RMB (RMB QIFI) at an initial scale of RMB50 bn. What's more, the Chinese government encourages domestic companies to apply RMB towards foreign investment and will allow foreign companies to issue RMB-denominated bonds inside China.

So far, loosening the restrictions on the RMB under the capital account has proceeded smoothly. As such, a new path for opening the capital account can be anticipated: when the domestic currency hasn't yet realized full convertibility, regulations on the domestic currency under the capital account can be loosened. This path is different from the traditional one that has been adopted by most developing countries. Following the traditional path, the capital account's opening should be based on the full convertibility of the domestic currency. Obviously, this

Table 5.2 Products of the offshore RMB market in Hong Kong

RMB-denominated products	Status quo
Deposit	The volume of the RMB-denominated deposits in Hong Kong has reached RMB990 bn
Spot	Daily trading volume: USD1 bn–1.5 bn; the bid-offer spread has been narrowed
Forward	Have established a curve for the offshore RMB deliverable forward; the forward with no more than one year maturity reports sound liquidity performance
Currency swap	Has priced for 1–5 year currency swap; has only a few transactions
Foreign exchange option	The duration can be as long as one year
Certificate of deposit	Many banks have issued the RMB-denominated certificate of deposit
Structured product	Bank of China (Hong Kong) and many other banks have launched the RMB-denominated structured deposit products
Bond	Have issued over RMB230 bn bonds (incl. certificates of deposit)
Fund	BOCHK Asset Management has launched the RMB-denominated bond fund
RMB-denominated REIT	Cheung Kong's Hui Xian RMB-denominated REIT has been listed

Source Bank of China (Hong Kong)

difficult situation has been defused under the new path, where the operation of currency applicability is both simple and feasible. Theoretically, this indicates Mundell's theory of Non-Corner Solutions to the aforementioned "Trilemma," marking the point at which China's economy has begun to transition from Portfolio (4) to Portfolio (5). Undoubtedly, the prerequisite for this transition is the RMB's global application. The development of the RMB offshore market in Hong Kong becomes an inseparable part of the RMB's internationalization overall (see Table 5.2).

5.3 New Challenges Faced by the Offshore RMB Financial Market in Hong Kong

Operating under a framework of "One Country, Two Systems" and by leveraging the exchange rate, Hong Kong's status as a global financial market has solidified. Assuming that any risks associated with the RMB can be mitigated, the offshore RMB market in Hong Kong can gradually be developed to a point where it offers an ideal financial infrastructure for further internationalization. Theoretically, this path may serve as a potential Non-Corner Solutions mentioned in Mundell's "Impossible Trinity," thus providing a fresh new solution to the "Trilemma."

Since Mundell's "Impossible Trinity" and the "Trilemma" are objective and irrefutable facts, however, all solutions, corner or non-corner, offer no possibility of escape from this "Trinity." From the perspective of Mundell's "Impossible Trinity," non-corner solutions can be expressed as M + E+K = 2 (capital flow + exchange rate stability + independent monetary policy = 2). As the Hong Kong offshore RMB market develops, we can apply the RMB towards opening the capital account. In Combination (5), the proportion of the exchange rate and that of the independent monetary policy should be around 2/3 after adjustment. In other words, this challenge has subjectively different meanings for Hong Kong and the Chinese mainland. As previously mentioned, under the currency board system, Hong Kong's exchange rate arrangement is to maintain a fixed rate of exchange against the US dollar (1 USD = 7.8 HKD). As the Hong Kong offshore RMB market develops, a parallel market covering the RMB, the Hong Kong dollar, and the US dollar will be established. In this parallel market, because the RMB is a currency that is not fully convertible within the Chinese mainland while being fully convertible in Hong Kong, the difference in the exchange rate formation mechanism might bring profound consequences to Hong Kong's linked exchange rate regime. The function proceeds s follows: the RMB is regarded as one of several foreign currencies extant in Hong Kong and can conduct all business that foreign currencies are capable of conducting under the law. This means that, under both the current account and the capital account, the RMB is convertible in Hong Kong. The exchange rate is totally determined by the supply-demand relationship between the RMB and foreign currencies. The exchange rate of the CNH market has, for its part, adopted a many-to-many pricing model. But restricted by the consideration of an independent monetary policy, however, the RMB, as a domestic currency, does not have a fully liberalized exchange rate. The CNY market adopts a one-to-many mechanism. The exchange rate of the RMB is controlled by the PBOC. Since the pricing mechanism of the CNH market and that of the CNY market are different, the RMB of these two markets will have different exchange rates. Arbitrage might occur between the RMB and the Hong Kong dollar as well as between the RMB and the US dollar. If there is a large difference in the exchange rate, arbitrage will occur more frequently and to a greater degree. The frequent inflow and outflow of capital will not only cause disorder within the Hong Kong financial market, but will also trigger inflation. In order to prevent this situation, the interbank lending rate must be increased. As a result, any action undertaken to mitigate arbitrage will further trigger arbitrage activities. Consequently, the linked exchange rate system will keep experiencing excessive difficulties, as previously seen in the 1997 Asian financial crisis.

As for the Chinese mainland, the different exchange rates under the two formation mechanisms have the potential to impact the PBOC's independent monetary policy. Even when the offshore RMB market in Hong Kong had yet to be established, an NDF market for overseas investors to predict the trend of the RMB's exchange rate had already existed for some time. Under various circumstances, due to the significant difference between the developmental path of the NDF exchange rate and that of the RMB exchange rate, frequent inflows and outflows of global short-term capital took place, disturbing the existing independent monetary policy.

As the offshore RMB market continues to develop and as the corresponding inflow mechanism evolves and stabilizes, China's capital account has basically been open in the form of the RMB. The issue of dual exchange rates in earlier years is now an issue of dual interest rates, which also have the potential to impact the country's monetary policy.

Such a mechanism operates as follows: under the framework of two-tiered exchange rates, an arbitrage of exchange will occur, which will further force China to open the capital account and to unify the existing exchange rates, thus further eliminating the possibility of an arbitrage of exchange. Under such circumstances, it is true that the capital account's opening will eliminate the possibility of an arbitrage of exchange. Since the RMB is not fully convertible, however, and according to the principle of interest rate parity, exchange arbitrage will eventually become interest arbitrage. This situation will impact the financial market in Hong Kong. If the gap between the interest rate in Hong Kong and that of the Chinese mainland is too large, the above-mentioned exchange arbitrage will cause market disorder and go on to trigger inflation.

Exchange and cash-based arbitrage are mutually convertible. Especially now, when China still has a rapidly-increasing economy while still being at the stage of industrial and urban development, the RMB will continue to show a trend of appreciation. Working under the expectation that the RMB will appreciate, the RMB might be unilaterally purchased by the offshore RMB market in Hong Kong. If so, the market might lose counterparties and further lose liquidity. If the expectation for the RMB's appreciation changes, moves might be made towards another "unilateral direction" (that is, selling the RMB) and the market will also lose liquidity.

In fact, the above situation occurred in September 2010 and again in September 2011. In September 2010, as the Hong Kong financial market purchased large amounts of RMB, the exchange mechanism between the Chinese mainland and Hong Kong was nearly even. In September 2011, as the Hong Kong financial market sold large amounts of RMB, the RMB's backflow increased significantly. Both of these actions triggered drastic fluctuations in the exchange rate, but indifferent directions.

In some sense, adequately addressing the aforementioned challenge traps us in a trilemma as described by Mundell's "Impossible Trinity". This is the gray zone discussed in Chap. 6. In order to accumulate adequate reserves of the RMB in overseas markets, especially in Hong Kong, the RMB must have a stable outflow mechanism and certain regulations should be set under the capital account in order to serve as a dam for the RMB. With this dam, any RMB that flows to the "reservoir" will be greater in volume than the RMB that flows out. In this way, the RMB will accumulate and the market will be saturated, creating further conditions for the wider application of the RMB in various financial products. If the RMB is able to smoothly flow back into the country, it indicates that the RMB will be convertible under the capital account. A backflow without a reservoir, however, is just like a round trip along a pipe, which will not aid in the expansion of the RMB's international application. Because a dam has been built under the capital account, the liberalized exchange rate and interest rate of the domestic RMB market and those of the offshore RMB market are likely to be different. As the RMB accumulates in the overseas market, the difference in the exchange rate and interest rate will grow. In fact, over the past two years, we have witnessed significant differences between the non-deliverable forward (NDF) exchange rate and savings rate of the Hong Kong offshore RMB market and those of the domestic RMB market, which have hinted at potentially quite dissimilar trends in development from the domestic market. On the one hand, due to higher expectation for the RMB's appreciation, the NDF exchange rate of the Hong Kong RMB market has performed higher than that of the domestic RMB market. On the other hand, since the RMB's application is currently still too narrow, the interest rate of the Hong Kong RMB market has performed lower than that of the domestic RMB market. This dual track facilitates speculation and increases the difficulties of implementing monetary policies for the RMB. Domestic companies expect to obtain RMB-denominated funds with lower costs in Hong Kong, while, for their part, Hong Kong financial institutions expect to invest the RMB in the domestic market with higher returns, thus boosting the RMB's backflow. The RMB's backflow not only challenges the tight monetary policy for managing the excess liquidity of the domestic market, but also indicates that the backflow mechanism can and should adapt to the changing economic environment. It is also possible that the RMB will flow back into the black market due to the gap in the exchange rate and the interest rate, thus attacking the validity of the capital controls. The question of whether to keep traditional capital controls in place or to encourage backflow is a new look at a still-challenging old problem.

International experience can serve as historical reference for addressing this challenge. In addition, the prior financial cooperation between the Chinese mainland and Hong Kong can also be assessed for future reference.

In the short run, any inconsistencies in the interest rate are unlikely to trigger larger risks. The interest rate of the US dollar in Europe, for example, was once inconsistent with that in the United States without triggering any large problems. Contemporarily, the interest rate of the RMB in Hong Kong is inconsistent with that of the RMB in the domestic Chinese market. For instance, a 0.5% deposit rate has almost been achieved by the financial market. At the same time, the US dollar market in Europe/the RMB market in Hong Kong hasn't had any substantial impact on the monetary policies or regulatory capabilities of the US dollar/the RMB, because compared to the huge domestic market, the offshore market is still too small to decide or influence the interest rate of the domestic currency. Given this situation, inconsistency in the interest rate is acceptable, with the only cost being that certain financial institutions will undergo arbitrage from the resultant fluctuations of the Hong Kong RMB market.

Inconsistency in the exchange rate brings with it higher risks. When the capital account is under regulation, many factors will impact the exchange rate, with the largest influence coming from tradable goods and services. Since the tradable part of the economy overall is relatively small, it will be easier to "leverage" this aspect in particular. The exchange rate, then, is more volatile than the interest rate. It is just for this reason that the current NDF can more or less exert pressure on the RMB's exchange rate. The practice in both the Chinese mainland and in Hong Kong indicates that regulation and solutions put into place by institutions and industries can help alleviate certain difficulties. The experience of the Chinese mainland in the 1980s is illustrative, in which multiple foreign exchange rates co-existed. Hong Kong's current differential treatment also offers valuable experience. In Hong Kong, those financial institutions under strict regulation have been differentiated from those operating under fewer regulations; for certain products or across certain industries, "designated merchants" have been differentiated from "non-designated merchants"; pooled investment has been differentiated from individual investment. This ensures that they will have different levels of access to the RMB market. The largest accompanying risk is a potential "one-sided trend" and the RMB's excessive appreciation. Since China's economy is now experiencing sustainable growth, the RMB will continue to appreciate. Yet this risks a potential "one-sided trend" of purchasing the RMB in which more pressure will be piled onto the RMB's excessive appreciation. Under such circumstances, the currency swap mechanism between the Chinese mainland and Hong Kong can be leveraged in order to use the RMB for necessary interventions, thus stabilizing the exchange rate. Because of the RMB's flowing out under the current account through multiple channels and the RMB's flowing back under the capital account through Hong Kong, however, the risks will be collectively revealed in one regional market only, and it will be easy to identify and to subsequently mitigate the potential risks. Working under the "One Country, Two Systems" concept, the effective cooperation between the Chinese mainland and Hong Kong will facilitate both timely and moderate operations. In addition, the Chinese financial institutions in Hong Kong (e.g. the affiliates of the Bank of China in Hong Kong) will be responsible for facilitating arrangements and economic coordination.

As for Hong Kong's linked exchange rate system, despite the fact that in recent years the economic relationship between Hong Kong and the Chinese mainland has grown closer, Hong Kong's economic links with overseas markets are still far stronger than its link with the Chinese mainland. Hong Kong's economic cycle is still subject to the world's economic cycle, especially that of the United States. This closeness is particularly evident in Hong Kong's financial market, in which overseas investors occasionally actually prefer to use the US dollar. For instance, in Hong Kong's financial market, the proportion of the US dollar-denominated deposit is as high as 35%, second only to the proportion of HKD-denominated deposits. As long as Hong Kong's economic relations with the overseas market don't experience upheaval, there is no reason for the HKD to unhook the US dollar. It is projected that it will take around ten years for Hong Kong's economic relationship with the Chinese mainland to become closer than Hong Kong's economic relation with the overseas market. This means that in the short run, at least, it is not necessary to peg the HKD to the RMB. In fact, if the HKD is pegged to the RMB, the RMB's trend of appreciation will encourage investors to speculate that the HKD will also appreciate. This is similar to the excessive appreciation of the RMB mentioned above: leveraging the currency swap mechanism between Hong Kong and the

Chinese mainland would increase the RMB's support for the HKD for stabilizing the exchange rate of the HKD, itself.

In the long run, in order to address this challenge, China should make long-term arrangements for its monetary policies and its corresponding floating exchange rate regime. In this process, every step or every link between steps requires delicate management, which is ongoing. The PBOC announced that the floating band for the RMB exchange rate had expanded from ±0.5 to ±1% on April 8, 2012, and further to ±2% on March 17, 2014. On June 8, 2012, the PBOC announced that the floating band for the RMB deposit rate and that of the RMB loan rate had expanded. On November 22, 2014, the upper limit of the floating band for the RMB deposit rate was adjusted from 1.1 times the benchmark to 1.2 times, and, further, to 1.3 times on March 1, 2015, indicating that the process of liberalizing the exchange rate and the interest rate has been initiated. Correspondingly, it was announced that the financing scale management has become the new operational goal of the monetary policy outlining any further development of the RMB.

Chapter 6
The Opening of the Capital Account and the Full Convertibility of the RMB

According to Mundell's "Impossible Trinity," the three corner solutions to the "Trilemma" are equal. This theory explains that one of the three corner solutions must be abandoned for the remaining two to remain. This theory does not, however, explain the reasons behind this choice. As previously mentioned, due to variations among countries' differing social and economic developments, different choices will arise. Developed countries can select a financial portfolio as they like, but there is one pre-condition for most developing countries: they should have a controllable capital flow. In other words, opening the capital account and enabling the free movement of capital is of deep significance to developing countries. The process of pursuing domestic industrialization, however, is restricted by the larger goal of achieving a low capital cost. The opening of the capital account has therefore become a historical difficulty.

Because of the RMB's overseas application, China's capital account can be opened without the corresponding need to realize the full convertibility of the RMB. Developing countries do not face the problems arising from opening the capital account and realizing the full convertibility at the same time—such as a currency mismatch, maturity mismatch, or structural mismatch. This, however, does not mean that the process is without problems altogether. A typical capital account opening should be an opening of both the domestic currency and foreign currencies. Only when the domestic currency becomes fully convertible can obstacles to the free movement of capital be completely eliminated. From this perspective, the opening of the domestic currency (RMB) under the capital account is only a transitional stage in the overall process of realizing the full convertibility of the country's domestic currency. Its significance lies in the fact that this transitional arrangement is different from the traditional path undertaken by most other countries. Therefore, we need to analyze and explore the path available to the RMB's full convertibility in a more comprehensive way, thus laying a solid foundation for the internationalization of the RMB.

© Social Sciences Academic Press and Springer Nature Singapore Pte Ltd. 2018

Y. Cao, *Strategies for Internationalizing the Renminbi*, Research Series on the Chinese Dream and China's Development Path,
https://doi.org/10.1007/978-981-13-0800-0_6

6.1 The Unique Significance of Opening the RMB Under the Capital Account

Internationalized sovereign currencies, in their highest form, are reserve currencies, meaning that these currencies have been widely applied in the balance sheets of governments, financial institutions, non-financial institutions, and families, thus creating reserve assets. Currently, the classification of global reserve assets is based on the type of currency used. For details of this distribution, please refer to Fig. 8.1 in later chapters. Following the collapse of the Bretton Woods system, the proportion of the US dollar remained volatile but maintained at a level of 50–75%. This proportion continuously dropped in the 1980s, but rose again in the 1990s. After entering the 21st century, the proportion of the US dollar again registered a downward trend.

The changing trend of the euro is different from that of the US dollar. After the euro was born in the 21st century, the proportion of the euro to total international reserves overall has continually increased, reaching around 11% and thus forming a threat to the global status of the US dollar. In a certain sense, the euro serves as a substitute for the US dollar. The Japanese yen, in the 20th century, held a large proportion of the world's total international reserves, peaking at 7%. After entering the 21st century, however, the proportion of the Japanese yen dropped continually, and now holds steady at around 3%. The proportion of other currencies is lower than 5%, among which, the proportion of the pound sterling maintains at 3–4% and the proportion of the Swiss franc has dropped from 2% to the current 0.2%. According to the *Geography of Money* (Chen 1998), a sovereign currency's status as an international reserve is a result of earning wide recognition in international commodity trade and asset exchange. The precondition for this must be the full convertibility of the domestic currency. After realizing full convertibility, the domestic currency can be applied in valuation and settlement for international trade and financial exchange. As a result, the domestic currency will earn recognition and report statistically-stable data. Even after the collapse of the Bretton Woods system, the US dollar has always been a top currency, accounting for over 50% of the international currency reserves. The euro and the Japanese yen are currencies of honor, which have both been widely recognized. The pound sterling and the Swiss franc are what are considered extraordinary currencies. The proportions of these two currencies are not high, but they always account for a certain percentage of total international funds. Excepting the above-mentioned currencies, other currencies might be used in one country's reserves, or even widely enter into the balance sheet of non-residents. This type of currency holding offers no guarantees of stability, however, nor is it likely to last for any significant duration. For instance, the Soviet ruble, before the end of the Cold War, was once held by most of Eastern Europe and some developing countries. Following the end of the Cold War, however, as the Soviet Union broke up and the Council for Mutual Economic Assistance collapsed, the Soviet ruble was no longer held by any country as a reserve asset.

The above global experience indicates that the precondition for the internationalization of a given sovereign currency to be recognized must be its full convertibility. The domestic currency should be convertible both under the current account and the capital account. The truth of the matter is, however, that the full convertibility of the domestic currency is only one of the necessities for international recognition, but is not in and of itself the only prerequisite. According to global precedent, most countries' currencies are convertible, but only several currencies have become global currencies—namely the US dollar, the euro, the Japanese yen, and the Swiss franc. Only these currencies have historically been widely applied in valuation, settlement, and reserves for international trade, investment, and financing. This indicates that the opening of the capital account, the full convertibility of the domestic currency, and the internationalization of the domestic currency are three interrelated but distinct concepts. The opening of the capital account does not in and of itself necessarily lead to the full convertibility of the domestic currency, because the current account is yet to be open; the full convertibility of the domestic currency does not necessarily lead to the internationalization of the domestic currency, because it also requires that the domestic currency be widely recognized in international trade and asset exchange. The relationship between these concepts is progressive. In fact, a majority of the world's countries and regions open their capital account based on the opening of their current account. Only when the capital account is open can a given country's domestic currency be fully convertible. Accordingly, only when the domestic currency becomes fully convertible can this currency be internationalized. Based on this line of reasoning, the traditional path towards internationalization follows a linear axis of progression. When the current account is open, the domestic currency will be convertible under the current account, and overseas non-residents will have the chance to hold offshore currencies; when the offshore currencies held by non-residents can be converted to the domestic currency, it means that this domestic currency has already been considered fully convertible in foreign countries. In addition, the trade in physical goods has been transformed into a purely financial trade. After the 1990s, frontier trade and stall banks became more common. When this currency can be converted to other currencies in foreign countries, it means that this currency has been widely applied in international trade and is recognized by financial exchanges. As a result, it is very likely that this currency will enter into the balance sheet of non-residents, or at least the government's balance sheet, as a reserve currency (for example, the current offshore RMB market in Hong Kong).

We can see from the above that as far as internationalization goes, the opening of the domestic currency under the current account and that under the capital account are progressive processes that must coordinate to achieve any degree of success. After the initial conditions have developed, the RMB will begin to be internationalized. As this process continues, new conditions are created. The RMB's path to internationalization is distinctive, and is fully reflected in this coordinative relation. The new conditions that arise as the path towards international applicability evolves form the typical "path dependence."

In fact, the initial performance of the RMB's overseas application has led directly to its contemporary performance, which is that the RMB's offshore market is growing faster than the onshore market. This result further creates further conditions for monetary evolution and presents new prospects for the RMB's internationalization.

First of all, the RMB's cross-border application, particularly after the emergence of the offshore RMB market in Hong Kong, separates the full opening of the capital account from the full convertibility of the RMB. Though the permanent separation of these two categories is impossible, for a significant degree of relative separation is possible at a certain stage—and in fact, China's opening of the RMB under the capital account represents the dawn of this particular stage. According to criteria established by the IMF, there are 43 items that exist under the capital account, most of which have been open or basically open in China. Only three of these items, all of which are related to capital behaviors, are under regulation. They include the fact that foreign direct investment requires investigation and approval; Chinese residents, in principle, are not allowed to hold foreign liabilities. If they are allowed to, the scale of foreign liabilities must be strictly regulated, but in principle, foreign capital does not have access to China's capital market except through special arrangement, namely the QFII. As the RMB's overseas application increases, China must continue to maintain the above regulation and subsequently adopt an open policy towards the RMB. Since the RMB is the country's own domestic currency, the existing regulations on the capital account can be relaxed to a large extent.

Secondly, the RMB's cross-border application, especially the development of the offshore RMB market in Hong Kong, helps form the balance of payments deficit, which will then be stabilized and institutionalized. The most recent three years have shown that the RMB's settlement under the current account is used more for imports than it is for exports. The reason why is quite simple: ignoring the fact that the RMB has a stable value and a tendency towards appreciation, the economic status of the importer is more important than that of the exporter when engaging in cross-border trade negotiations. As a result, the RMB's outflow is generally larger than its inflow. So far, the RMB's cross-border settlement under the current account has covered all the provinces of mainland China, and mechanism has been developed for the RMB's external payment. China still has a sound economy and the income of its citizens as a whole has continued to climb, laying a foundation for the further expansion of exports and stabilization of the trade deficit. At the same time, as China's economy develops, Chinese companies have begun to make overseas investments, which are facilitated by the RMB's application in said overseas investments. As a result, the proportion of foreign investment settled in RMB to the total foreign investment of China overall continues to reports a rising trend. For its part, the RMB boasts an expanding capital account deficit. Due to the above—and despite the fact that China's balance of payments is now reporting "double surpluses"—the RMB has already shown a trend of deficit. In the aspect of China's international balance of payments, a change in both geographical and currency structure has taken place. The US dollar has reported a surplus while the RMB registers a deficit. As such, economic structures are not only adapting to the rapid development of China's economy, but are also beneficial in meeting the standing requirements necessary for the RMB's overseas application.

Thirdly, the RMB's cross-border application, particularly the development of the offshore RMB market in Hong Kong, serves as a reference and point of direct guidance for the Chinese mainland to incubate its financial market and further develop its domestic financial system. The financial system of the Chinese mainland focuses largely on indirect financing, of which, the largest deficiency is the continued immaturity of its capital market. Hong Kong, however, possesses a mature financial market, which focuses on both direct and indirect financing. The financial industry in the Chinese mainland has always been concerned with the example provided by Hong Kong's economic experiences—and the development of the offshore RMB market has provided just the right opportunities and solutions to do so. Along with the opening of the RMB under the capital account, all types of financial instruments attached to the RMB are to be transmitted to the Chinese mainland, thereby stimulating and guiding the growth of its financial market. Foreign financial institutions are allowed to engage in the mainland's inter-bank bond market, which will directly or indirectly promote economic competition. By learning from the managerial experience of more established global financial institutions, the financial market in the Chinese mainland is able to enhance its own competiveness and accelerate further financial innovation. One visible effect of all this is that the liberalization of the interest rate and the process of enabling the flexibility of the exchange rate have both accelerated, which provides a solid foundation for enhancing the validity of the PBOC's monetary policies. In addition, the PBOC is now increasingly able to undertake the obligation of global liquidity management.

It's worth pointing out that the new conditions created during the RMB's internationalization will, on the one hand, open up new prospects for the RMB's overseas application, but on the other hand create a new problem all of their own. The outline of this problem arises from the intersection of the RMB's convertibility and its movement under the capital account. As to the RMB's convertibility, overseas markets—represented by the Hong Kong international financial market—have realized the RMB's full convertibility both under the current account and under the capital account, while in the Chinese mainland itself, the RMB is not convertible under the capital account. Both inside and outside China, however, the RMB is open under both the current account and under the capital account (see Tables 6.1 and 6.2).

The intersection between the convertibility of the RMB and the opening of the RMB lies in China itself. Under the capital account, the RMB can flow both

Table 6.1 RMB's convertibility

	Domestic	Overseas
Current account	+ (convertible)	+ (convertible
Capital account	- (inconvertible)	+ (convertible)

Table 6.2 RMB's movement

	Domestic	Overseas
Current account	+ (movable)	+ (movable)
Capital account	+ (movable)	+ (movable)

domestically and internationally, but cannot be converted. What, then, is the meaning of this intersection?

Macroeconomic theory dictates that the demand for money can be divided into two categories: L1 and L2. L1 represents people's demand for money in actual trade and investment. L2 represents people's demand for money under the motivation of capital. In finance, the background to L2 is speculation. L2 is not sensitive to actual trade and investment, but, rather, to price changes (e.g. the price of assets, the interest rate, and the exchange rate). Economically speaking, the so-called capital account opening covers the undifferentiated opening of both L1 and L2 for non-residents. In other words, all sub-items under the capital account and the financial account in the international balance of payments (which are denominated in domestic currency or foreign currencies), can move freely and without restriction among different countries. For China, the RMB is required to be open under the capital account while remaining inconvertible under the capital account in the Chinese mainland. This indicates that non-residents' L2 is still regulated under the capital account of China. It is subsequently easy to speculate that the purpose of this regulation is to alleviate anxieties surrounding international capital, especially the impact of short-term capital on the domestic currency. The tradeoff for this, however, is a currency mismatch in international balance of payments. This mismatch will impact the central bank's monetary base (the independency of the monetary policy) and increase the exchange rate's torsion resistance (the distortion of the anchor currency).

6.2 The Opening of China's Capital Account: The Process and Experience

The opening of China's capital account took place alongside the implementation of domestic economic reform and its opening-up policy. By reviewing this journey and summarizing the experience and lessons learned from history, we can deduce how to realize the RMB's full convertibility and to subsequently draft a roadmap for the future internationalization of the RMB.

The management of the capital account has historically been one of the most important components of China's management of foreign exchanges, and is one of the primary restrictions imposed on cross-border capital transactions (including transfers and payment) and foreign exchange activities. Historically, capital account management in China has gradually shifted away from tilting in favor of inflow over outflow of foreign currencies and become more balanced. According to some scholars, existing regulations on capital in China can be divided into three phases: the phase taking place from 1978 to 1996 was the first, during which, regulations on capital account were loose, with great improvements being made in the absorption of foreign direct investment. Reforms being enacted at that time focused on the regulation on the current account. The years between 1997 and 1999 constituted the second phase, during which, the process of opening the capital account was postponed due to the Asian financial crisis. Furthermore, the regulation of certain areas was strictly reinforced. The third phase took place from 2000 to 2010. As China entered into the WTO, the process of opening the capital account accelerated (Huang 2010).

Before reform and opening-up, China held no foreign or domestic debts. Foreign companies were not allowed to engage in direct investment in China, and the capital account was strictly regulated. After the national policy of reform and opening-up was adopted, however, China began to loosen regulations governing the absorption and utilization of foreign capital and began the gradual process of opening the capital account. Chinese companies, for their part, began to raise funds in the overseas market by issuing securities. The management of the capital account has manifested in a policy-based tendency towards encouraging the inflow of funds but restricting their outflow. In order to absorb foreign capital, China has carried out a series of policies outlining certain aspects of the capital market, direct investment, and foreign exchange trading management, in order to encourage the influx of capital. As the policy of reform and opening-up proceeded, an official exchange rate and liberalized exchange rate were established for the RMB in China in 1994, and, further, a managed floating system was adopted for the RMB based on existing market supply and demand. In December 1996, China realized the RMB's convertibility under the current account. Neither quantitative nor institutional restrictions outlining the use of foreign currencies were in use at this time. Later, the focus of national policy shifted towards the opening of the capital account.

When China loosened its regulations on capital inflow, it simultaneously adopted strict regulatory policies towards direct investment, securities investment, and foreign debts management, in order to control the potential flight of capital. For instance, any domestic company planning to make overseas investments must have its source of funding reviewed by the country's foreign exchange authority; the foreign exchange funds raised by the issuing of securities by domestic companies on the overseas market must flow back into China; domestic banks operate under strict regulations when extending loans to foreign institutions/individuals; non-banking financial institutions are not allowed to extend loans to foreign institutions/individuals; domestic residents are barred from opening foreign exchange accounts in foreign countries/regions, and more. The management of the capital account—as established in the mid-nineties—was strict in its regulation of the capital outflow but loose in regulating capital inflow. The primary focus of these regulations was first on foreign investment and only later shifted to foreign debts, with the investment of securities explicitly prohibited. After the outbreak of the financial crisis in Southeast Asia in 1997, China further consolidated its regulations on capital outflow in order to maintain the stability of the macro-economy and the country's financial industry.

The 1997 Asian financial crisis heavily affected both foreign trade and the utilization of foreign capital in China, and both the capital account and the financial account registered slight deficits. Expectations that the RMB would depreciate rose. But at the same time, the capital flow began to reverse. 1998 registered a USD6.3 bn net capital outflow, while the net outflow under other investment items was as high as USD43.7 bn. In order to deal with the situation after the Asian financial crisis, to maintain the stability of the RMB's exchange rate, and to prevent the flight of capital, China adopted a series of strict measures to regulate its capital. For instance, repurchasing repayments in advance was forbidden; purchasing foreign currency by deceitful means was illegalized and subsequently punished; evading foreign exchanges and the illegal trading of foreign exchanges was also outlawed; purchasing foreign exchanges for the purpose of investing in overseas equities and creditor's rights was forbidden, as was purchasing foreign exchanges in order to repurchase stocks and bonds in foreign currencies; while under the capital account, if the payment for purchasing foreign exchange equaled or exceeded USD10 mn, it was required to be filed with the State Administration of Foreign Exchange. The management of the capital account during this stage is, in essence, the strict control of the capital outflow with an effort to maintain the stability of the RMB's exchange rate. After adopting a series of measures for strictly regulating foreign exchange, China's international balance of payments has reported increased performance and the issue of excessive foreign exchange outflow has been alleviated.

After the outbreak of the Asian financial crisis, as the movement of foreign capital took a turn for the better, China adjusted its policy on the capital account in response, gradually deregulated foreign exchange and decentralizing the power of approval for foreign exchange to facilitate the movement of capital. After 2000, in order to meet the necessary prerequisites for China to join the WTO and the needs of economic globalization, China began to accelerate and promote the opening of its capital account. Compared to the previous stage of development, the primary features characterizing capital account management after 2001 are revealed in two aspects: first, the focus on opening the capital account has shifted; and second, the management of the capital account has gradually turned from the "Easily In, Strictly Out" model to a more balanced one.

The management of China's direct investment has proven itself quite mature and, as such, the opening of the capital account has almost been accomplished; in terms of securities investment, though management was initially insufficient, it has since developed to an appropriate level. Especially as the scale of the international capital flow has expanded, regulators have had to face the following questions: how best to engage in the global financial market in order to share the fruits of the development of the international capital market? How best to effectively utilize the global financial market in order to prevent and deal with financial risks? And so on. In light of these questions, in 2002, China launched the QFII system, under which overseas investors were allowed to invest in China's capital market; soon afterwards, China carried out policies designed to loosen the existing regulations on banks, securities, insurance companies, and other financial institutions using proprietary capital to make overseas securities investment or to engage in the corresponding brokerage business.

Since 2002, China's current account and capital account have reported persistent surpluses with rapidly increasing foreign exchange reserves. In 2002, the Bank for International Settlements explicitly noted, in response to the liberalization of China's capital account: "firstly, even though China still has regulation on foreign exchange, this country, to a great extent, enables the free movement of the international capital. So to speak, China has already been more open in foreign direct investment than some OECD members, especially in the aspect of resources and technologies. According to the errors and omissions in the balance of payments statement, there has been massive capital flight and cross-border capital activities in China. The scale of cross-border settlement in cash between China and its neighboring countries is also expanding. As a result, the RMB has been regarded by its surrounding countries as one of the hard currencies. During the process of liberalizing the finance in China, the most distinct symbol could be the enlarging deposits of foreign currencies in China. The deposits of foreign currencies in China held by Chinese families and companies have reached 8% of the total deposits, partly because the yield rate of depositing the US dollar in China is the same with that in the rest of the world. The monthly deposit change is more sensitive to the interest rate spread and the expectation for the exchange rate. Along with the process of liberalizing the finance, the capital account can be liberalized. In this aspect, China has made many adjustments." In July 2005, a mechanism designed to reform the RMB's exchange rate was put forth. Since then, the RMB has experienced a slight appreciation. Such a process consolidated previously-held expectations for the RMB's appreciation, as significant amounts of capital flowed in and the independency of the existing monetary policy was constantly affected. Because of this, the management of the capital account focused on encouraging the orderly outflow of capital and preventing speculative capital inflow, all with the purpose of promoting the international balance of payments equilibrium. In order to encourage capital outflow, the regulator reformed the management of foreign exchange in overseas investment, facilitated the "going out" of domestic companies, authorized the investment of overseas financial products via QDII, and allowed individual citizens to transfer their capital.

As China encouraged the outflow of capital, it simultaneously reinforced its management of the influx of overseas capital, particularly the influx of short-term capital. In order to stop the expansion of the real estate bubble and to prevent the real estate market from becoming a channel for speculation, China strictly managed direct investment in the real estate market by increasing the time required for transferring overseas financing into China. In 2005, the period of time required for overseas public firms to recall foreign exchanges, as well as the service life of the special foreign exchange account, were increased to six months and two years, respectively. In August 2008, the State Council revised the *Regulations on Foreign Exchange* and canceled the existing requirement that foreign exchange revenue should be compulsorily recalled.

In 2011, the IMF investigated China's 36 capital account items across four categories and commented that over 80% of items were open while fewer than 20% of items were under strict regulation. The items under regulation were mainly those pertaining to securities investment and the movement of short-term capital, but few items were related to the movement of international capital. The capital account was quite open. To be specific: seven items (19.4%) were fully convertible; 13 items (36.1%) were under loose regulation; nine items (22.5%) were more limited; and seven items (17.5%) were under strict regulation (see Table 6.3).

The IMF's *Annual Report on Exchange Arrangements and Exchange Restrictions* (AREAER) has been published every year since 1997. The AREAER adjusts the statistical indicators for capital regulation, classifies the capital account transactions into eleven different categories, and marks whether or not its members have imposed regulations on certain types of transactions. Every year, the IMF will make certain adjustments to the items in the AREAER based on the evolution of the financial market. As for the classification of the items in question, frequent regulations (including temporary regulations) include those pertaining to direct investment, securities investment, and credit management.

6.2.1 Direct Investment

Continuing rapid growth of the Chinese economy is closely related to the prospect of boosting foreign direct investment. Since 1993, the Chinese government has carried out many preferential policies to encourage the investment of foreign business in China, including tax credit policies and a list of industries that to which foreign capital is made accessible. During the early 1990s, among all developing countries, China was the one that attracted the most FDI. In fact, even compared to domestic companies in China, many foreign companies still enjoy preferential policies, rendering FDI quite convenient. For instance, after 2009, it has not been necessary for FDI to go through pre-examination in the process of foreign exchange management, enabling FDI to be "supplied as needed." In 2011, RMB-denominated FDI was promoted by China. In October 2011, the Ministry of Commerce published the *Notice on Related Issues of Cross-Border RMB-Denominated FDI*, which facilitated overseas investors (including Hong Kong, Macao, and Taiwanese investors) to legally apply offshore RMB in direct investment. The PBOC published the *Administrative Measures on the RMB Settlement Business Relating to Foreign Direct Investment*, allowing overseas investors to do RMB settlement business with banks. Furthermore, China reformed the management of foreign exchange applied in the trade of goods. In September 2011, the State Administration of Foreign Exchange, the State Administration of Taxation, and the General Administration of Customs co-published a document, establishing that from December 1, 2011 on, pilot programs for the management of foreign exchange applied in the trade of goods would be established in seven provinces/municipalities. The State Administration of Foreign Exchange published the document, *Guidance and*

Table 6.3 Capital account opening in China

Category	Full opening	Partial opening	Many restrictions	Strict restrictions	Remarks
Capital market and monetary market					
1. securities trading in the capital market					
A. Stock					
Purchased by non-residents in China			√		QFII (supervised by the CSRC)
Issued by non-residents in China				√	(International Board)
Purchased by residents outside China			√		QDII(supervised by the SAFE)
Issued by residents outside China			√		Requirement for profits' inflow (supervised by the CSRC)
B. Bond					
Purchased by non-residents in China		√			QFII, available in the bond market
Issued by non-residents in China			√		Should be approved by the Ministry of Finance, the PBOC and the National Development and Reform Commission
Purchased by residents outside China		√			Allow insurance companies, securities companies, banks and QDIIs
Issued by residents outside China			√		Allow offshore RMB bond issuance (Require the approval from the NDRC and the SAFE)
2. Money market instruments					
Purchased by non-residents in China			√		Allow QFIIs to purchase securities fund and money market fund
Issued by non-residents in China				√	

(continued)

Table 6.3 (continued)

Category	Full opening	Partial opening	Many restrictions	Strict restrictions	Remarks
Purchased by residents outside China		√			Allow insurance companies, securities companies, banks and QDIIs
Issued by residents outside China		√			Approved by the SAFE
3. Financial derivatives					
Purchased by non-residents in China				√	Prohibited
Issued by non-residents in China				√	Prohibited
Purchased by residents outside China			√		Supervised by the CBRC and the SASAC
Issued by residents outside China			√		Supervised by the CBRC and the SASAC
External credit loan business					
1. Commercial credit loan					
Provided by residents for non-residents	√				Agreed by the CBRC
Provided by non-residents for residents	√				Application is required for over one-year loan.
2. Financial credit loan					
Provided by residents for non-residents		√			Agreed by the CBRC
Provided by non-residents for residents		√			Application is required

(continued)

Table 6.3 (continued)

Category	Full opening	Partial opening	Many restrictions	Strict restrictions	Remarks
3. Guarantee, pledge and alternative financing facilities					
Provided by residents for non-residents		√			Approved by the SAFE
Provided by non-residents for residents		√			Allow foreign-funded enterprises
Direct investment					
1. Foreign direct investment		√			Only require the approval from the SAFE
2. Internal direct investment	√				Application is required for (over USD200,000) foreign investment
3. Investment settlement	√				Should be approved by the SAFE
4. Real estate					
Purchased by residents outside China		√			Approved
Purchased by non-residents in China		√			(Over USD50,000) purchase should gain approval from the SAFE.
Sold by non-residents in China		√			Should be authorized by the SAFE
Individual asset trading					
1. Loan				√	Prohibited
2. Gift, donation and heritage					
Provided by residents for non-residents	√				Approved (with maximum quota)
Provided by non-residents for residents	√				Approved (with maximum quota)

(continued)

Table 6.3 (continued)

Category	Full opening	Partial opening	Many restrictions	Strict restrictions	Remarks
3. Foreign debt settlement				√	Prohibited
4. Asset transfer					
Transfer assets to foreign countries			√		Can transfer pension and old-age allowance to foreign countries; others should be supervised
Transfer assets to China				√	Prohibited
5. Gambling revenue transfer		√			Application is required
6. Savings of non-residents	√				
Total	7	13	9	7	
Weight (%)	19.4	36.1	22.5	17.5	

Source State Administration of Foreign Exchange, Mizuho Securities

Operating Procedures for Pilots Regarding the Management of Foreign Exchange Applied in Trade of Goods (*Version for Banks and Enterprises*) and finalized the corresponding enforcement regulations. On May 10, 2013, in order to promote and facilitate foreign investors' direct investment in China, and, further, to regulate the corresponding management of foreign exchange, the State Administration of Foreign Exchange published the *Administrative Regulations on the Management of Foreign Exchange Applied by Foreign Investors in Direct Investment in China* and supporting documents.

Compared to domestic FDI performance, China's ODI has experienced relatively slow growth. Over the past decade and guided by its "Going Out" policy, the Chinese government has loosened its restrictions on overseas investment and has provided governmental fund support to facilitate companies making overseas investments. At present, China's overseas investment mainly focuses on neighboring countries, particularly Southeast Asian countries and other developing countries. In2014, the total amount of FDI and ODI settled in RMB reached RMB1048.58 bn, accounting for 76% of the total amount of FDI and ODI overall. According to preliminary calculations, over 60% of ODI was transferred via Hong Kong. From this, we can conclude that the offshore RMB market in Hong Kong greatly facilitates the extant ODI settled in RMB.

On the whole, the opening of FDI comes prior to that of ODI when couched in terms of direct investment. Nevertheless, the regulations outlining ODI are stricter than those for FDI, creating a trend towards unidirectional regulation. This situation is changing, however. In order to deal with the "hot money" brought in by the direct investment, many provisional regulatory measures have been carried out, including strengthening the enforcement efforts surrounding foreign exchange management and improving existing regulatory details. Relevant authorities have conducted numerous timely investigations into foreign exchange and have strictly prevented the inflow of fraudulent "hot money." These authorities persistently and heavily attacked "illegal private banks" and "online speculation in foreign exchange," and have also prompted foreign exchange trading entities to obey the country's laws and regulations; relevant measures have been introduced to reinforce the management of foreign exchange business. Provisional policy adjustments were made in seven distinct aspects, including the balance of banks' foreign exchange for settlement and sale, the foreign exchange earned from export, short-term foreign debts, FDI, overseas listings, round-trip investment, and foreign exchange penalties, all of which have reasonably guided the flow of cross-border capital.

6.2.2 Securities Investments

In order to prevent the short-term flow of capital, China has tended to take a relatively reserved and prudent attitude towards investment by foreign investors in the domestic securities market. In 2002, qualified overseas institutional investors were allowed to make an investment in the domestic securities market, though at the same time, the State Administration of Foreign Exchange, together with relevant authorities, increased the maximum quota for one single QFII, narrowed the locking period for the QFII's principal, and simplified the approval procedures necessary for opening an account and transferring funds. As a result of the above efforts, in 2003, QFIIs were allowed to make an investment in China's RMB-denominated A-share market. As of December 2010, 97 QFIIs had gained the approval of the State Administration of Foreign Exchange, contributing a total investment of USD19.72 bn into China's domestic market. As of 2011, 107 foreign institutions had gained the qualifications necessary for QFII. In 2012, when the number of foreign currency-denominated QFIIs grew, the scale of RMB-denominated QFIIs reached 50bn. In 2013, QFIIs were allowed make investments in stock-index futures. In 2014, the quota further increased, with 33 new QFIIs and a new quota of USD17.2 bn. This quota reported a year over year increase of 40%. By the end of 2014, 261 QFIIs were allowed to make securities investment in China, totaling USD66.9 bn.

In 2006, QDII was launched in China. Since that time, domestic financial institutions have been allowed to invest in the overseas market. Similar to QFIIs, QDIIs are not controlled by existing or potential capital. Domestic investors are allowed to make an investment in the overseas market via qualified asset management institutions, insurance companies, securities companies, and other asset management institutions. In 2007, China's foreign investment seemed to be developing stably, however, under the impact of the global financial crisis, this development slowed considerably. Since China's savings ratio is relevantly high, however, foreign companies' investment in China's stock market and bond market has confirmed Chinese predictions for growth.

In 2010, overseas funds developed by domestic securities grew rapidly, with 13 new funds by the 3rd quarter of 2010. By the end of 2014, an additional 127 QDIIs had gained approval, fora total quota of USD83.3 bn in securities investment.

Due to worries outlining the risk of currency speculation, China has and continues to set quite strict regulations on cross-border financial derivative instruments. Global "speculators" illegally engaging in Chinese securities investment face huge risks. For this reason, no global "financial magnate" willing to speculate in China or witness the inflow of a large amount of capital has appeared. This situation guarantees that the trading volume of China's overseas securities investment account (including the associated assets and liabilities of the securities investment in question) will sustain steady economic growth. For example, in2010, net inflow reached USD35.5 bn (excluding the USD40 bn net domestic payment by RMB), accounting for 7.6% of the overall increase in foreign exchange reserves.

In general, the regulations on securities investment are stricter than those outlining direct investment. The current opening of the QFII and QDII is similar to the concept of "cutting holes in a high wall," or, rather, finding loopholes around a difficult problem. In terms of monetary direction, the inflow almost equals the outflow.

6.2.3 *Credit Management*

The regulations on capital accounts are, by and large, currently focused on credit management. The large number of detailed rules in this area are also intricately linked to the management of and regulations on foreign direct investment and portfolio investments. Taken as a whole, credit management evinces the following features:

First of all, foreign-funded companies in China are allowed to engage in debt financing on the overseas market without restriction, while, conversely, Chinese institutions are not allowed to do so until they have obtained the necessary qualifications, and, furthermore, the amount that they can borrow is subject to approval by the State Administration of Foreign Exchange (SAFE). In addition, domestic financial institutions are not allowed to issue loans within overseas markets unless the loans in question have been approved by relevant authorities and meet existing foreign exchange liability/asset ratio requirements. Domestic Chinese non-financial institutions are prohibited from issuing loans in overseas markets altogether.

Secondly, China is currently encouraging the development of the interbank bond market as well as the issuance of offshore bonds in RMB in an effort to facilitate cash inflow. At the same time, China has been promoting related trade financing and project financing pilot programs. These not only provide a channel for the offshore flow of onshore funds, but also aid the RMB's transition from an account settlement currency to one used for investments. In July 2009, the Bank of China (Hong Kong) began offering cross-border trade financing in RMB, thus providing a vital payment service for RMB-denominated cross-border trade. At the beginning of 2010, all Hong Kong banks launched their own RMB cross-border trade finance packages, though at varying, non-standardized rates.

Third, China is expanding the scale of its cross-border lending and promoting a convertible credit business. In 2009, in an attempt to mitigate the pressure on companies' financing and liquidity, the SAFE allowed qualifying institutions, within a set quota, to issue loans in overseas markets using their own foreign exchange and/or by purchasing foreign exchange. Issues related to opening foreign exchange accounts, the domestic transfer of funds, and the purchasing of foreign exchange all must be handled by banks authorized to manage foreign exchange. Additionally, since 2010, Chinese companies have, within set quotas, been allowed to take on short-term foreign debt (see Table 6.4).

Fourth, China is simplifying the process of foreign exchange as a whole and cutting back on extensive bureaucratic red tape. According to *the Notice on Cancelling and Adjusting Powers of Approval and Administrative Measures for Some Foreign Exchange Businesses using Capital Accounts* promulgated by the SAFE, from June 1, 2011 on, the registration for payments previously deferred beyond the agreed-upon payment deadline, as well as the authorization outlining there-exchange of advance payments for goods, were both cancelled as part of the system for the registration and management of trade credit. What's more, the powers of approval for certain foreign exchange businesses using a capital account,

Table 6.4 Structure and growth of China's long-term and short-term foreign debts (2002–2014)

Project/Year	2002	2003	2004	2005	2006	2007	2008	2009	2010	2011	2012	2013	2014
Outstanding external debt (Unit: USD1 bn)	202.63	219.36	262.99	296.55	338.59	389.22	390.16	428.65	548.9	695	736.99	863.17	895.46
Long-term													
Outstanding amount (Unit: USD1 bn)	115.55	116.59	124.29	124.90	139.36	153.53	163.88	169.39	173.2	194.1	196.06	186.54	212.1
YoY growth (%)	−3.3	0.9	6.6	0.5	11.6	10.2	6.7	3.4	2.3	12.0	1.0	−4.9	13.7
Proportion to the total balance (%)	57.0	53.2	47.3	42.1	41.2	39.4	42.0	39.5	31.6	27.9	26.6	21.6	23.7
Short-term													
Outstanding amount (Unit: USD1 bn)	87.08	102.77	138.71	171.64	199.23	235.68	226.28	259.26	375.7	500.9	540.93	676.63	683.36
YoY growth (%)	4.0	18.0	35.0	23.7	16.1	18.3	−4.2	14.6	44.9	33.3	8.0	25.1	1.0
Proportion to the total balance (%)	43.0	46.8	52.7	57.9	58.8	60.6	58.0	60.5	68.4	72.1	73.4	78.4	76.3
Proportion to foreign exchange reserves (%)	30.4	25.5	22.7	21.0	18.7	15.4	11.6	10.8	13.2	15.8	16.3	17.7	17.8

Source State Administration of Foreign Exchange Annual Report 2014

along with certain administrative trade credit management systems, were adjusted. To some extent, therefore, the *Notice* enhances the convertibility of the capital account as a whole.

Fifth, China is reinforcing its regulations outlining risk prevention and improving the management of capital inflow. Since 2010, in order to deal with the problems such as the international balance of payments disequilibrium, the upward pressure on RMB, and the ongoing attacks from "hot money," China has launched a series of administrative measures aimed at improving oversights on the authenticity of exchange earnings and settlements for export; on the process for adjusting banks' metrics in regards to short-term foreign debts; to regulating the management of the foreign exchange being applied in the real estate market; to attacking the illegal flow of cross-border capital; and to strengthening its monitoring of the existing cross-border capital flow. In terms of credit management, many aspects are complicated. Furthermore, with a view towards the existing domestic regulations, we can predict the ultimate destination of China's capital account: the free movement of the RMB under the capital account without corresponding convertibility under the domestic capital account. The combination of these two factors has increased the difficulty of regulation. While China has imposed frequent regulations on credit management, the scale of China's foreign debts has continued to climb and short-term foreign debts have reported rapid growth. By the end of 2014, the balance of China's foreign debts had reached USD89.546 bn (not including the foreign debts held by Hong Kong, Macao, and Taiwan, registering a year-on-year growth of 3.75%). Short-term debts also saw persistent growth (see Fig. 6.4), accounting for 76.32% of the total foreign debts held.

After reviewing the process of opening the capital account, the following features are apparent:

First and foremost, this is a gradual process that follows the development of the real economy, and, further, this process is restricted by China's existing financial structure. For developing countries in the process of industrialization, the low cost of capital often becomes the primary requirement for accelerating its accumulation. The development of commercial banks for which the fundamental business is credit loans constitutes an indirect financing-based financial structure, and such a structure can meet this requirement for low-cost capital. Therefore, the priority of any potential capital account regulation must be credit management. As the process of industrialization proceeds apace and the real economy develops, both the process of credit management and the country's existing financial structure will change accordingly, thus promoting the gradual opening of the capital account.

The path towards the opening of the capital account is as follows: at first, the opening of the flow of long-term capital must be enabled, with a particular emphasis on loosening the restrictions on FDI; then, the flow of short-term capital should be opened; in terms of long-term capital, the opening of direct investment should take place prior to the opening of securities investment; while in terms of securities investment, the opening of the bond investment process should occur prior to the process of opening up stock investment; as for all categories of capital flow, at the emphasis should first be on opening the capital inflow and only then on opening the capital outflow.

Secondly, as the world's second-largest economy and the country with the greatest degree of trade, China demands the internationalization of the RMB. Internationalization would not only accelerate the opening of the capital account in RMB, but also highlight the limitations inherent to the traditional method of regulating the capital account. Because of the growing cost of the process itself, it is becoming increasingly difficult to depend on the traditional method of regulating the capital account. The increase in China's foreign debts, especially the increase in short-term foreign debts, is indicative of the issue at hand. This newly-applied international pressure is the key force accelerating the process of opening the capital account.

Currently, the RMB is not convertible under the domestic capital account. The main worry surrounding this issue comes from the potential for attack from international capital, especially short-term capital on the domestic currency. The difficulty with opening the capital account is being able to enable the convertibility of the RMB under the domestic capital account, which is also the point of greatest emphasis in China's current economic policy. To loosen the existing regulations, China must liberalize the exchange rate and the interest rate. This, however, depends on the degree of maturity of the domestic financial infrastructure and on the financial market, most notably the fixed income market.

6.3 Methods and Steps to Realize the Full Convertibility of the RMB

The RMB is convertible outside China but is not convertible inside China. In the long run, this represents a transitional status in the process of enabling the full convertibility of the RMB. Due to the RMB's cross-border movement (generated by the opening of the capital account in RMB), the regulations on the capital account will be partially invalidated. Over time, the cost of maintaining the inconvertibility of the RMB under the capital account inside China will be grow. This alone indicates that such a transitional status cannot be sustained indefinitely. In this sense, it is necessary to simultaneously accelerate the RMB's cross-border movement and the RMB's full convertibility.

As previously mentioned, under the capital account, the RMB is convertible outside China but is not convertible inside China. The purpose for this is to meet the international community's demand for RMB. This status, however, is also established by and predicated upon the degree of maturity of China's financial system and market, with all its attendant restrictions. The market mechanism for both the interest rate and the exchange rate has yet to be developed. In order to realize the RMB's cross-border movement and full convertibility, China must be able to harness the RMB's global application, which will, in turn, accelerate the development of China's financial system and market. Based on the degree of maturity and the pace of improvement, China can then gradually realize the convertibility of the RMB inside China under the capital account. This is an important element to constituting the RMB's full convertibility.

Following the above line of logic, the RMB's full convertibility will only be realized by taking small but decisive steps. According to previous international experience [especially the experience of emerging markets (e.g. South Korea, Taiwan, Indonesia, and Malaysia)], in order to demonstrate the convertibility of their currencies under the capital account, the bond markets of the economy in question must have an average openness of 8% (that is, overseas funds occupy 8% of the domestic bond market) while the openness of the stock markets must reach an average level of 11%. Based on this degree of openness, the inflow of foreign capital almost equals its outflow. As such, the risk of capital flow on a large scale will be reduced as the country further opens its capital account (see Table 6.5).

Therefore, when we compare China to other emerging economies, if the target for the first stage is to realize an 8% openness of the bond market, opening the capital account should follow these subsequent steps: (1) increase the quota of the RMB that can be converted to foreign currencies by individuals and companies; (2) accordingly, allow individuals and companies to transfer the same amount of RMB to the overseas market; (3) increase the quota of the RMB that's made available for overseas institutions to enter into the inter-bank market; (4) increase the quota of foreign exchange investment for QFIIs in the domestic capital market; (5) gradually allow overseas non-resident companies to raise funds in the domestic market (including panda bonds), and allow these companies to convert their RMB-denominated funds to foreign currencies; (6) gradually allow non-residents to invest in more domestic RMB products (via the NRA account) at a pace that should be consistent with that of the product development taking place in the offshore RMB market in Hong Kong (see Table 6.6).

The purpose of the above arrangements is, at first sight, to loosen the existing regulations on the capital account. The actual purpose, however, is to develop the domestic financial market, especially the capital market. Similarly to the introduction of foreign capital after the1980s, the central aim is to introduce technologies

Table 6.5 Openness of the capital market at the preliminary stage of capital account opening in emerging markets

	Stock (%)	Bond (%)
South Korea (1998)	5	7
Taiwan (2003)	12	6
Brazil (1993)	27	8
India (2000)	9	2
Malaysia (2000)	11	11
Turkey (2000)	6	16
South Africa (1994–1997)	6	9
Avg.	11	8

Source WIND, IMF, World Bank, BIS

Table 6.6 China's capital market openness compared with that of other capital markets (2009–2011)

	Stock (%)	Bond (%)
China (not incl. Chinese securities listed in the overseas market)	0.8	0.8
China (incl. Chinese securities listed in the overseas market)	8.3	1.5
South Korea	31	11
Taiwan	28	8
Brazil	27	9
India	20	3
Malaysia	25	28
Russia	14	18
Vietnam	8	3
South Africa	12	14
Argentina	9	14
Thailand	52	8
Turkey	19	17
Mexico	28	12
Germany	51	45
Japan	21	4
USA	13	17
UK	47	39
Avg. of 13 emerging markets (excl. China)	25.9	13.1
Avg. of 17 countries (excl. China)	27.6	16.2

Source Deutsche Bank, IMF (CPIS), World Bank, BIS, CEIC

and managerial experience. The domestic market has been enriched with the introduction of foreign capital designed to bring financial products, managerial technologies, and investment concepts into the country, all of which will further create conditions for opening the domestic capital account. Based on the development mentioned above, the country should proceed to make decisions about its economic future by capitalizing on existing opportunities for development and by canceling the restrictions on quotas.

For now, China has met the basic requirements for realizing the RMB's convertibility under the domestic capital account, as indicated in the following sections.

First, the RMB's mechanism outlining foreign exchange has already been improved, but in 2005, China further reformed the existing mechanism. In addition to an appreciation of 2%, the RMB's spot exchange rate was allowed to float against the US dollar by ±0.3%. In 2010, this range expanded to ±0.5%. On April 14, 2012, the PBOC announced that from April 16 on, the floating range would expand from ±0.5 to ±1%. On March 15, 2014, the PBOC published an announcement on its website stating that beginning March 17, 2014, this range will further expand to ±2%. Since 2005, the RMB has appreciated by 30% against the

US dollar. One obvious piece of evidence for this is that the exchange rate of the CNH is now almost consistent with that of the CNY (see Fig. 6.1).

Secondly, the process of liberalizing the RMB's interest rate is accelerating. Since 1996, when China implemented a uniform inter-bank offered rate, the process of liberalizing the interest rate proceeded in earnest, moving from the monetary market to the bond market to the credit market. Till now, the interest rate of the bond market, the inter-bank lending rate, and the discount rate have all almost been fully liberalized. The interest rate of foreign currency-denominated loans and that of foreign currency-denominated deposits have, in fact, been fully liberalized. Regulations only exist for the minimum loan rate and the maximum deposit rate.

Because China's financial structure is still based on indirect financing, credit loans remain the main source of funds. The regulations constraining the deposit and loan interest rate still serve as obstacles for enhancing the efficiency of resource allocation and for improving the macro-adjustment mechanism. In 2011, an almost-unnoticed—but significant—change took place, which was the adoption of a "dual-track approach" in the credit loan market. The difference not only exists in the deposit and loan rates between banks and non-banking institutions, but also exists between banks' deposit rate and the yield rate of wealth management products.

When the deposits held in banks have been injected into wealth management products, the regulation on the maximum deposit rate has been be loosened, and the dual-track mechanism has been adopted for both the sources funding and for the interest rates, then the RMB's loan rates will indirectly bypass their bottom line. In this same vein, a trend of loans securitization has been taking place. Additionally, this same dual-track mechanism has been adopted in fund sourcing. In recent years, bond financing has gradually become one of the important channels for what are considered high quality companies. In China, however, commercial banks are still the major players on the bond market. Corporate bond financing is, in essence, an

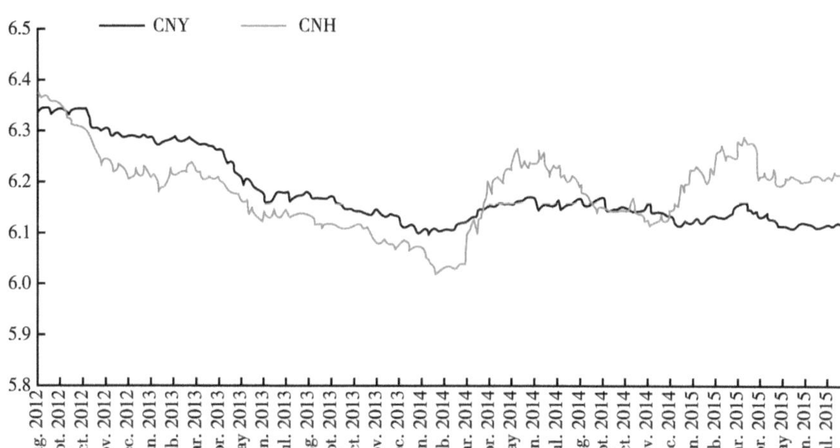

Fig. 6.1 CNH & CNY price trend *Source* Bloomberg

indirect channel for raising funds via banks. Even though the bank is the most common source of funds, they each possess different rates. According to previously-published statistics, the issuing rates of Chinese bonds tend to be lower than the loan rate of the same term. Take middle/short-term notes (with an inter-bank credit of AAA) for example. Their average yield rate will be around 80% of the benchmark interest rate for loans of the same term (see Table 6.7). Therefore, for one common client and in one common bank, the interest rate could still vary significantly due to the different types of bonds and loans available. As a result, two tracks exist for the interest rate in the loan market.

The development of the financial market in China today is consistent with the reform of the pricing system in the 1980s: the planned prices are similar to banks' minimum loan rates and maximum deposit rates, which are themselves determined by the government; in addition, the yield rates of banks' wealth management products are similar to the planned prices in the past. They will face intervention from the government, but despite this banks still hold the pricing power; the interest rates for private lending are similar to the liberalized prices in the past, which depend totally on the supply-demand relationship present in the market at a given point in time.

As seen in the price reforms taking in the 1980s, the revolutionary significance of the reform itself is not reflected in the dual tracks between the planned price and the liberalized price across different systems, but rather, is reflected in one system's dual tracks between the planned price and the planned referential price (see Fig. 6.2). From this perspective, it is worth paying attention to the development of banks' wealth management products. As for principal-protected products, both the fixed type and the floating type are similar to the business of banks' traditional deposits, evincing only some small degree of innovation. In this aspect, non-principal-protected products have made a breakthrough. They are qualitatively different from the traditional deposit business, the principal of which is protected and interest is fixed. Non-principal-protected products are risky to a certain degree and exist "out of the planning." Yet there have been many non-principal-protected products on the market, which shows that the marginal guiding function of the liberalized interest rate is being strengthened.

Table 6.7 Avg. yield to maturity (%) of AAA middle- and short-term notes in 2014

Maturity	Avg. yield to maturity of AAA notes (%)	Benchmark interest rate of RMB-denominated loans (%)	Avg. yield rate/ benchmark interest rate of loans (%)
6 months	4.58	5.60	81.79
1 year	4.59	5.60	76.50
3 years	4.61	6.00	76.83
5 years	4.71	6.00	76.59
7 years	4.81	6.15	78.21

Source Wind, Institute of International Finance, Bank of China

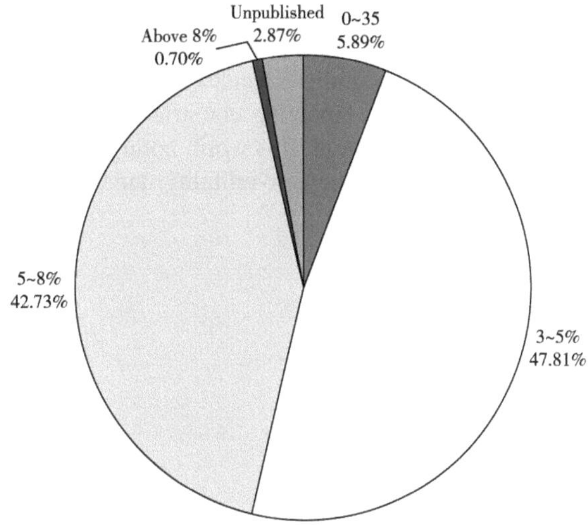

Fig. 6.2 Expected annual percentage rate (%) for Certificate of Deposits (Dec. 2014–Jun. 2015) *Source* Wind Information

Further observations show that the yield rates of banks' wealth management products diverge wildly from the interest rate on banks' deposits, but gradually tend to converge with the yield rates of trust products.

Banks' wealth management products and trust products now share a single common yield curve, which not only shows that banks' wealth management products have been significantly impacted by liberalized interest rates, but also indicates that the liberalization of the interest rates themselves is maturing.

Accordingly, it is possible to predict that as the country's bond products and fixed income products develop, any changes in the interest of the loan market will be similar to those of the deposit market. Faced with an ongoing trend of the liberalization of the interest rate and the pressure of market competition, it is very likely to follow existing international rules insofar as pricing (shibo + BP). This signifies that the dual-track mechanism is moving towards becoming a market-oriented mechanism.

The above indicates that the exchange rate formation mechanism has undergone gradual improvement, enabling the continued flexibility of the exchange rate. The accelerated process of liberalizing the RMB's interest rate has allowed the financial market to deal with the price impacts. The growing market—as marked by a variety of financial products, particularly in corporate bond financing—reflects these two aspects. The proportion of corporate bond financing has increased from less than 10% for 2010 to 15% now. This growth is taking place at a much more rapid rate than that of traditional bank loans, which indicates that the focus of China's financial structure is transforming from indirect financing to direct financing. Additionally, as previously mentioned, significant conditions have been created for fostering the RMB's full convertibility. Experts usually believe that, assuming these conditions hold, the openness of the domestic capital market will increase by one percentage point every year. Within five years, the openness of the fixed income market as represented by bonds has the potential to reach 6%. The capital market of a large country won't be as open as that of a small country, of course. In this sense, the 6% openness is similar to an 8% openness in a small country. In other words, it has already met the emerging countries' requirements for realizing convertibility under the capital account. It is worth noting that this requirement is consistent with the goal of realizing the convertibility under the capital account mentioned in the 12th Five-Year Plan.

Chapter 7
A Method for Accelerating the RMB's Internationalization

The previous chapters' discussion of methods for promoting the RMB's internationalization was only a kind of forecast with a focus on its inevitability and necessity. In more concrete and less theoretical terms, however, the RMB's internationalization proceeds as it will, resulting in the development of the offshore market to proceed faster than that of the onshore market—a situation further responsible for consolidating the model of "offshore market + settlement bank." This path is entirely contrary to the one it was presupposed the RMB would follow. What's more important, the "dependence on this path" not only brings new challenges but also new opportunities.

7.1 Creating the Conditions for Realizing the Convertibility of the RMB Under the Capital Account—Shanghai Pilot Free Trade Zone

As previously mentioned, the 2008 global financial crisis revealed the "original sin" of money and intensified the urgency for each country to enable trade financing using its own domestic currency. China—as the major trading partner for many countries in East Asia—is significant in this aspect. Aside from the European Union and the United States, five of the top seven global trading countries belong to this region, and their imports generally exceed their exports. For this reason, the RMB has become a preferred currency in trade financing.

In order to meet growing international demand, on July 2, 2009, the internationalized RMB was applied in cross-border trade settlement with China using two different methods, namely, via the agency bank (Shanghai Model) and via the settlement bank (Hong Kong and Macao Model). The Shanghai Model was the first applied, however, significant deviation from the original design took place over the following seven years. The volume of settlement taking place via the agency bank

© Social Sciences Academic Press and Springer Nature Singapore Pte Ltd. 2018

Y. Cao, *Strategies for Internationalizing the Renminbi*, Research Series on the Chinese Dream and China's Development Path,
https://doi.org/10.1007/978-981-13-0800-0_7

was much smaller than that via the settlement bank. As a result, the global application of the RMB in the offshore market is much greater than that of the onshore market.

While the RMB is the sovereign currency of China, international experience has shown that the internationalization of a sovereign currency within the onshore market is typically a faster process than that taking place in the offshore market. As such, the government should guide development in the offshore market. In the process of internationalizing the RMB, however, the actual performance was just the opposite from what was predicted. Development in the offshore market took place prior to that of the onshore market, and the development in the onshore market had to passively adapt to that of the offshore market. These two separate markets have different exchange rates and interest rates. This financial evolutionary inconsistency not only triggered interest and exchange arbitrage, but also disrupted the stability of the financial market and the consistency of China's monetary policy. In fact, this phenomenon has become increasingly prominent since the second half of 2015. At the beginning of the 2016 fiscal year, as the exchange rate of the RMB in the offshore market dropped, the exchange rate of the RMB in the onshore market correspondingly reported a downward trend. Even though the ascending overnight rate of the RMB in the offshore market curbed the fall of the RMB's exchange rate overall, it also triggered the RMB's flowing back, thereby squeezing the liquidity of the offshore market and further impacting the RMB's worldwide application. Therefore, to further internationalize the RMB, it is important to establish why a dual track has been fostered for the offshore market and the onshore market, and how to speed up the incorporation of these two tracks.

If we compare the Shanghai offshore RMB market to the Shanghai onshore RMB market, for example, the underlying causes for utilizing a dual-track system become obvious. As for the Hong Kong offshore market, in addition to the fact that the RMB is fully convertible under the current account, the RMB's backflow mechanism (as represented by the settlement bank) shows that the RMB is also convertible under the capital account. A loop therefore takes shape for the RMB's cross-border transactions. Specifically, the RMB will flow out under the current account and will flow in under the capital account. With such a loop, a connection is established among the RMB's overseas application, the RMB's application in domestic trade financing, and the domestic RMB-denominated financial market. What's more, a parity relation between the interest rate and the exchange rate is established. Overseas investors are enthusiastic about holding the RMB, especially considering that China's rapid economic development has lifted the interest rate and the exchange rate of the RMB. The volume of cross-border trade settled in RMB will skyrocket as a result. Since more RMB-denominated currencies have been deposited by overseas investors recently, it is increasingly necessary to make arrangement for the RMB's overseas cash position. Furthermore, the capital account's connection to the domestic market via the RMB is foundational to the establishment of the RMB's offshore financial market. At the same time, the mature infrastructure of Hong Kong's financial market is accommodating to the development of the offshore financial market, thus fostering positive feedback from the

RMB's application under the current account and under the capital account. The scale of RMB applicability is expanding.

As opposed to the offshore RMB market in Hong Kong, the onshore market in Shanghai has an open current account. Due to the existing regulations on the capital account, however, the RMB is not convertible. If an overseas trader applies the RMB in valuation and settlement, it means that when this trader exports goods to the Chinese mainland, it must also immediately *import* goods from the Chinese mainland. Failing that, arrangements for the RMB's cash position will be impossible. Naturally, this results in a greater reluctance to use the RMB, and the settlement volume will subsequently be lower than that existing under the Hong Kong and Macao model. In addition, since Shanghai's financial infrastructure and financial market remain as-yet undeveloped, the supply of financial products—especially the supply of fixed income products—is far from adequate. Even if domestic investors hold supplies of the RMB, it remains difficult to maintain and appreciate its value. For this reason, the concept of an onshore RMB market is alien to the RMB's international application. In fact, the ongoing joke is that "the water of Shanghai's onshore market is too shallow. Big fish cannot live here."

The above indicates that the core reason for the divergence between the RMB's international application in the onshore market and that of the offshore market can be found in two aspects: the opening and convertibility of the RMB under the capital account on one hand, and the development of RMB-denominated financial products in the onshore market and the further expansion of the market on the other. If the reform of these two aspects cannot achieve substantive progress, any progress surrounding either the exchange rate or the interest rate will not be incorporated into further financial progress, and the frequent movement of short-term international capital triggered by either interest or exchange arbitrage will occur. Furthermore, the stability of the financial market will become a source of potential anxiety. For this reason, if no other, China must rapidly connect the offshore market to the onshore market and, in doing so, create the conditions necessary for eliminating the dual-track system. This entails the financial reform of the Shanghai Free Trade Zone.

The financial reform policies include, specifically, the following four major aspects: the RMB's cross-border application, the reform of the existing policy outlining foreign exchange, the convertibility of the RMB under the capital account, and the liberalization of the interest rate. The first three policies have corresponding enforcement regulations that were previously separately drafted by the Shanghai Headquarters of the PBOC and Shanghai Branch of the SAFE from 2014 to2015. These regulations are the *Notice on Facilitating the Chinese (Shanghai) Free Trade Zone to Expand the RMB's Cross-Border Application*, the *Notice on Facilitating the Chinese (Shanghai) Free Trade Zone to Develop Enforcement Regulations on Foreign Exchange,* and the *Enforcement Regulations on the Prudent Management at the Macro Level of Overseas Financing and the Cross-Border Capital Movement of Separate Accounting in the Chinese (Shanghai) Free Trade Zone (Tentative).*

The purpose of instituting these financial reform policies is to solve three problems: first, they constitute a trial for realizing the RMB's convertibility under the capital account. By regarding the Shanghai Free Trade Zone as a portal to international exchange, China will not only expand the RMB's cross-border application under the current account and the capital account, but also will explore the convertibility of the RMB under the capital account. Second, it will help boost Shanghai's financial market. By lowering the threshold for the financial services industry, China will encourage financial institutions to engage in trading RMB-denominated financial products drawn from the onshore market, further facilitating the development of the RMB's interest rate system. Third, due to the mutual promotion of the above two aspects, the parity between the RMB's exchange rate and interest rate will become more market-oriented and consolidate further, which will facilitate the RMB's internationalization. It is worth noting that according to the *Enforcement Regulations on the Prudent Management at the Macro Level of Overseas Financing and the Cross-Border Capital Movement of Separate Accounting in the Chinese (Shanghai) Free Trade Zone (Tentative)* (February 2015), any companies (foreign or domestic, financial or industrial) registered in the Free Trade Zone can automatically own two accounts: the general account and the free trade account. The only limitation is that any RMB-denominated funds raised from the overseas market are not allowed to be used in the domestic A-share market. Aside from this limitation, companies do not face any other limitations when applying these two accounts under the current account or under the capital account. On the basis of the RMB being open under the capital account, the Free Trade Zone serves as a pilot program for realizing the RMB's full convertibility.

As such, the *Enforcement Regulation* defines all aspects pertaining to the scale, the application restrictions, and the business procedures for financial institutions and companies registered in the Free Trade Zone in the process of raising funds from the overseas markets via FTU and/or FTA (see Tables 7.1 and 7.2).

Financial institutions in Shanghai, enterprises and non-banking financial institutions within the Free Trade Zone are allowed to leverage the separate accounting system to do overseas financing business (Figs. 7.1 and 7.2).

The maximum amount for overseas financing by financial institutions or intra-zone enterprises through separate accounting unit is as follows:

Table 7.1 The account system for the Shanghai free trade zone

Account holder	FTU Shanghai branch		Original account system of Shanghai branch
	Other branches	Free trade zone branch	
Residents living within the region	Free trade account for residents		Basic account, general account, special account, temporary account
Non-residents	Free trade account for non-residents		
Residents living outside the region			Basic account, general account, special account, temporary account

Table 7.2 Procedure for conducting separate accounting for overseas financing business

	Entity	Department in charge	Procedure	Turnaround time
1	Enterprises or non-banking financial institutions within the region (through settlement bank)	PBOC (Shanghai HQs)	Overseas financing business declaring	After signing the overseas financing contract, but no later than 3 work days ahead of time
2	Entity within the region > foreign currency-denominated overseas financing >Non-fund-transfer domestic/foreign currency-denominated overseas financing	PBOC (Shanghai HQs)	Foreign debt registration or filing	Turnaround time required by the management policies for foreign debts
	>RMB-denominated overseas financing (leverage a settlement bank to set up a free trade account)	PBOC (Shanghai HQs)	Reporting of information on financing by relevant systems of the PBOC (Shanghai HQs)	When handling the overseas RMB-denominated loan settlement business
3	Settlement bank	PBOC (Shanghai HQs)	Inquire the basic information on financing entity's separate accounting for overseas financing and check whether the overseas financing meets the compliance requirements	When conducting separate accounting for overseas financing business

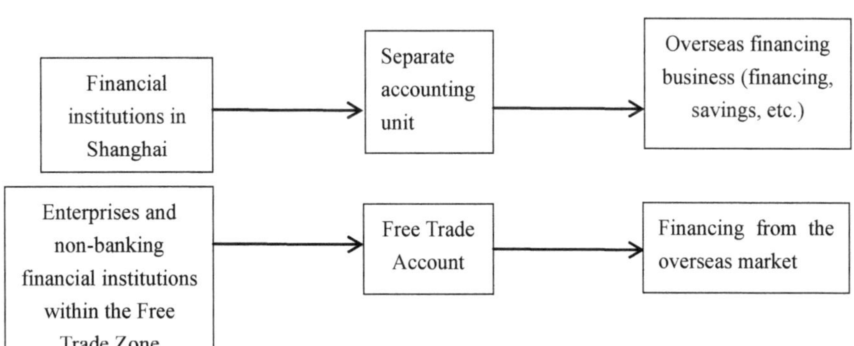

Fig. 7.1 Overseas business by financial institutions in Shanghai

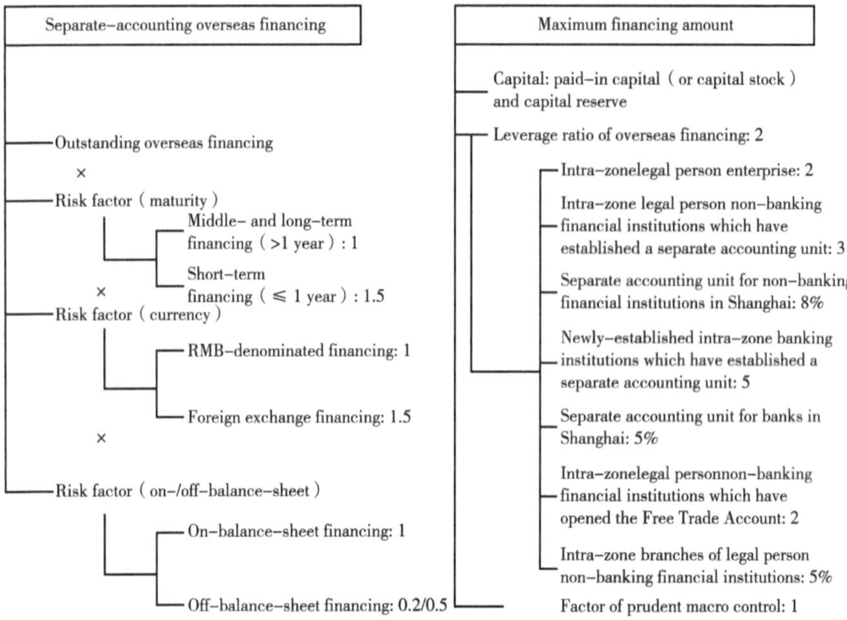

Fig. 7.2 Maximum amount for overseas financing by financial institutions or intra-zone enterprises

Business types which should be included into the separate -accounting overseas financing:	Business types which shouldn't be included into the separate-accounting overseas financing:
√Foreign currency-denominated trade financing √Off-balance-sheet financing (contingent liability) √Other types of external liabilities	×Deposit taken ×Trade credit loan, non - financing guarantee, RMB-denominated trade financing ×Panda bond ×Fund transfer within the Group ×Overseas financingtransferred or deducted

Fig. 7.3 Eligible and ineligible business types for separate-accounting overseas financing

Figure 7.3 shows business types which should be included into the separate-accounting overseas financing and which shouldn't be (Fig. 7.4).

For overseas financing by financial institutions or intra-zone enterprises through separate accounting unit or free trade account, the following requirements should be met:

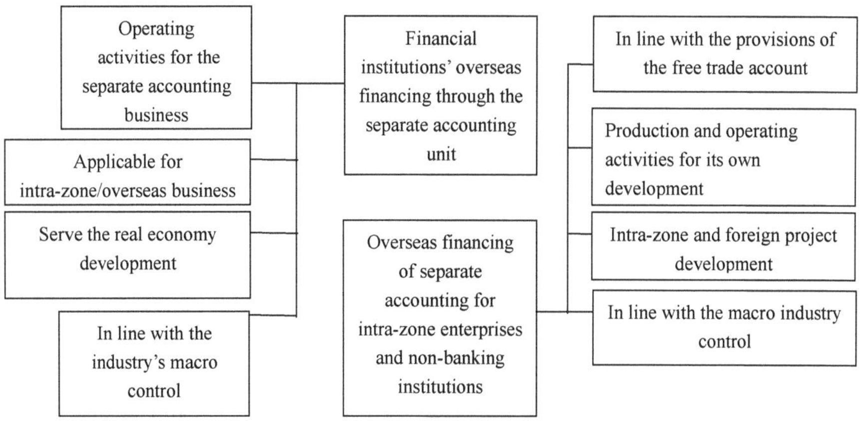

Fig. 7.4 Requirements for using separate accounting unit or free trade account

The following procedures should be followed when financial institutions or entities within the region conduct separate accounting for overseas financing business.

The above clearly indicates that the "Free Trade Account System" is both the very foundation of the pilot program and is an important step towards realizing the RMB's opening and convertibility under the capital account. For this reason, the "Free Trade Account System" plays a central role in China's financial reform. The establishment of this "Free Trade Account System" is of particular significance because it helps foster a financial environment that is separate from other domestic markets while remaining closely connected to the global financial market.

The *Enforcement Regulation* has been effective for over a year and has brought with it measurable and obvious achievements. According to relevant regulations, financial institutions and companies registered in the Free Trade Zone can engage in overseas financing activities and calculate financing costs independently; in this way, institutions registered in the Free Trade Zone will raise more funds from the overseas markets via a greater number of channels and their financing costs will be reduced. It should be noted that the Shanghai Free Trade Zone is an experimental Chinese pilot program initiated with the intent of improving the trading experience.

The precedent set by the Shanghai Free Trade Zone establishes that China is expanding its experimental reach—a program that not only covers the whole of Shanghai, but also establishes new Free Trade Zones in Guangdong, Fujian, and Tianjin. The policies and measures initiated in the Shanghai Free Trade Zone to encourage and to support the RMB's wider cross-border application are also applicable to other pilot zones. Additionally, the capital pool for the RMB's two-way cross-border application has been extended to the country as a whole.

7.2 Establishing a More Stable Mechanism for Generating the Capital Account Deficit—"The Silk Road Economic Belt and the 21st-Century Maritime Silk Road" (The Belt and the Road)

According to statistics, as of December 2015, 80 companies registered in the Free Trade Zone had already conducted intensive management of the foreign exchange fund. By promoting self-discipline in terms of the ratio of foreign debts, the scale of foreign debts filed by companies was close to USD5 bn, while the actual scale of foreign debts reached USD750 mn. A total cost of roughly RMB400 bn was saved for the companies in this manner. As of January 2016, the balance of RMB-denominated loans to foreign countries that were covered by the policies of the Shanghai Free Trade Zone and issued by Shanghai's financial institutions reached RMB74.732 bn, among which, RMB38.317 bn outstanding loans fell under the umbrella of direct investment. Furthermore, since the 1990s, China has gradually developed its export-oriented economic model. The scale of imports and exports had, at one time, reached 70% of the national GDP. It was at that time that China became the "world's factory." The current account surplus increased steadily, peaking in 2007 (the current account surplus as a percentage of GDP peaked at 7.2%). At the same time, due to China's rapid economic growth and low factor cost, China has become the primary destination for foreign direct investment. Due to the regular influx of foreign capital, China's capital account continues to grow. As a result, China has become one of the few countries in the world which reports "double surpluses" and holds the world's largest foreign exchange reserves—a figure that peaked at USD4 tn. To put it mildly, Chinese companies have experienced rapid growth. In 2013, China's foreign direct investment exceeded USD100 bn (7% of the world's total) and the scale of its domestic inventory surpassed USD600 bn (2.3% of the world's total). In 2014, the total amount of foreign direct investment in China, for the first time, exceeded the amount of foreign capital introduced originally. For this reason, China has become a net capital exporter. In 2015, the capital account deficit reached USD504.4 bn, among which, FDI reached as high as USD16.7 bn, with a year-on-year growth of 108%.

7.2.1 The Significance of "The Belt and the Road" in Terms of the Sustainable Development of China's Economy

Geographically, "the Belt and the Road" is an area representing a channel to the West, reaching Central Asia, South Asia, Southeast Asia, West Asia, North Africa, Russia, and some Central and East European countries. In the future, "the Belt and the Road" might conceivably also reach other European countries and develop further as the longest and most potentially profitable economic corridor. This extensive geographic range indicates that most emerging markets and developing economies are in the stage of rapid economic development coupled with a significant "second-mover" advantage.. It is urgent that these countries address what are currently ongoing difficulties in transportation, electricity, information, and other infrastructures. According to estimates offered by the Asian Development Bank, "the Silk Road Economic Belt" will generate USD8 tn infrastructure in investment demand over the next ten years, which would go a long way towards addressing these issues.

Considering that the imports and exports of China only reported a growth of 2.3% in 2014, any exports aimed towards countries along "the Belt and the Road" increased by over 10%, with a focus on infrastructure (see Table 7.3). Half of the service export contributed by China's engineering companies focused on this area.

On March 28, 2015, the Chinese government published the tract, *Vision and Actions on Jointly Building the Silk Road Economic Belt and a 21st-Century Maritime Silk Road,* making clear that the connectivity of its associated facilities is of the utmost priority when implementing the initiative. The measures included encompass promoting policy coordination, facilities connectivity, unimpeded trade, financial integration, and people-to-people bonds. The countries involved are called upon to improve regional infrastructure and put into place a secure and efficient network of land, sea, and air passages, thus improving their connectivity; further enhance trade and investment facilitation; establish a network of free trade areas that

Table 7.3 Overview of some published infrastructure projects

Field	Projects (in the pipeline)
Cross-border high-speed rail	• Eurasian high-speed rail (Line 1: From London to Kazakhstan via Paris, Berlin, Warsaw, Kiev and Moscow; Line 2: from London to Manzhouli of China via Paris, Berlin, Warsaw, Kiev, Moscow and Russian Far East) • Central Asia high-speed rail (From Urumchi to Germany via Uzbekistan, Turkmenistan, Iran and Turkey) • Pan-Asia high-speed rail (From Kunming of Yunnan to Singapore via Laos, Vietnam, Cambodia and Malaysia; from Kunming of Yunnan to Thailand)
Infrastructure	• D Line of China-Central Asia natural gas pipeline • Railway upgrade in India • Port and Port industrial park in Sri Lanka
Overland cross-border oil and gas pipeline	• Line 3, Line 4 and Line 5 of West-to-East natural gas transmission project • Line D of China-Central Asia natural gas pipeline • East Line and West Line of China-Russia natural gas pipeline
Communications & electricity	• China–Myanmar, China–Tajikistan, China–Pakistan cross-border communications line • Submarine communications cable projects of Southeastern Asia • Electricity pipeline of Southwestern China, China-Russia electricity pipeline (construction or upgrade)

meet previously-established high standards; maintain closer economic ties; deepen political trust; and enhance cultural exchange.

Against this background, a financial system constituted by financial institutions such as the BRICS Development Bank, the Asian Infrastructure Investment Bank, and the Silk Road Fund has been established. The original intent of setting up the BRICS Development Bank was to build a common financial security network and capital pool, with which, BRICS countries would be able to solve the problem of a currency mismatch and to regulate the international balance of payments. The Asian Infrastructure Investment Bank was established in order to solve the problem of a maturity mismatch in this region, to provide long-term funding support for infrastructure construction, and to invite member states to share the USD800 bn annual infrastructure investment demand in Asia. The Silk Road Fund will finance "the Belt and the Road" countries in terms of high-speed rail construction and resource exploration. The goal of arranging these financial facilities is to encourage the application of local savings in local investment and to correct the savings/investment structure mismatch. As a result of having rectified the currency mismatch, the maturity mismatch, and the structural mismatch, the process of localizing foreign currencies accelerated and the existing financial cooperation within this region grew deeper and more interlinked. In the process of localizing foreign currencies, the RMB has recently been the preferred choice. It not only indicates the need to further internationalize the RMB, but also shows that the RMB has both a stable mechanism for generating a deficit under the arrangement of "the Belt and the Road" and a stable outflow under the capital account.

History has shown that the RMB's outflow mechanism under the capital account —as it takes place against the background of "the Belt and the Road"—is similar to the US dollar's outflow mechanism in the European Recovery Program (the Marshall Plan) after the end of WWII. Because of their perceived similarity, the RMB's outflow mechanism has been dubbed "the Marshall Plan of China." "The Belt and the Road" is different from "the Marshall Plan," however, at least in terms of intention and arrangement. "The Marshall Plan" was expressly political, with the United States aiming to support the European recovery process following WWII in order to prevent the spread of communism—a move that ultimately ended up triggering the Cold War. For its part, however, "the Belt and the Road" adopts the trade concept established over 2000 years ago by the Silk Road, with the express intent of carrying on the mutual exchange of needed goods and fostering peace through consultation, negotiation, compromise, seeking commonality in difference, and expanding existing common ground. The ultimate goal is to foster a mutually-beneficial community through common development and production.

From the above, the unique feature of "the Belt and the Road" are apparent, especially insofar as they differ from the Marshall Plan. Some jokingly have claimed that "under this mechanism, using money is encouraged; without money, goods and future revenue are also available in exchange." This principle is fully reflected in China Railway's external cooperation. For example, in 2012, China granted a USD7 bn loan to Laos for use in constructing a China-Laos railway to Vientiane. As for Thailand, this country exchanged rice for a railway. Thailand exported rice to China for the purpose of repaying the loan. In Central Asia, China spent RMB20 mn on technical verification of the China-Kyrgyzstan-Uzbekistan Railway. Obviously, the concept of "do unto others as you would have them do unto you" is a guiding factor in what makes the development of "the Belt and the Road" sustainable while fostering a stable mechanism for the RMB to generate a deficit.

7.3 Developing China's Financial System to Target the Global Economy—The RMB Joins the SDR

On November 30, 2015, the IMF officially announced that the RMB would join the SDR basket and would become the 5th currency in use, along with the pound sterling, the euro, the Japanese yen, and the US dollar.

To deal with the US dollar crisis, the SDR was created in the 1960s and 70s for the purpose of regulating the international balance of payments. The SDR organically became each country's official reserve. After the RMB joined the SDR, this indicated that the status of the RMB as a reserve currency had been firmly consolidated. In addition, the weight of the RMB in the SDR basket is 10.92%, while the weight of the other four currencies has decreased: the weight of the US dollar fell from 41.9 to 41.73%; the weight of the euro decreased from 37.4 to 30.93%; the weight of the Japanese yen dropped from 9.4 to 8.33%; and the weight of the pound sterling fell from 11.3 to 8.09%. Even though the actual weight of the RMB is still far from the estimated 14–16%, the weight of the RMB has surpassed the Japanese yen and that of the pound sterling. As a result, the RMB has become the third-largest currency in the SDR basket, which signifies the rising significance of the RMB as a reserve currency.

In the short run, the mere fact of a sovereign currency's joining the SDR basket is neither essential nor sufficient as a condition of becoming a reserve currency. The Australian dollar and the Canadian dollar have not joined the SDR basket, but their shares in terms of international reserves are still far higher than the share of the RMB. Due to the RMB's joining the SDR basket, the share of the RMB in each country's official reserves will go up, but this does not necessarily indicate that the RMB will immediately have the same share in international reserves. Currently, the SDR accounts for 2.5% of the global official reserve assets. Based on the assumption that the weight of the RMB in the SDR basket is 10.92%, it can be calculated that around USD30 bn worth of global official reserve assets will be directly allocated to the RMB.

In the long run, however, the RMB's entry into the SDR basket will be of great significance, because the RMB is the first newly-added sovereign currency of a developing country meeting the criteria first established by the Bretton Woods system in1976. On the one hand, the RMB meets the criteria of the Bretton Woods system, which indicates that China has accepted the existing international monetary system and its corresponding rules. On the other hand, China's role here is as a developing country. China is not content with the current situation in which the system is dominated by developed countries, particularly the unfair rules governing developing countries. China currently advocates for systemic reformation and seeks economic international development (with the purpose of making the international monetary system more aligned with the current global economic trends), to make the system more sustainable, and to develop the system to a point at which it can connect all countries' finances and economies.

Now that the RMB has joined the SDR basket, China must accelerate its proposed development of a financial system targeting the world at large. The RMB's successful entry into the SDR basket indicates that the international financial system has officially recognized China's economic and financial reform over the past 30 years. This recognition also spurs China to continue its own development, however, due to the fact that the qualifications for inclusion as an SDR require currencies to follow the market-oriented principle. If any currency affects the stability of the SDR, this currency will be weeded out. As such, China will insist on reforming the economic and financial system with an eye towards the RMB's internationalization.

As the RMB joins the SDR basket, China will be further encouraged to engage in the global system of economy, trade, investment, and finance and, what's more, to initiate a new round of reform and opening-up, especially in regards to the liberalization of the financial system and the opening of the RMB under the capital account. China has also been encouraged to positively engage in improving the structure and mechanism of global governance. According to the Chinese government's 13th Five-Year Plan, spurred by the RMB's internationalization, the opening-up of China's financial system will proceed over the next five years. Initially, the internal opening-up of the financial industry is likely to accelerate. Access to the banking market, the insurance market, the securities market, and the annuity market will be relaxed, and the capital market will open both internally and externally. The existing restrictions on the quota of domestic and overseas investment will gradually be cancelled out. Secondly, the liberalization of the exchange rate and that of the interest rate will proceed apace, and the foreign exchange market will attract a greater number of participants and feature more products. The RMB's two-way volatility will become more apparent, and the process of liberalizing the interest rate will, itself, run smoothly and without hiccups. Alternative deposit or loan products will develop rapidly, and the PBOC's system for regulating interest rate policies will be established over a period of several years. Third, the opening and convertibility of the RMB under the capital account will proceed as previously scheduled. Negative lists will be adopted in foreign exchange management and restrictions will be loosened on overseas institutions issuing RMB-denominated bonds on the domestic market. Furthermore, the convertibility of the RMB under the capital account for individuals will be enhanced. As a result, "the Belt and the Road" will continue to be developed and existing and future cooperation with international financial institutions promises to grow in strength. Fourth, if China takes the RMB's entry into the SDR basket as the opportunity it is, the RMB's internationalization process will rapidly accelerate and China will be able to more actively engage in the global economic and financial governance system. Both the bilateral and multilateral monetary and financial systems of cooperation will be reinforced. By establishing different categories of free trade zones and providing services for "upgrading the trade, investment, and industrial chains," China will evolve from a position of consolidating the RMB's status as a currency for valuation and settlement to one for transactions and international reserves.

In an effort to promote reform and liberalization, China's attitude towards the global market has been one marked by recent openness. The RMB's entry into the SDR basket will continue to help stabilize the international financial market's expectations for the RMB; enhance its competitiveness; inject more RMB-denominated capital into the global stock market, the bond index market, and central banks' reserve assets; and will expand the global market's demand for RMB-denominated assets. This, in turn, will stimulate the process of internationalizing the RMB, enhance the international market's confidence in it, and promote the status of the RMB within the extant international monetary system.

At present, the average share of the RMB in each country's official reserve assets ranks No. 7 (1%), the share of the Canadian dollar ranks No. 6 (2%), and that of the Australian dollar ranks No. 5 (2.3%). If the share of the RMB were to catch up with that of the Canadian dollar, a supply of RMB570 bn in assets would be available. If the share of the RMB should catch up with that of the Australian dollar, this figure would represent a supply of RMB670 bn in assets. We predict that, in the next five years, as the supply-side reform requested by China's 13th Five-Year Plan is put into action, the ratio of cross-border payment in RMB to that using foreign currencies will increase from around 1% in 2015 to 5–7% in 2020. In other words, in the next five years, we predict a supply of USD50 bn–100 bn (RMB300 bn–700 bn) in RMB-denominated assets. Concurrently, the RMB is likely to play a larger role in the international market, and China's economy can make a greater contribution to the global economy overall.

As per the requirements of the IMF, the RMB will be officially included into the SDR basket in October 2016. At that time, the RMB will become one of the most important currencies used for calculating the value of the SDR basket as a whole, and the volatility of China's exchange rate and interest rate will begin to affect the SDR itself. Since the SDR is a unit of accounting among the IMF members, the SDR will, of course, require that the volatility of the RMB and that of other currencies in the basket should remain unaffected by domestic governmental intervention.

Therefore, the reform on the RMB's interest rate and exchange rate will be China' stop priority in the coming years. The process of establishing an in-depth financial market targeting the whole world and represented by fixed-income products should accelerate. It will be a challenging task for China to improve the existing financial system.

From the perspective of the interest rate, after the RMB is included into the SDR basket, the requirement is for the RMB's interest rate to be liberalized. This also signifies that the ability of the government to regulate the interest rate is less applicable. Currently in China, even though regulations on the upper and lower limits of the deposit and loan interest rates have been completely invalidated, the mechanism for generating a curve of the liberalized interest rate will be further improved, and, as a result the interest rate will gradually draw close to what can be observed at the freely-floating level. The potential risks of liberalizing the interest rate haven't been totally analyzed, however, for the significant reason that, under an easy monetary environment, commercial banks and other financial institutions have plenty of money. Neither the deposit interest rate of commercial banks nor the lending interest rate in the market has, up until this point, faced any obvious upward pressure. If the inflationary pressure increases in the future, however, tightening the existing monetary policies might trigger commercial banks and other major financial institutions to raise their interest rates for the purpose of competing for funds. Typically, since the risks posed to small commercial banks are higher than those of big banks, their deposit interest rates have the potential to significantly increase. As a result, commercial banks might face higher debts and greater operating difficulties. We cannot exclude the possibility that some small commercial banks may potentially face critical operating risks.

From the perspective of the exchange rate, the RMB's entry into the SDR basket might force the reformation of the path towards liberalization to accelerate. Yet the question as to whether the RMB's exchange rate can be considered close to the level of equilibrium has not yet been answered. This is, in fact, a difficult point to objectively judge. If the RMB would like to maintain its competitiveness in the SDR basket, then any reform regarding the RMB's exchange rate market should be further promoted. This would result in further uncertainties about the RMB's exchange rate, however. The volatility triggered by the reform of the RMB's exchange rate in August 2015 indicates that China should pay greater attention to the exchange rate risks caused by the RMB's inclusion into the SDR basket.

In terms of the stability of the financial system, the RMB's inclusion into the SDR basket might trigger an increased scale of cross-border capital flow, and will further increase the systematic risks undertaken via the stock market, the real estate market, and other channels. The stock market volatility that has existed since June 2015 and the exchange rate market volatility that has taken place since August 2015 are early warning signs, indicating that China's ability to prevent financial risks must be shored up. If the domestic or overseas environment undergoes acute changes, the cross-border flow of the capital in the stock market or real estate market might accelerate, with a correspondingly negative impact on the financial market and the macro economy. Under the circumstances that China continues to utilize a separate system of oversights, the potential systematic risks triggered by the large scale of cross-border capital flow cannot be overstated.

Perhaps more importantly, according to theoretical research and practices, as the process of internationalizing a sovereign currency proceeds, a sovereign country's status within the global community will, on the one hand, rise in terms of economic scale, cross-border trade, and the financial system; on the other hand, however, the process is unsustainable without the stability of the macro economy, the maturity and openness of the financial market, cross-border trade, the convertibility of the domestic currency, and some basic guarantees, such as "the lender of last resort," deposit insurance, and the protection of investors. Investors, for their part, hold several key requirements when evaluating an international currency: the currency must have a great deal of liquidity (traded freely with low costs), free convertibility (convertible under most trading programs), and security (low credit risks). These requirements hold that the country's financial market must be mature to a certain degree, and that the currency should be convertible under the capital account. In addition, the monetary policies and the exchange rate system should be clear, transparent, and above all, legal.

Despite the huge challenges it faces, China knows that its domestic economy is an organic component of the world economy as a whole. Over the past 30 years, the development of China's domestic economy has benefited greatly from the integration of China's economy into the world. China has duties and obligations to make contribution to the sustainable development of the global economy. Especially now, during the gloom of the global financial crisis, China should face the world with an open attitude. It was for this reason, specifically, that the RMB chose to join the SDR basket during tough times, rather than prosperous ones. Actually, it has been just seven years since July 2, 2009, when the RMB was officially applied to be considered in the valuation and settlement of cross-border trade. The RMB's internationalization has achieved amazing progress in that time. Currently, over one fifth of all trade with China is valued and settled in RMB, and the RMB has become the second-largest currency for trade finance, second only to the US dollar. China has signed bilateral currency swap agreements with over 32 central banks, totaling RMB3.3 tn. The RMB-denominated domestic assets held by foreign residents have reached RMB4.4 tn. The scale of the assets in the offshore market has drawn close to RMB2 tn. The RMB is gradually becoming the reserve currency for assets held by other countries. In October 2015, 38 countries reported that their international reserves included the RMB. Accordingly, the trading of RMB-denominated financial assets has become increasingly active. Excluding offshore RMB-denominated loans, the RMB-denominated bonds issued on the international market have exceeded USD500 bn (over RMB3 tn). In the offshore market, there have been RMB-denominated stocks, ETFs, and other derivatives. Until now, 14 offshore RMB markets have been recognized by bilateral governments. In addition to the traditional Asian markets like Hong Kong and Singapore, London has become the second-largest offshore market behind Hong Kong. Following in London's steps, Frankfurt and Paris are also prospering in their use of the RMB. In the past seven years, the RMB has achieved great progress. But the RMB is a new sovereign currency in the international monetary system, and China —as the largest developing country in the world—is now in the process of transformation. All these aspects ensure that the path towards the RMB's internationalization will not be smooth. Therefore, it will be necessary to look into the future of internationalizing the RMB.

Chapter 8
The Prospect of Internationalizing the RMB

8.1 The Sustainable Development of China's Economy Is the Foundation for Internationalizing the RMB

The rapid growth of China's economy since its reform and opening-up is, to put it bluntly, a miracle. Across Chinese history, the last thirty years have been the period with the fastest economic development; globally, China has rapidly outpaced other countries in terms of the economy. China's GDP in 1990 was USD404.5 bn, while the GDP in 2014 was 25.66 times that of1990. This means that the yearly growth has been equal to China's GDP in 1990. Similarly, in 2014, Guangdong province's GDP exceeded USD1.1 tn alone. This number is equivalent to the whole country's GDP in 2000.

China's GDP ranked No. 10 in 1990, trailing after Brazil. In 2006, the GDP of China surpassed that of the UK, and China became the fourth-largest economy in the world; in 2007, the rank of China was higher than even that of Germany, and China became the world's third-largest economy; in 2009, China surpassed Japan, and thus became the world's second-largest economy. China's economic performance is continually and rapidly progressing. The GDP of China surpassed that of the UK in 2006 and reached twice that of the UK in 2010 (Note that the UK ranked No. 5 in the world at that time and China took only four years to reach this achievement). In 2011, China's GDP was twice that of Germany (Note that Germany ranked No. 4 in the world at that time and China took only four years to reach this achievement, as well). In 2014, China's GDP was twice that of Japan (Note that Japan ranked No. 3 in the world and China took five years to reach this achievement). In 1990, China held1.78% of the world's GDP. In 2014, this ratio increased to 13.4%. Behind the United States, China has become the second-largest economy in the world, with a GDP surpassing USD10 tn.

China's economic miracle after the reform and opening-up serves as the primary foundation for internationalizing the RMB. On November 30, 2015, the IMF agreed to include the RMB into the existing SDR basket, marking the fact that China's

© Social Sciences Academic Press and Springer Nature Singapore Pte Ltd. 2018
Y. Cao, *Strategies for Internationalizing the Renminbi*, Research Series on the Chinese Dream and China's Development Path,
https://doi.org/10.1007/978-981-13-0800-0_8

economic achievements over the past 30 years since the reform and opening-up have been internationally recognized, and China's status in international economy, trade, investment, and finance had been also been duly recognized. Therefore, the sustainable development of China's economy is another foundation upon which the internationalization of the RMB moves forward.

In recent years, despite the fact that China's economy still has an average growth rate of 7–8%, it has already said goodbye to the rapid progress marked by double-digit growth. In the future, it seems that China's economy is likely to face extensive negative pressure. People have focused on whether China's economy will be able to maintain its previously-sustainable development and whether the economic downturn will result in a "hard landing." As for the RMB's internationalization, its very foundation and future prospects are threatened.

Seen in terms of historical epochs, China's economy has entered into a new stage. The factors that once facilitated the rapid growth of China's economy in the past have changed radically in the following four aspects:

First, similar to other Asian economies, since the 1990s, China has embarked on the road towards an export-oriented economy. Exports boosted investment, which, in turn, turned around and promoted further exports. As a result, the scale of China's imports and exports reached around 70% of the GDP and, at one time, the current account surplus accounted for 7.2% of the total GDP. After the 2008 financial crisis, however, the global economy remained weak, causing total demand to remain low. At the same time, the growth rate of China's exports kept falling, from 30% in 2010 to negative growth in 2015. As for the economic development trend in the future, the growth of the global economy promises to continue to be slow, and the low level of inflation is apt to be the norm. This signifies that China's export-oriented economy has come to an end, and the existing excess production capacity will continue for the foreseeable future.

Second, China's economic growth model one that is typical of Asian economies. Since the rural sector possesses a surplus of labor, the marginal labor productivity will be close to zero. Attracted by the high salaries offered by the industrial sector, the surplus labor forces of the rural sector typically start to flow into the industrial sector. As a result, China will embark on a road towards industrialization. Furthermore, since the rural sector has such a significant source of surplus labor—with the attendant fierce competition and low level wage maintenance—these low-cost labor forces create a competitive advantage for the manufacturing industry. For this reason, China has grown to be the "world's factory." As the process of industrialization continues and the labor forces evolve, the surplus supply of labor is no longer abundant. Statistics show that nearly 50% of able-bodied laborers (i.e. those younger than 45 years old) have been employed by non-rural working units. For this reason, the minimum wage level keeps rising with an average growth rate of over 100%. As a result, the competitive advantage of China's low-cost manufacturing industry is no longer as evident as it once was.

Third, for a long time, China's rapid economic growth was based on the rapid growth of investment. According to statistics, over the past 20 years, investment's average annual growth in China has been as high as 20% at various points in time.

Now, however, China is becoming an aging society, and as a result, the country's demographic dividends are beginning to disappear. For this reason, the savings ratio of society as a whole has begun to decline. Since savings are the source of investment, the falling savings ratio signifies that the investment-driven economic growth is unsustainable. In fact, since 2014, the growth rate of investment in China has dropped to around 10%. It is projected that growth will drop to single digits very soon.

Fourth, in the past, China's economic growth has depended on consuming resources—a model that is not exactly environmentally friendly. As the Earth's natural resources (earth, minerals, energies, etc.) decrease daily and as the environmental pollution becomes a more serious issue, an economic growth model based on reckless consumption has almost come to an end. At the 2015 Climate Conference in Paris, the Chinese government pledged to adopt the toughest environmental protection measures possible with the purpose of greatly reducing carbon emissions after they peak in 2030. To fulfill this commitment, China has to close certain companies to remove their capacity for pollution.

We can conclude from the above that the export-oriented economic growth model is not sustainable. The low-level manufacturing industry has been challenged. What's more, this unsustainable investment-driven economic growth and a growth based on the consumption of resources have evolved. The factors which once facilitated China's economic growth have experienced radical changes. As a result, the potential growth rate of China's economy will drop. Naturally, people will worry that China's economic growth is not sustainable and might, in the future, face the aforementioned "hard landing."

China's history of economic development, however, shows that China is propelled by the reasons given to initiate its transformation: total demand in the past depended purely on the overseas market, but now it depends on both the domestic market and the overseas market, with a focus on expanding domestic demand. The key to expanding domestic demand is to expand residents' consumption, and the method for achieving this is to increase residents' income. In the aspect of structural adjustment, past growth mainly depended on industrial growth. Now, however, it has come to depend on the primary, secondary, and tertiary industries, with a particular focus on developing the service industry. This aim was proposed by the Chinese government in ots12th Five-Year Plan (2010–2015), and compulsory measures have been adopted to press ahead with this economic transformation. The measures included are: when allocating labor and capital, wages must be aligned with labor productivity; increase the proportion of residents' income to the national income overall so as to align residents' income to GDP; and more. With the support of this policy, in the past five years, China's economic structural adjustment has already achieved some initial success and the economic growth model has been preliminarily transformed.

In terms of the measures discussed above, the growth of Chinese residents' income in the past seven years is now almost aligned with the growth of overall GDP. The growth of rural residents' income in China, however, has grown above 10% yearly, exceeding the growth of GDP. If, in the next five years, the growth of

Chinese residents' income is to fully align with the growth of GDP, it must meet or exceed over 6.5% yearly. From 2010 to 2020, both the GDP of China and Chinese residents' income will double. China is a large country with a population of 1.3bn, or more than a sixth of the total global population. If residents' income can be doubled within ten years, China will become the world's largest market. In fact, since residents' income grows quickly, consumption has replaced investment and exports to become the main engine of China's economic growth. Over the past seven years, the share of consumption to GDP has jumped from 35 to 50%. As the income of more than 900mn rural residents rapidly increases, the rural market will significantly boost consumption. China once had excess production capability in heavy industry, but in the industry of consumer goods (TV sets, refrigerators, washing machines, etc.), China has never encountered poor sales.

Additionally, China's service industry has exceeded manufacturing to become the pillar of the national economy. In 2013, the proportion of the service industry to GDP reached 46%, exceeding that of the manufacturing industry for the first time. In 2015, the proportion of the service industry to GDP surpassed 50%. If such a level of growth continues, we predict that, by 2020, the growth of the service industry will not only be reflected in the growth of restaurants and hotels, but also in the growth of high-end servers. In addition, the growth of the service industry will also be reflected in the rapid growth of health care, education, finances, the internet, and the aged care industry. Between 2013 and 2015, these industries have averaged an annual double-digit increase, with the average annual growth of the health care industry rising as high as 30%.

Third, during the 11th Five-Year Plan (2005–2010), the Chinese government stated its expectations that the proportion of research expenses to GDP would reach 2%; however, this target had yet to be reached when the period came to an end. This figure reached 2% for the first time in 2012 and increased to 2.2% in 2015. In the past five years, China's technical input has continued to increase, bringing up the productivity of China's manufacturing industry in the process. This is especially true for China's auto industry. The launch of new auto types is in line with the progress taking place in the rest of the world; however, Chinese auto prices are decreasing—during the period from 2013 to 2015, 1/5 of all industrial robots in the world were sold in China. This indicates that China's manufacturing industry is to one based on the quality of technological progress, which itself is put in the service of economic growth.

Fourth, China has experienced significant and detrimental regional differences in the past. The eastern coastal region is economically developed, while the western region is generally regarded as underdeveloped. In the past five years, the economic growth of the western region has progressed much faster than the national average, including that of the eastern region. In addition, technical improvement has contributed significantly to this growth. At present, excluding those in Shenzhen and in Beijing, most Chinese high-tech enterprises are based in Chengdu. What's more, China's most advanced textile technology was born in its westernmost region, Xinjiang. The rapid economic growth of the western region is indication of the opening of China's economy towards the West and serves as an economic foundation for "the Belt and the Road" policy.

As such, some vibrant and new economic elements can be seen to be emerging in China. The trend has been to integrate new technologies with traditional industries. Terms such as "internet plus," "cloud computing," and "functional innovation" are often bandied about these days. While the new economic elements for growth are currently relatively week, they will soon grow in scope and strength. As these elements mature, China' per capita GDP will increase. For instance, China's per capita GDP exceeded USD800 bn in 2015. If the growth rate of China's GDP for the next five years is over 5%, China's per capita GDP will reach USD12,300 in 2020 and China will become what is considered a "high-income" country.

Following this economic transformation, China's domestic economic growth has become sustainable and its domestic demand continues to expand. China has now become the world's largest market, which is not only reflected in the country's robust import of energies and raw materials, but is also reflected in the import of manufactured products, particularly the import of consumer goods and service goods. According to statistics, China was the world's largest importer in 2013. During this year, China's total volume of goods, both imported and exported, ranked No. 1 in the world. In 2014, the total import and export volume of China exceeded USD43 tn, which was 54 times that in 1990 and accounted for 11.19% of the world's total; in 2014, the proportion of the current account surplus to GDP was lower than 2%. In 2015, 120mn outbound Chinese citizens contributed a total consumption of USD215 bn to the overseas market. It is worth noting that China, with its strong domestic demand, is now contributing to rebalancing the world economy.

Since July 2009, the RMB has been officially applied in cross-border trade settlement. As the process of rebalancing the global economy proceeds rapidly, the process of the RMB's internationalization has been smooth beyond all expectation. The ever-expanding application of the RMB on the overseas market not only challenges China's financial system and accelerates the country's further reform and opening-up, but also raises a new question about whether the RMB's internationalization will cultivate China's "exorbitant privilege." Under circumstances such as the ones seen in the RMB's internationalization, the currency issuer possesses an asymmetrical advantage over foreign countries. If this "exorbitant privilege" is abused, the resultant disequilibrium in the global political pattern will form the so-called "China Threat."

The concept of "exorbitant privilege" refers to the advantage a currency issuer has over other countries based on its "seigniorage" revenue. Such an asymmetrical advantage results in privilege. This concept derives from international politics, with the earliest known use of the term being by former French president Valéry Giscard d'Estaing. As France's Minister of Finance, he once critically noted that the United States had "exorbitant privilege" and that the US dollar was highly internationalized. He did not, however, explain what the privilege in question was, only implying that such a currency would have huge advantages once it was internationalized. In 2015, Robert McCauley of the Bank for International Settlements researched the issue, reaching the conclusion that the previously-identified "profits" or "advantages" of such an arrangement really existed, but were quite small. He analyzed five of the six potential profits that could have been considered a "privilege" in the time of Giscard d'Estaing (the temporal fixity is important here, in that the United States once revealed that the yield rate of its overseas investment had exceeded the current account surplus. At the time when Giscard d'Estaing criticized the privilege owned by the United States, however, this phenomenon had already disappeared forever). According to McCauley's research, any resultant privilege is only a drop in the bucket of overall profit, and is not closely connected to any inherent international advantage. Some advantages, for example, were and are not directly derived from the US dollar's international status. In other words, this "privilege" has almost been shared by many countries, and fears about the contemporary currency issuer enjoying special profit or privilege are largely unfounded.

We cannot deny the fact that the first potential privilege resulting from such a situation is that the United States can use its own currency to supplement its current account deficit. Many other countries can also do so, however, like Australia, despite of the fact that the international application of the Australian dollar is not as widely utilized as the US dollar. The second potential privilege is that the United States can obtain interest-free loans from countries holding the US dollar. This is inarguable. Because the interest rate has, in recent years, been extremely low, however, even if the United States was to do so, it would not save much. In addition, Eurozone countries can also enjoy this privilege. Since the euro is highly valued, the euro can be widely applied in non-Eurozone countries, including those of the European Union. The third potential asymmetrical profit is that the United States Department of Treasury can raise funds at a low cost. This privilege can be traced back to the T-bond market of the United States with its high liquidity, rather than from the international status of the US dollar. The fourth potential unfair profit is that the interest paid by the United States for external debts is lower than the interest earned from external assets. This is also true. But this profit has been fostered as a result of US investors' portfolio selection and investment, however, rather than the international status of the US dollar. US investors are inclined to shoulder high risks to invest in products with high yield rates. The fifth potential privilege is that US financial institutions can reap the benefits from US dollar-denominated valuation when widely applying the US dollar. This benefit may exist, but its payoff is negligible. In addition to US financial institutions, London and other markets that apply the US dollar in trading can also share this particular profit.

Another focus is the asymmetric advantage related to this concept of "exorbitant privilege." Some believe that if a country's sovereign currency is not one of the primary, dominant international currencies, the economic management capability of this country is likely to be weaker when compared to those countries with more dominant international currencies. This viewpoint is very popular among emerging markets like China, because these countries are often strongly affected by the monetary policies issued by the US Federal Reserve. The monetary policies issued by the US Federal Reserve, however—which are often based on the macro-economic performance of the United States—can't be counted on to take care of other countries. This refers to the so-called "spillover effect." Other countries' monetary authorities can only passively respond to changes, while the US Federal Reserve is always the controlling party manipulating the changes themselves. Such an effect really exists. But this asymmetry is not completely due to the international status of the US dollar. Instead, it is mainly due to the huge economic scale of the United States (which makes up 1/4 of the world's total) and the country's huge financial market (which represents more than 1/2 of the world's securities market).

Even if the international reserves held by each government are all SDRs, the US dollar and the euro will be isolated and lumped into one "alternative account." Since the United States has a huge financial market and its financial products possess adequate liquidity, many transactions occur in the United States. The issue is that the yield rate of the SDR is slightly lower than that of the US dollar or the euro, because the low interest rate of the Japanese yen (one of the components of the SDR) drives down the yield rate of the SDR as a whole. Regardless of whether the international reserve currency only consists of the SDR or consists of both the US dollar and other currencies, the direction of flow and the scale of international hot money will be similar. The impacts of the U.S. monetary policies on emerging economies are basically the same.

Third, the US dollar is currently the dominant international currency, accounting for 63% of each country's foreign exchange reserves. The exorbitant privilege enjoyed by the United States as a currency issuer is far from any expectation currently held about the future of the RMB, even after its internationalization (note that the RMB currently only accounts for around 1% of each country's foreign exchange reserves). In fact, even if the RMB accounts for 10.92% of the SDR as a whole, it will not exactly be influential. While many people in China believe that applying the RMB in offshore trade and investment is beneficial because it reduces Chinese residents' foreign exchange risks, research shows that these perceived foreign exchange risks are unaffected. Instead, the risks are merely transferred. Chinese residents have, in fact, transferred the risks to their foreign trading partners, while, for their part, the foreign trading partners in question must consider the foreign exchange risks when pricing products—a consideration effected largely by increasing the prices when exporting goods to this country or lowering the prices when importing goods from this country. Chinese residents have indirectly borne the costs of transferring the exchange rate risks, namely, lowering the export prices and increasing the import prices. In this sense, the exchange rate risks, as premiums of exporting and importing products, have been hedged entirely, resulting in a neutral outcome.

While it is believed by some that the exorbitant privileges stemming from the RMB's internationalization will bring many profits, this line of reasoning is ultimately misguided and unsustainable. In this sense, what is the significance of internationalizing the RMB? What does it stand for? We believe that the target is to develop a world economy that shares a common financial and cultural destiny.

As previously mentioned, China's is now the second-largest economy and the largest trading entity in the world. The economy is still reporting sustainable growth and the average income continues to increase. At the same time, China's dependence on the world grows deeper and more intertwined. For instance, China is now the largest importer of oil. In 2015, 62% oil consumed in China was imported. China depended highly on having access to a stable and sustainable supply of oil from the international market. We predict that in the next five years, China's import volume will exceed USD10 tn. For China, a world economy with stable growth, an open international trade and investment system, and a peaceful and orderly international environment are of the utmost importance.

8.2 To Develop a Global Economic Community with a Shared Destiny Is to Meet the Requirements for Internationalizing the RMB

The 2007 international financial crisis reflected many problems inherent in the world economy, including aspects of the economic development model, global economic structure, and financial structure. This international financial crisis resulted from ongoing internal conflict within the international division system. What's more, during this period, the systematic risks caused by the global economic disequilibrium were revealed. The growth of the world economy slowed at the same time that the pattern of global demand changed. The world economy is now undergoing the arduous process of rebalancing.

This problem of global economic disequilibrium is reflected in two aspects. The first aspect is the trade surplus (against the United States) and the rapidly-accumulating foreign exchange reserves of emerging Asian countries—as represented by China—and the petroleum exporting countries of the Middle East. The economic imbalance between East Asia (represented by China) and the United States, in fact, constitutes the core of the global economic disequilibrium, while the trade surplus over the past decade of the petroleum exporting countries benefits mainly from rising oil prices and the global demand for energies. The second aspect is the growing trade and fiscal deficit, the huge current account deficit, and rapidly rising net indebtedness. In recent years, the net debt ratio of the United States has remained steady at a high level. In order to fight against the shock from international capital and to maintain the security and value of the foreign exchange reserve assets, enormous amounts of capital from Asian countries has flowed back to the United States (the most developed financial market in the world) to purchase the T-bond issued by the United States, thus maintaining the balance of payments equilibrium within the United States. The disequilibrium of the world economy undergoing "double cycles" is superficially reflected in trade. In fact, this indicates the nature of disequilibrium between savings and investment, and the disequilibrium between savings and consumption.

In recent years, in terms of the international financial crisis, the world economy has gradually begun to recover thanks to support from each country's government and facilitated by their assistance policies. Since the underlying problem leading to the disequilibrium of the global economy in the first place remains intact, however, the economic recovery of many countries will depend on additional financial stimulus, and, even so, growth in the real economy is unlikely to be significant. In the short run, the effects brought about by these stimuli will be limited. In the long run, too, unintended side effects will emerge. The global economy has entered into an era of low growth, low inflation, and low interest rates. The risk of reaching the bottom a second time still exists.

Since the United States, Europe and Japan have high debt ratios and are experiencing economic downturns, abundant demand is unlikely in the near future. The excess capacity of the emerging economies will not be absorbed in the short run, which would facilitate the future prosperity of the world economy. Over the next few years, the world economy will experience slow economic growth and frequent fluctuations. During this period, decentralized global demand will be the key to maintaining a balance between the global demand structure and economic development. China and other emerging economies will be the most important consumers of global products. While they depend on sustainable and rapid economic growth, increasing per capital income, and a huge population base, emerging economies—particularly China's potential market—will largely support the trade of global goods and services in the future, thus generating increased global demand for internationalizing the RMB. The process of the RMB's internationalization stems from trade valuation and settlement and, this sense, the RMB's internationalization is an important tool for rebalancing the world economy.

Nevertheless, considering the sagging economy, financial turbulence, and the high geopolitical risk involved, the outlook for future peaceful development remains gloomy. The current financial situation indicates that, as a result of the system of governance established after WWII and associated polito-economic restrictions, adequately addressing economic challenges has been and will continue to be a point of difficulty globally. The world needs to be reformed. Particularly in the area of international finance, the world needs to reform the international monetary system.

During the 2007 global financial crisis, the fundamental defects of the US dollar-centric international monetary system were collectively exposed. Under the current monetary system, as the deficits of the United States continue to increase and as the disequilibrium of the world economy becomes graver, it will be increasingly difficult to maintain the stability of the currency value of the US dollar. Therefore, the US dollar, as a major currency for valuation and settlement in international finance and trade, cannot actually overcome the "Triffin Dilemma." The following inner contradictions and limitations of the international monetary system have been fully revealed as a result.

First, the US dollar's flooding leads to frequent outbreaks of globally-extensive financial crisis. One of the important reasons for this is that the macro-economic policies of the United States lack institutional restraints. In recent years, for example, for the purpose of promoting domestic economic development, the Federal Reserve of the United States has adopted easy money policies with low interest rates. Under such policies, a significant amount of US dollars flooded the global marketplace in the form of a current account deficit. The expanding issuance of the US dollar boosted the US economy and brought worldwide excess liquidity and inflation. The asset bubble expanded such that the virtual economy was, in a very real sense, separate from the real economy. As a result, the real estate bubble burst and triggered the subsequent global financial crisis.

Second, the Bretton Woods system has defects in terms of policy design. The major currency for adjusting the international balance of payments is the US dollar, while adjustments are often made to emerging economies. The adjustment method is often the tightening of the fiscal policy and the monetary policy, which causes economic downturn and stagnation. It is not helpful for maintaining economic stability. Before the global financial crisis, the liquidity of the US dollar was sufficient. Even though the above adjustment was not ideal, it was still effective at that time. At this time, however, the United States—the originator of the global financial crisis—has gone wrong. Due to the liquidity shortage of the US dollar, the IMF does not have adequate adjustment methods or capabilities. Given this governance vacuum, the G20 Summit and other new governance mechanisms have been established, reflecting the fact that the original international monetary system, after a long period of development, has and will gradually deviate from its function of correcting and regulating market failures. To a large extent, such failures deepen the global economic disequilibrium and disorder and intensify the systematic risk inherent in the global financial system.

In the wake of the global financial crisis, all countries have fully recognized the significance and necessity of reforming the existing international monetary system. To reform the current international monetary system and to develop material constraints for the US dollar, however, going back to the gold standard or gold exchange standard will be useless. A more practical method is to diversify the available international currencies and to foster competition among international currencies already in use. Compared to the gold standard or a single world currency, a diversified international monetary system is a sub-optimal but practical arrangement. As a result, an important consensus has been reached by all countries: the world community would be best served by reducing global dependence on the US dollar and establishing an equal, fair, and mutually-beneficial international monetary system. Many countries and economists have called on the world community to actively promote the internationalization of sovereign currencies already in circulation and for the diversification of existing reserve currencies for the purpose of reducing global dependence on the US dollar, enhancing the status and function of other currencies, and establishing an international monetary system dominated by several key currencies. Because China has a sound economy and plays an increasingly important role in rebalancing the world economy, the RMB is increasingly regarded as a currency which can serve as a restraint for the US dollar and can make contribution to the stability of the international monetary system in the ongoing call to diversify international currencies. In the process of meeting the needs for internationalizing the RMB, since China has already experienced positive economic development for a significant period of time and has played an increasingly important role in rebalancing the global economy, the RMB is regarded as a currency which might have the ability to counterbalance the US dollar and to enhance the stability of the international monetary system. The internationalized RMB is no longer a valuation instrument, a means of circulation, ora payment instrument for a certain country or a certain region only; instead, it is poised to become an important method for improving global governance.

Even though more than eight years have passed since the end of the global financial crisis, the shadow of the crisis has not vanished completely and continually threatens the stability of the global economy. It has been a common challenge for the international community to prevent a future global financial crisis. In Asia, China has appealed to every regional country to establish a security network for its finances, to consolidate and update the "Chiang Mai Initiative", and to set up an Asian financial complex, among other initiatives; globally, China's initiative is to press ahead with "South-North Cooperation," especially multi-level and comprehensive cooperative agreements with developed economies such as the United States, the European Union, and Japan, in the aspect of trade, finance, and currency. This is to establish bilateral/multilateral free trade zones, strengthen mutual trust, and to enhance the global governance mechanism through negotiation and coordination, thus establishing a more harmonious economic and financial global order and forming a shared politico-economic community.

8.3 World Economic Prospects and an Outlook on the RMB's Internationalization

Over the last century of economic history, the global industrial structure has undergone three significant transformations. The first transformation occurred in the late 19th century, when industrialized European countries transferred the remainder of their manufactured goods, technologies, talents, and funds to the United States; the second transformation occurred after WWII, when European countries and the United States largely transferred their manufacturing industry and electronic industry to Asian countries (particularly Japan). Japan's economy and industry developed rapidly, and Japan quickly became the world's second-largest economic power. The third transformation occurred in the 1970s. European countries, the United States, and Japan transferred their labor intensive industries and technology intensive industries to Asia, thus facilitating the development of what became known as the "Four Asian Tigers."

The global economy now finds itself at the eve of a new technological revolution, the evidence of which is already appearing. Emerging industries, such as shale gas exploration, nanometer manufacturing, and "the life project" have begun to spring up. As the revolution approaches, the world economy seems poised to recover its growth after a period of depression, and a new round of change for the global industry structure will emerge as a result. In this sense, countries possessing a large market, such as China or India, will most benefit from the process of rebalancing the world economy. In this arena, China is no doubt the leading actor.

According to the trend towards development evinced by the world economy at large, the RMB's global application holds a great deal of potential. The model of quantitative development that has been adopted was designed by Chinn and Frankel. Based on the historical data of major international currencies, this model uses several variables to explain the rule of change as it applies to international reserves:

$$\mathrm{Yj} = \sum \beta\mathrm{i} \times \mathrm{Xij} + \varepsilon \tag{8.1}$$

In the above formula, Y is a ratio that explains the currency's degree of internationalization (e.g. the ratio of savings); X is an explanatory variable (e.g. economic aggregate, monetary stability); i marks different explanatory variables; j marks different types of currencies; but there is only one common explanatory coefficient β_i in the regression equation; while ε is the error term.

We hold a prudent attitude towards selecting an explanatory variable. After comparison, we have selected an optimal model as follows:

The ratio of international reserves = −0.2743 + 0.967*inertia + 0.068*GDP ratio − 69.80* movement ratio of exchange rate

$$(0.0126)\quad(0.0319)\qquad\quad(18.9955)$$
$$[\mathrm{F} = 14181.2,\quad \mathrm{Adj\ R\^{}2} = 0.9986]$$

Based on the above model, a mid-term estimate has been made for the RMB-denominated international reserves, with efforts advanced towards future extrapolation. At first, an initial value must be set for the independent variable. When calculating the ratio of GDP, IMF standards should be adopted. The exchange rate movement ratio is calculated based on the five-year average. The initial value of the RMB-denominated international reserves is calculated based on the current volume of the RMB-denominated international settlement, with a proportional ratio between US dollar-denominated reserves and the US dollar-denominated settlement. Under the circumstances that existing requirements for serving as an international currency have been met, an estimated value and an extrapolated value for RMB-denominated international reserves can be extrapolated.

According to estimates, if in all aspects the RMB initiates the process of internationalization, the proportion of the RMB to international reserves overall will reach around 3% within five years. By 2030, this percentage will exceed 10%. and the RMB will become the world's third-largest international currency (Table 8.1).

On this basis, we can predict the performance of the RMB's application in terms of international settlements. For instance, over the past ten years, a stable proportional relationship has existed between US dollar-denominated international settlements and US dollar-denominated international reserves. From 2001 to 2010, this range has fluctuated between 1.49 and 1.59, with an average proportion of 1.52. Working under the assumption that the proportion of RMB-denominated settlements and RMB-denominated reserves are the same, the volume of the RMB-denominated international settlements for 2016 is projected to reach USD2.25 tn.

Table 8.1 Estimated ratio of Chinese Yuan and other major international currencies

Year	US dollar	Euro	Japanese Yen	Chinese Yuan
2011	60.86	26.45	4.14	0.76
2012	60.28	26.58	4.51	1.07
2013	59.74	26.65	4.87	1.45
2014	59.25	26.65	5.21	1.91
2015	58.79	26.62	5.55	2.43
2016	58.27	26.62	5.91	2.93
2020	56.38	26.29	7.27	5.15
2025	54.06	25.76	8.29	8.32
2030	51.85	24.97	8.99	11.87

Unit %

Since many factors exert pressure on international bonds, solid predictions are difficult to make. For this reason, any predictions about the future prospects of RMB-denominated bonds are predicated upon the data published by the Bank for International Settlements (BIS). In Fig. 8.1, we can see that the issuance of RMB-denominated international bonds has reported a stable trend of linear growth. The conservative estimate is now that the issuance of the RMB-denominated international bonds will eventually reach RMB450 bn.

In terms of volume, the RMB's internationalization is likely to proceed sequentially, from trade settlement under the current account and investment under the capital account to inclusion by sovereign economies into their international reserves. As demonstrated in Fig. 8.2, the RMB serves as a currency for valuing and settling international trade. Due to the rapid development seen over the past few years, a sufficient overseas liquidity pool has been provided for the global applicability of the RMB. As the RMB is widely applied in international trade settlement, the financial market has begun to provide for RMB-denominated investment and financing products. Its investment applicability is predicted to develop rapidly over the next five years, after which, it will steadily adapt to trade developments.

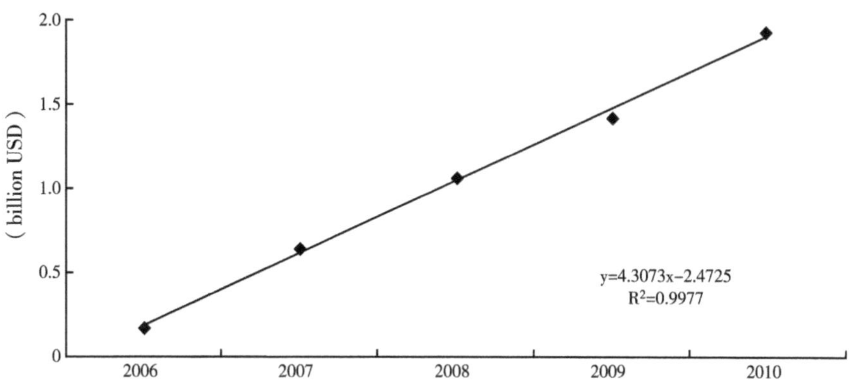

Fig. 8.1 Changes in the amount of RMB-denominated international bonds *Source* BIS

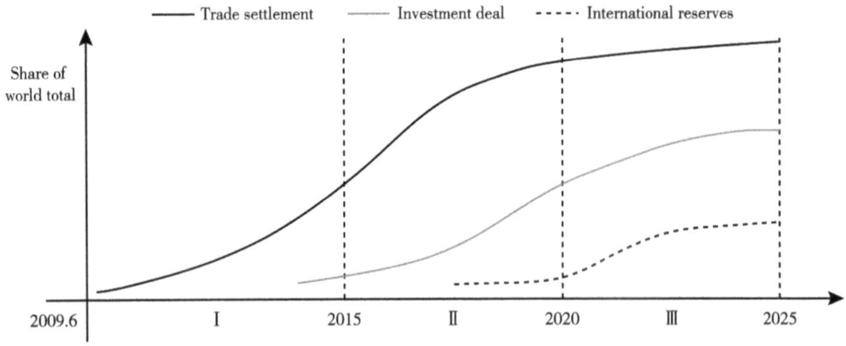

Fig. 8.2 Roadmap of RMB internationalization *Source* Institute of International Finance, Bank of China

Following the widespread applicability of the RMB's towards international trade and within financial markets, third-party countries and regions will be more willing to bring the RMB into their international reserves so as to deal with existing problems related to the balance of payments. The proportion of the RMB to the total international reserves will thus continue to increase gradually.

The above forecast opens up broad prospects for the internationalization of the RMB, the application of which is likely to attain a considerable volume in the future. Several trillion yuan are predicted to become reserves for other countries or to be widely applied in third-party trade, finance, and settlement. There is a popular belief among foreign experts and scholars that by 2025, China's economic volume is expected to rank first in the world. At that time, based on advanced technology, stable geopolitics, and a harmonious culture exchange, the RMB will be widely applied to the balance sheets of non-residents (companies and families) and will become the third-largest international currency, functioning in the same vein as the US dollar and the euro. The RMB's internationalization is one of China's primary contributions to the world.

Ultimately, we may use a quote from President Xi Jinping's 2015 Asian-African leaders' meeting both as a summary of the internationalization of the RMB and as the conclusion of this book: "we will develop a community of a shared destiny and embark on a new path toward security by all, of all, and for all."

Afterword

The internationalization of the RMB is currently a globally-central economic phenomenon. It is not only the result of adjustments to the international economic structure, but also indicates a new international economic order. Only seven years have passed since the RMB was officially applied towards valuing and settling the cross-border trade of goods on July 2, 2009, yet its internationalization has already achieved extraordinary progress. At present, over one fifth of all trade with China is valued and settled in RMB, and the RMB is now the world's second-largest currency for trade and financing, second only to the US dollar. China has signed bilateral local currency swap agreements with over 32 overseas central banks on a scale of RMB3.3 tn. The RMB-denominated domestic assets held by foreign residents have reached RMB4.4 tn. The asset scale of the offshore market is close to RMB2 tn, with offshore RMB financial markets in Hong Kong, London, and Singapore. This trend inexplicably exceeds expectations. For this reason, academic, business, and political circles have paid careful attention to the RMB's internationalization, and explanations for and arguments around this topic have poured forth unceasingly. The purpose of writing this book is to discuss the path towards development and the significance of internationalizing the RMB from both theoretical and practical perspectives, thereby predicting future trends in development and their potential impact on global economic patterns.

Led by Cao Yuanzheng, former chief economist with the Bank of China and President of the BOC International Research Corporation, this book was compiled through the joint effort of numerous contributors. Authors include Lin Hui, postdoctoral researcher with the National Information Center; Dr. Lu Peng and Dr. Hao Zhiyun with the HQ of the ICBC; Dr. Ji Jianjun, with the Foreign Economic Research Institute of the National Development and Reform Commission; Zhen Feng, postdoctoral researcher with the Bank of China; and Dr. Chen Shibo, Founder Fubon Asset Management Co., Ltd. They are all researchers and drivers of the RMB's internationalization. In addition, they are teachers and students.

The internationalization of the RMB is still an ongoing process. One year into it, this writing aims not only at identifying issues deserving of further research, but

© Social Sciences Academic Press and Springer Nature Singapore Pte Ltd. 2018

Y. Cao, *Strategies for Internationalizing the Renminbi*, Research Series on the Chinese Dream and China's Development Path,
https://doi.org/10.1007/978-981-13-0800-0

also is a process of teaching and learning. In putting this collection together, we've tried very hard to elaborate upon and to summarize existing practices and future prospects, but, of course, certain aspects remain unexplored. Our team's hope is that this book can serve as a good introduction for further discussion. The RMB's internationalization indicates a great opportunity for China's development and its future contribution to the global economy.

References

Adam K (2009) Monetary policy and aggregate volatility. J Monetary Econ (Supplement 1):S1–S18

Akay OC, Emre Alper C, Karasulu M (1997) Currency substitution and exchange rate instability: the Turkish case. Eur Econ Rev 3:827–835

Alami TH (2001) Currency substitution versus dollarization: a portfolio balance model. J Policy Model 4:473–479

Andersson M, Dillén H, Sellin P (2006) Monetary policy signaling and movements in the term structure of interest rates. J Monetary Econ 8:1815–1855

Ba S (2007) The Renminbi's internationalization and its impacts on China's financial market. Securities Times, 15 June 2007 (A03)

Beckworth D (2010) One nation under the fed? The asymmetric effects of US monetary policy and its implications for the united states as an optimal currency area. J Macroecon 32:732–746

Bergin PR (2000) Fiscal solvency and price level determination in a monetary union. J Monetary Econ 1:37–53

Bernasconi M, Kirchkamp O (2000) Why do monetary policies matter? An experimental study of saving and inflation in an overlapping generations model. J Monetary Econ 2:315–343

Bian D, Rao H, Bian M, Chen J (2010) Solve the Triffin Dilemma and reform the current international monetary system. China Money (11)

BIS Annual Report 2009-10 (2010) Bank for International Settlements Communications, Basel

Bullard J, Mitra K (2002) Learning about monetary policy rules. J Monetary Econ 6:1105–1129

Bulmer-Thomas V (2010) Economic development of latin America after independence (trans: Feng Z et al.). China Economy Press, China, p 422

Canzoneri M, Cumby R, Diba B (2010) The interaction between monetary and fiscal policy. Handb Monetary Econ 3:935–999

Cesarano F (2006) Monetary theory and Bretton woods. Cambridge University Press, Cambridge

Chen H (2004) Path for the Japanese Yen's internationalization. World Econ Polit (5)

Chen Z (2006) Study of regional economic integration in Northeast Asia—from transaction cost theory perspective. Jilin People's Press, Changchun

Chen B (2010) Settlement in sovereign currency: terminating US Dollar's supremacy. China Financial Publishing House, Beijing

Chinn M, Frankel J (2008) Why the euro will rival the dollar. Int Financ 11:49–73

Chown JF (2002) A history of money: from AD 800 (Chinese edn). The Commercial Press, Beijing

Chu H (2009) Study of the Renminbi's internationalization. Fudan University, Shanghai

Clark P, Polak J (2002) International liquidity and the role of the SDR in the international system. IMF Staff Papers 51 (April)

© Social Sciences Academic Press and Springer Nature Singapore Pte Ltd. 2018

Y. Cao, *Strategies for Internationalizing the Renminbi*, Research Series on the Chinese Dream and China's Development Path,
https://doi.org/10.1007/978-981-13-0800-0

Cohen WI (2000) East Asia at the center: four thousand years of engagement with the world. Columbia University Press, New York
Consolo A, Favero CA (2009) Monetary policy inertia: more a fiction than a fact? J Monetary Econ (6):900–906
Curtis ES, Waller CJ (2000) Search-theoretic model of legal and illegal currency. J Monetary Econ 1:155–184
Damjanovic T, Damjanovic V, Nolan C (2008) Unconditionally optimal monetary policy. J Monetary Econ 3:491–500
Daniels JP, Van Hoose DD (2003) Currency substitution, seigniorage, and currency crises in interdependent economies. J Econ Bus 3:221–232
Ding Y (2004) Selection of exchange rate regime in economic development. Jilin University, Changchun
Duncan R (2009) The dollar crisis: causes, consequences, cures. Dongbei University of Finance & Economics Press, Dalian
Eichengreen B (2008) Globalizing capital, a history of the international monetary system, 2nd edn. Princeton University Press, Princeton
Ekvall NL, Jennergren P, Slund BN (1997) Currency option pricing with mean reversion and uncovered interest parity: a revision of the Garman-Kohlhagen model. Eur J Oper Res 1:41–59
Elliott WB, Huffman SP, Makar SD (2003) Foreign-denominated debt and foreign currency derivatives: complements or substitutes in hedging foreign currency risk? J Multinational Financ Manage 2:123–139
Engineer M (2000) Currency transactions costs and competing fiat currencies. J Int Econ 1:113–136
Erceg CJ, Henderson DW, Levin AT (2000) Optimal monetary policy with staggered wage and price contracts. J Monetary Econ 2:281–313
Feng Y (2007) Path and policy for the Renminbi's gradual internationalization. Southwestern University of Finance and Economics, Chengdu
Feng B (2008) The Renminbi's strong strategy in the process of internationalization. Economic Science Press, Beijing
Feng Y (2009) Path and policy selection for the Renminbi's gradual internationalization. China Financial Publishing House, Beijing
Fu L, Liu L (2003) The internationalization of the Japanese Yen and its implications for China's participating in the monetary cooperation in East Asia. Jpn Study Forum (3)
Gao H (2008) The Renminbi exchange rate: policy options and risk prevention from global perspective. China Financial & Economic Publishing House, Beijing
Garber PM (2011) What currently drives CNH market equilibrium. Presented at the Council on Foreign Relations/China Development Research Foundation Workshop on the Internationalization of the Renminbi
Garfinkel MR, Oh S (2005) When and how much to talk credibility and flexibility in monetary policy with private information. J Monetary Econ 2:341–357
Gaspar V, Smets F, Vestin D (2010) Inflation expectations, adaptive learning and optimal monetary policy. Handb Monetary Econ 3:1055–1095
Ge Z (2009) Reform of the international monetary system and the Renminbi's internationalization. J Shanghai Financ Univ (6)
Gilpin R (2006) The political economy of international relations. Shanghai Century Publishing Group, Shanghai
Goldsmith RW (1994) Financial structure and development. Shanghai Joint Publishing, Shanghai
Gong Z, Liu C. Study of APEC's development towards Asia-Pacific region's free trade. Nankai University Press, Tianjin
Guan T (2002a) Status quo of China's capital account management and prospect for the Renminbi's capital account convertibility. J World Econ (4)
Guan T (2002b) Status quo of China's capital account management and the prospect for the Renminbi's capital account convertibility. J World Econ (3)

Hamilton JD (2008) Daily monetary policy shocks and new home sales. J Monetary Econ 7:1171–1190
Han Q (2007) Financial deepening and China's financial stability. Jilin University, Changchun
Han W (2011) The RMB's development towards internationalization. Economic Science Press, Beijing
Hartmann P (1998) The currency of denomination of world trade after european monetary union. J Jpn Int Econ 12:424–454
Hartmann P (1998) Currency competition and foreign exchange markets: the dollar, the yen and the euro. Cambridge University Press, Cambridge
Hayek FA (1970) The denationalization of money, 2nd ed. Institute of Economics Affairs, London
He H (2006) Monetary cooperation in East Asia and the Renminbi's internationalization. Soc Sci J (4)
He H (2007) Model and path arrangement for the Renminbi's internationalization. Econ Manage J (5)
He F, Zhang B, Zhang M, Xu Q, Zheng L (2011) Status quo, prospect, problems and risks of HK's offshore Renminbi market. Int Econ Rev (3)
Heimonen K (2008) Substituting a substitute currency. Int Rev Econ Financ 1:66–84
HKMA (2011) Hong Kong: the premier offshore Renminbi business centre. http://www.hkma.gov.hk
Hong Y (2010) Japanese Yen's effective exchange rate, net export ratio and trade terms—time series analysis based on the intrinsic economic growth model. Contemp Econ Jpn (6)
Honghui C, Shen W (2007) East Asia's selection of exchange-rate regime and the RMB's strategy. Rev Econ Res (46)
Huang Z (2001) The Japanese financial system. East China Normal University Press, Shanghai
Huang Y (2010) Research on the effectiveness of capital control in China. Forty Voices in China Finance Forum, 2010
Hunag J, Li Z (2004) A review and empirical study of currency substitution theory. J Shandong Univ (2)
Ingram JC (1969) Comment: the currency area problem. University of Chicago Press, Chicago
Jiang L (1997) Theory and practice of the Renminbi's internationalization. J World Econ (4)
Kaminsky GL, Lewis KK (1996) Does foreign exchange intervention signal future monetary policy? J Monetary Econ (2):285–312
Kannan P (2009) On the welfare benefits of an international currency. Eur Econ Rev 53:588–606
Keen BD (2004) In search of the liquidity effect in a modern monetary model. J Monetary Econ 7:1467–1494
Kenen PB (1969) The theory of optimum currency areas: an eclectic view. University of Chicago Press, Chicago
Keynes JM (1997) A treatise on money. The Commercial Press, Beijing
Kim S (2001) International transmission of U.S. monetary policy shocks: evidence from VAR's. J Monetary Econ 2:339–372
Koenda E, Hanousek J, Engelmann D (2008) Currencies, competition, and clans. J Policy Model 6:1115–1132
Kosuke A (2003) On the optimal monetary policy response to noisy indicators. J Monetary Econ 50(3):501–523
Krugman P (1990) Policy problems of a monetary union. Longman, London
Krugman PR (1999) The return of depression economics. China Renmin University Press, China
Li J (2002) The choice of the Renminbi's exchange rate regime: literature review. J World Econ (3)
Li H (2003a) Strategy for internationalizing the Renminbi based on the nature of the currency. Econ Manage J (2)
Li Y (2003b) Non-internationalized currency, currency internationalization and capital account convertibility. J Financ Res (8)

Li H (2008a) International monetary coordination under economic globalization. China Metallurgical Industry Press, Beijing
Li J (2008b) China's capital account opening under the background of weak US dollar. Asia Pac Econ Rev (6)
Li W (2008c) International experience analysis: capital account opening, financial development and economic and financial instability. J World Econ (3)
Li D (2009a). *The Renminbi's Cross-border Settlement: Problems and Solutions*. Beijing: China Financial Publishing House
Li J (2009b) Impacts of the Renminbi's regionalization on China's economy and solutions. China Financial Publishing House, Beijing
Li J (2009c) Study of the path for the Renminbi's internationalization. Jilin University, Changchun
Li W (2010a) Process of internationalization of the world's major currencies: comparison and lessons. J Financ Dev Res (7)
Li X (2010b) Why does the monetary cooperation in East Asia suffer setbacks? —the Renminbi's internationalization and its impacts on the monetary cooperation in East Asia. Int Econ Rev (7)
Li C (2011) Study of the Renminbi's regionalization. China Financial Publishing House, Beijing
Li X, Ding Y (2006a) Preeminence of Asia—regional monetary system in East Asia and the Renminbi's asianzation. Contemporary China Publishing House, Beijing
Li X, Ding Y (2006b) Asia's leap forward—develop East Asia's regional monetary system and realize the Renminbi's asianization. Contemporary China Publishing House, Beijing
Li X, Ding Y (2010a) Study of problems from the Renminbi's regionalization. Tsinghua University Press, Beijing
Li X, Ding Y (2010b) Regional monetary cooperation in East Asia and reform of the Renminbi's exchange rate regime. Economic Science Press, Beijing
Li F, Lin S (2009) History and status quo of the international monetary system—choice of the Renminbi's internationalization. J Financ Res (5)
Li D, Liu L (2008) The Renminbi's internationalization: quantitative research and policy analysis. J Financ Res (11)
Li Y, Pang D (2009) Economic globalization and regional economic cooperation in Northeast Asia. Jilin People's Publishing House, Changchun
Li X, Takao K (2010) Renminbi, Japanese Yen and monetary cooperation in Asia. Tsinghua University Press, Beijing
Li W, Zhang Z (2008) Effects of capital account opening in different ways; actual change in exchange rate and economic growth. J World Econ (10)
Li Y, Chen Z, Yin L (2006) Study of Northeast Asia's innovation in regional economic development and cooperation mechanism. Jilin People's Press, Changchun
Lindset S (2005) Valuing the flexibility of currency choice in multinational trade with stochastic exchange rates. J Multinational Financ Manage 2:137–153
Liu Z (2006) Study of East Asia's monetary cooperation and the selection of the RMB's exchange rate regime. China Economic Publishing House, Beijing
Liu R, Liu H (2009) Risk assessment and risk management for the Renminbi's internationalization. Social Science Academic Press, Beijing
Lothian JR (2002) The internationalization of money and finance and the globalization of financial markets. J Int Money Financ 21:699–724
Lotz S (2004) Introducing a new currency: government policy and prices. Eur Econ Rev 5:959–982
Ma J (2011) Impacts of the Renminbi offshore market development on domestic currency and finance. Deutsche Bank's research report
Ma J, Xu J (2012) The internationalization of the Renminbi: offshore market development and capital account opening. China Economic Press, Beijing
Makowiak B (2007) External shocks, U.S. monetary policy and macroeconomic fluctuations in emerging markets. J Monetary Econ 8:2512–2520
Mathieon (1994) The internationalization of yen and key currency questions. IMF working paper

McCauley R (2011) Renminbi internationalization and China's financial development model. Presented at the Council on Foreign Relations/China Development Research Foundation Workshop on the Internationalization of the Renminbi
McKinnon RI (2001) The international dollar standard and sustainability of the current account deficit. Brookings papers on economic activity
Meade JE (1951) The theory of international economic policy, vol I: The balance of payment. Oxford University Press, London
Melvin M, Peiers B (1993) On the possibility of a yen currency bloc for Pacific-basin countries: a stochastic dominance approach. Pac Basin Financ J 4:309–333
Mundell RA (1973) Uncommon arguments for common currencies. Harvard University, Boston
Mundell R (2000) Currency areas, volatility and intervention. J Policy Model 22(3):281–299
Mundell RA (2003a) Selected works on economics of Robert Mundell. China Financial Publishing House, Beijing
Mundell RA (2003b) Selected works on economics of Robert Mundell (trans: Xiang S). China Financial Publishing House, Beijing
Murase T (2010) Hong Kong RMB offshore market and risks to Chinese economy. Inst Int Monetary Aff (40)
Nakagawa T (2004) Internationalization of the Yuan and its impact on East Asia. Inst Int Policy Stud 2:1–21
Nelson E (2003) The future of monetary aggregates in monetary policy analysis. J Monetary Econ 5:1029–1059
Norgaard O (2007) Economic institutions and democratic reform. Shanghai Century Publishing Group, Shanghai
Ogawa E, Shimizu J (2006) Stabilization of effective exchange rates under common currency basket systems. J Jpn Int Econ 4:590–611
Oi H, Otani A, Shirota T (2004) The choice of invoice currency in international trade: implications for the internationalization of the yen. Monetary Econ Stud 3:27–63
Orphanides A (2001) Historical monetary policy analysis and the taylor rule. J Monetary Econ 2:339–372
Pan M, Miao H (2010) Promotion of non-regular monetary polices under economic recovery — theoretical analysis and China's choice. World Econ Study (12)
Pang L. Study of Binhai new area's financial innovation and the Renminbi's internationalization. Tianjin University Of Finance & Economics, Tianjin
Papaioannou E, Portes R, Siourounis G (2006) Optimal currency shares in international reserves: the impact of the euro and the prospects for the dollar. J Jpn Int Econ 4:508–547
Peng X (2010a) The evolution of international monetary system and China's choice in the process of global monetary diversification. Chin Rev Financ Stud (5)
Peng X (2010b) Evolution of the international monetary system and China's choice in the diversification process—analysis of the evolution of the international monetary system based on the 'Power of Money'. Chin Rev Financ Stud (5)
Qiyuan X, Liu L (2009) Study of exchange rates variation during Renminbi's internationalization. China Financial Publishing House, Beijing
Ravenna F, Walsh CE (2006) Optimal monetary policy with the cost channel. J Monetary Econ 2:199–216
Rich G (1997) Monetary targets as a policy rule: lessons from the swiss experience. J Monetary Econ (1):113–141
Robson P (1980) The economics of international integration. Allen & Unwin, London
Rodrik D (2011) The globalization paradox. China Renmin University Press, Beijing
Salvatore D (2007) The Euro, the US Dollar and the international monetary system. Fudan University Press, Shanghai
Shi J (2007) China's capital account opening: significance, progress and review. Int Econ Rev (11)
Sibert A, Liu L (1998) Government finance with currency substitution. J Int Econ 1:155–172

Smets F, Wouters R (2002) Openness, imperfect exchange rate pass-through and monetary policy. J Monetary Econ 5:947–981
Sun D (2008) Theoretical and empirical analysis of the Renminbi's cross-border circulation. University of International Business and Economics Press, Beijing
Sun H, Xie L (2010) Choice of international currencies: analysis based on the function of foreign exchange reserves. Stud Int Financ (12)
Tan Q, Guo Y (2007) Conflict and coordination: internal and external equilibrium under the Renminbi's internationalization—experience of other international currencies and its implications. Int Econ Trade Res (7)
Tootell GMB (1999) Whose monetary policy is it anyway? J Monetary Econ (1):217–235
Triffin R (1997) Gold and the dollar crisis (trans: Chen S, Lei D). The Commercial Press, Beijing
Uhlig H (2005) What are the effects of monetary policy on output? Results from an agnostic identification procedure. J Monetary Econ 2:381–419
Valev NT (2010) The hysteresis of currency substitution: currency risk versus network externalities. J Int Money Financ 2:224–235
Wan Z (2003) Study of the economic foundation for the monetary cooperation in East Asia. Nankai University, Tianjin
Wang Y (2008a) A review on McKinnon's theory of exchange rates under East Asia's US dollar standard. Jilin University, Changchun
Wang Y (2008b) Analysis of the monetary cooperation in East Asia from perspective of political economy. World Affairs Press, Beijing
Wang H (2010) International currency, international monetary system and the Renminbi's internationalization. Fudan Univ J (1)
Walker E (2008) Strategic currency hedging and global portfolio investments upside down. J Bus Res 6:657–668
Watanabe S, Ogura M (2010) How far apart are the two ACUs from each other? Asian currency unit and asian currency union. Emerg Markets Rev 2:152–172
Wu X (2006) Intrinsic decision for the time of opening the capital account: an optimal model for two-stage dynamics. World Econ Study (6)
Wu X (2009) Study of monetary cooperation in East Asia. Jilin University, Changchun
Xiong Q, Zhang X (2011) International experience for currency internationalization: comparison and lessons. Shanghai Financ (2)
Xu X (2006) Study of the Renminbi's internationalization: theory and empirical study. Fudan University, Shanghai
Xu X (2009) Major international currencies, offshore Renminbi market and the Renminbi's internationalization. Northern Econ Trade (5)
Xu Q (2010) Experience from the Japanese yen's internationalization and its implications to Renminbi. Chin Rev Financ Stud (2)
Xu Q, He F. Impacts of the Renminbi's Internationalization on China's macro economy—analysis based on the Renminbi's cross-border settlement. Soc Sci Guangdong (4)
Xu Q, Liu L (2009) Study of the exchange rate change in the process of the Renminbi's internationalization. China Financial Publishing House, Beijing
Xuan W (2009) Reform of the international monetary system and the Renminbi's internationalization. Shanghai J Econ (5)
Yang H (2010a) Thoughts on the Renminbi's internationalization—comparison with the US dollar, the Japanese Yen and the Euro. J Nanjing Audit Univ (7)
Yang X (2010b) An empirical study of the Japanese Yen as an international reserve currency. World Econ Stud (11)
Yin J (2011a) The Renminbi's internationalization: "Trade Settlement + Offshore Market", Or "Capital Export + Multinational Enterprise"—lessons from the Japanese Yen's internationalization. Int Econ Rev (4)
Yin J (2011b) Reflection on the model of the Renminbi's internationalization: lessons from Japan. Int Econ Rev (7)

Yu B (2000) The new contention of economy in Japan. Jilin University Press, Changchun
Yu Y (2011a) Have clear target and plan for the Renminbi's internationalization. Review of Finance and Economics, No. 2011042
Yu Y (2011b) About the path for the Renminbi's internationalization. Review of Finance and Economics, No. 2011056
Yu Y (2012) View on the Renminbi's internationalization from perspective of Renminbi's exchange rate fluctuation. Int Econ Rev (1)
Zhang Q (2006) Study of the Renminbi's internationalization. Fudan University, Shanghai
Zhang M (2011) Progress of the Renminbi's internationalization. Econ Perspect (12)
Zhang M, He F (2012) Study of onshore-offshore arbitrage in the process of the Renminbi's internationalization. Stud Int Financ (10)
Zhang C, Hu Z (2012) View on the Renminbi's internationalization from perspective of the internationalization of the world's major currencies. Asia Pac Econ Rev (3)
Zhang B, Xu Q (2012) Exchange rate and the Renminbi's internationalization under the capital account control. Int Econ Rev (4)
Zhang G, Zhang N (1993) On the Renminbi's full convertibility and internationalization. J Financ Res (10)
Zhang Y, Zhang J (2008) The nature of money and the Renminbi's choice in the future——monetary cooperation in Asia. J Contemp Asia Pac Stud (2)
Zhao D (2004) About the Renminbi's capital account convertibility. Financ Econ (5)
Zhao Q (2005) Study of the Renminbi's capital account convertibility and the RMB's internationalization. China Financial Publishing House, Beijing
Zhao Z (2006) Developing countries' capital account opening and its implications to China. Theor Res (7)
Zhao Q (2015) Study of the Renminbi's capital account convertibility and internationalization. China Financial Publishing House, Beijing
Zhao C, Li X (2007) Monetary cooperation and the Renminbi's core role in East Asia. J Contemp Asia Pac Stud (2)
Zhong W (2002) On the Renminbi's internationalization. J World Econ (3)
Zhong R, Yang L (2010) An empirical study of the currency substitution in macao. J Cent Univ Financ Econ (7)
Zhou C (1996) The endogeneity of money supply and monetary polices—analysis of Marx's theory of money and its implications. Contemp Econ Res (9)
Zhou X (2009) Reforming the international monetary system. China Financ 7:8–9
Zhou Z, Jiu S. A comparative study of western monetary theories against marx's theory of money. J Wuhan Train Cent Agric Bank China
Zhou L, Wen X (2001) Currency internationalization. Shanghai University of Finance and Economics Press, Shanghai
Zhou X, Xie P (1993) Towards the Renminbi's convertibility. Economy & Management Publishing House, Beijing
桥本寿朗, 长谷川信, 宫岛英昭 (2001) Contemporary economy of Japan. Shanghai University of Finance and Economic Press, Shanghai
(2015) Currency roles and currency internationalization: a typical case of Yen. Contemp Econ Jpn (5)

MIX
Papier aus verantwortungsvollen Quellen
Paper from responsible sources
FSC® C105338

If you have any concerns about our products,
you can contact us on
ProductSafety@springernature.com

In case Publisher is established outside the EU,
the EU authorized representative is:
Springer Nature Customer Service Center GmbH
Europaplatz 3, 69115 Heidelberg, Germany

Printed by Libri Plureos GmbH
in Hamburg, Germany